# ARGUMENTATION

**STUDIES IN LANGUAGE COMPANION SERIES (SLCS)**

The SLCS series has been established as a companion series to STUDIES IN LANGUAGE, International Journal, sponsored by the Foundation "Foundations of Language".



* * *

Volume 8

E.M. Barth & J.L. Martens (eds.)

*Argumentation: Approaches to Theory Formation*

# ARGUMENTATION

## APPROACHES TO THEORY FORMATION

Containing the Contributions to the
Groningen Conference on the Theory
of Argumentation, October 1978

edited by
E.M. BARTH & J.L. MARTENS

*University of Groningen*

JOHN BENJAMINS NORTH AMERICA, INC.
One Buttonwood Square
Philadelphia, PA 19130
DISTRIBUTOR

AMSTERDAM/JOHN BENJAMINS B.V.

1982

ISSN 0165 7763 / ISBN 90 272 3007 2

## CONTRIBUTORS

L. Apostel, formerly professor of philosophy, University of Gent, Belgium.

E.M. Barth, professor of philosophy, State University of Groningen, the Netherlands.

F. van Dun, lecturer of law, University of Gent, Belgium.

Arnold Günther, lecturer of linguistics, Technical University of Berlin, W. Germany.

Carl H. Heidrich, lecturer of linguistics, University of Bonn, W. Germany.

Jaakko Hintikka, professor of philosophy, Florida State University (Tallahassee), U.S.A.

Merrill B. Hintikka, professor of philosophy, Florida State University (Tallahassee), U.S.A.

Rüdiger Inhetveen, lecturer of philosophy, University of Erlangen-Nürnberg, W. Germany.

Erik C. W. Krabbe, lecturer of philosophy, State University of Utrecht, the Netherlands.

Ulrike Leopold-Wildburger, lecturer of mathematics, University of Graz, Austria.

Kuno Lorenz, professor of philosophy, University of Saarland at Saarbrücken, W. Germany.

P. Lorenzen, formerly professor of philosophy, University of Erlangen-Nürnberg, W. Germany.

Arne Naess, formerly professor of philosophy, University of Oslo, Norway.

# PREFACE

What can philosophers, linguists, and communications theorists do in order to promote a climate of discussion, preferably world-wide in the end, and improve the quality of discussions?

These were the questions and the long-term goals for the sake of which a number of scholars from other countries, as well as scholars from Dutch universities, were invited to come together at Groningen, The Netherlands, in 1978. The plan for such a conference met with immediate sympathy and support from the Groningen State University, and from the philosophical faculty there, for which we were, and are, very grateful.

Our short-term aspiration was to bring together a number of persons in a primarily non-combative and non-competitive atmosphere, in order to see whether some degree of synthesis between competing research programmes would be feasible. Obviously it is not possible to find that out in the course of a mere three days. We do hope, however, that the present volume will be of value in assessing the extent to which such a synthesis is feasible and, to be quite honest, we even hope that this collection of contributions may cause some of its readers to take steps in the direction of such a synthesis themselves.

The times being what they were, we had to make do with a very limited budget. To ensure that all types of contributions to the field were represented would not have been financially possible. Hence it was necessary to select a certain viewpoint from which to work in organizing the conference.

In the budding discipline that should, in our opinion, be called the Theory of Argumentation, three theoretical phases may be distinguished. Each new phase allows for another definition of the very word "argumentation". In explaining this, let us start from the influential research programme called phenomenology. Edmund Husserl himself was primarily, though not exclusively, interested in the -- his own term -- "pre-predicative" phases of cognition. His quest for "foundations" of cognitive content had nothing to do with argumentation even in the weaker sense. Phase One of the theory of argumentation consisted in taking the step from this search for a pre-predicative foundation of a conviction, belief, theorem, or point of view, to the *justification* of an overt position (cp. S.E. Toulmin 1958). In Phase Two the justification is related to the specific concessions of an *audience* (Ch. Perelman and L. Olbrechts-Tyteca 1952), however the verbal reactions of the audience are not yet considered in detail, and the interplay of locutions is not analysed. Let us call this *the rhetorical stage* of the theory of argumentation.

In Phase Three the justification is analytically related to the audience's verbal reactions, and vice versa. 'The audience' now figures theoretically as an active partner in a discussion between two (or more) parties or *dialectical roles*. The interplay -- or, as Kant says in his Table of Categories, the *Wechselwirkung* -- between the locutions of these two (or more) dialectical roles will be called *the dialectical stage* of the theory of argumentation.

The development can be described as one from Idea (and Judgement) *via* -- public -- Meaning, and later, Sentence (Alston 1964, Hacking 1975), to the focal notion of a *Sequent* or *ordered pair* (*triple*,...), of the sets of locutions that, at a certain stage of some dialogue, characterize the two (or more) parties, or their roles, in that dialogue. The third, or dialectical, phase in argumentational studies is that in which the theoretician, more or less conciously and more or less explicitly, is discussing *operations on sequents*. Such studies may be purely descriptive and empirical, in which case they may or may not be related to linguistic studies, or they may be normative, in which case they may be related to logic, ethics, and social affairs generally. Or they may be both at the same time.

We decided to devote the conference to the third, or dialectical, phase in argumentational studies. Even so we were not able to invite all the important contributors to the field, not even those within Europe. To our sincere regret, some of the invited speakers were, for one reason or another, unable to attend the conference. One of them was Arne Naess. Since the conference quite possibly would never have been thought of, had it not been for his inspiring influence, years before, it may seem strange that we went along with our preparations rather than wait another year; however, the financial situation at the universities being as it was, we deemed it wiser to carry out the plan immediately.

During the conference one of the participants emphasized that whereas there is no possibility of overlooking the practical importance of truth (or, we take it, of competing notions, such as agreement - eds.), truth alone is not enough. In philosophy as well as in daily life we also need a second value, viz. *relevance*. Argumentation is a human activity and instances of argumentation are, as all human activities, more or less "good" or "bad" (for someone, or, mediately, for something). When, in the discussion that followed, one of the participants pointed out that the sub-formula principle is a principle of relevance, the former speaker retorted that as a principle of relevance in her general sense (of moral, of epistemic, and of general cultural relevance), the sub-formula principle is hardly of importance. Apart from the problem of the relevance of instances of argumentation to ethical goals she also threw up the still more involved topic of *creativity* in argumentative communication. The notion of a sentence which, given a certain argumentative situation, is in all respects appropriate, relevant in the technical sense of the word, yet *novel* in a sense in which a sub-sentence is not, certainly seems to be a realistic one.

This conference did not itself contribute to an analysis of what constitutes "appropriate, but novel and valuable" arguments. However, several among its participants have, in one way or another, demonstrated in writing that their involvement with other theoretical questions concerning argumentative uses of language is deeply rooted either in moral concerns, or in epistemic concerns, or in both. These earlier -- in a couple of cases, later -- publications should be seen as the background of the Groningen conference, or as connected with that background. These publications may be found in the bibliography at the end of this volume.

A small number of persons who had been invited to this conference and who had expressed their interest in participation were, for various reasons, unable to come. Two of them -- Arne Naess and Frank van Dun -- sent us their contributions afterwards. We decided to treat their contributions as if the authors had been present in person.

The papers have been put into five relatively coherent groups. With respect to the first of these groups, which we have called *Re-modelling logic*, we finally decided to put the papers in the order in which the authors' first contributions to argumentational studies (or to closely related studies) appeared in print. A chronological bibliography, which is intended to be complete (concerning argumentational studies) with respect to the contributors to this volume, but not with respect to other authors, is added at the end of the book (pp.295-333). It was compiled by Mr. A. van Hoof, graduate student of philosophy and argumentation theory in the University of Groningen, and for this we are very grateful to him. Our thanks are due also to Ms. C.A.M. Roy and especially to Mr. R. North, who went through the English texts from a linguistic point of view.

E.M. Barth

J.L. Martens

The editors of the series in which this volume is appearing, and the publishing house as well, have requested some kind of introductory text connecting the papers. I am glad to comply with their wish. In order not to dominate the volume too much I have kept these pieces as short as possible, but have arranged that a chronological bibliography was compiled which shows the development of the field better than I could do. By grouping the papers together in what I hope is a systematic manner (there are, of course, strong overlaps between the groups), and by asking those authors who had not done so already to produce clarifying subtitles throughout their papers, it was possible to keep the introductions short.

E.M.B.

CONTENTS

# PART ONE:

# RE-MODELLING LOGIC

## INTRODUCTION TO PART ONE: RE-MODELLING LOGIC

The name of this largest batch of papers may speak for itself, but let me try to unpack it anyway. Contrary to what some writers on questions of argumentation seem to imply, in the present writer's opinion there can be no kind of theory of "rational" argumentation that does not take systematic account of the science called formal logic. On the other hand, formal logic in its present representations has not yet had the broad cultural value-in-use one could hope for. The papers in this batch all deal with or refer to this fact, in one way or another.

### *Pro et contra dicere*

In the nineteen-forties, Arne Naess wrote the first version of a book he called, in Norwegian, *En del elementaere logiske emner* - "Some elementary topics in logic". More recently it was published in English under the title *Communication and Argument* and later also in German and Dutch, under similar titles. The Swedish translation, however, was called *Empirisk semantik*, "Empirical semantics". These shifts of title, from "logic" to "semantics", "communication" and "argumentation", indicate that the author considers not only communication, but also the more specific phenomenon of *argumentation* as a topic, and even as perspective, in *semantics*. His pretensions as he describes them in this little book were, however, modest: "It is not my intention to introduce the readers to a new field." The description of his general outlook that I am giving here is, I believe, nevertheless quite adequate. His oeuvre as a whole permits one to speak of an argumentational, or argumentative, outlook on semantics. This "argumentational semantics" has two main goals: *understanding* through a clarification of language, and *penetration to the center of a conflict of opinions*, through elimination of pseudo-conflicts and through analysis of arguments *pro et contra* as well as *pro aut contra* the competing standpoints (c.q. the competing attitudes to a standpoint).

In his preface to a recent edition of this book Naess wrote: "I still am of the opinion that elementary logic is most fruitfully studied when it is undertaken as a study of the role played by language in the pursuit of a logically clear exchange of opinions." His conclusion: in a textbook on elementary topics in logic, "one ought to focus on sources of misunderstanding in practice, rather than on cases of sinning against the rules of formal logic. For this reason rules for 'pleading for and against' (*pro et contra dicere*) are discussed extensively...". In the nineteen-forties, and even in most contemporary textbooks and monographs, formal logic was one thing and *pro et contra dicere* another.

In 1959 another event took place which changes this situation at least in principle: the birth of Paul Lorenzen's dialogue approach to first-order predicate logic ("elementary formal logic"). This was preceded by E.W. Beth's method of semantic tableaux in 1955, followed by his (Beth's) method of deductive tableaux (1959).

Since then, formal logic can be studied in terms of *pro et contra dicere*. Nevertheless, Naess' work and that of Lorenzen and Lorenz are complementary, in the following sense. Whereas Lorenzen and Lorenz are concerned with those sentence constituents which are called "logical constants", such as connectives and quantifiers, Naess' rules and recommendations either pertain to whole sentences, to non-logical constants, or to components of sentences containing non-logical constants. In addition to *pro et contra dicere,* he is concerned with problems of interpretation and clarification. In their analysis on "dialogue logic" Lorenzen and Lorenz are exclusively concerned with criticism and defense, on the basis of fixed meanings-in-critical-use, formulated for the first time by Lorenzen in 1958, 1959, of the logical constants. Obviously each of these pursuits is not only "legitimate", as one says, but absolutely indispensable in a comprehensive Argumentology. To (mis)interpret is no less, and no more, important than to criticize, and to find more precise formulations so as to prevent or eliminate certain interpretations of a locution is no less, and no more, important than to defend it against certain critical moves. Both interpretation/clarification and criticism/defense must be based on a semiotics whose fundamental notion, or *Leitmotif,* is, or can be, related to a sequent (Con,T) -where T is a thesis and Con a class of concessions- as well as to a pair of users of language, in short to what Barth and Krabbe call a "conflict of avowed opinion" (1978,1982).

*What is semantics?*

Jaakko Hintikka distinguishes between *dialogue games* and *semantical games*. Dialogues are, as he says, intra-linguistic activities, hence dialogue games are parlour games, or "indoor games". A semantical game, however, is not a parlour game at all, but an "outdoor game" more like hide-and-seek, and should not be studied as a variety of conversation. Rather conversation, at least part of conversation, should be understood as rooted in *semantic activities* (my term -E.M.B.) constituting non-verbal games against Nature.

What Hintikka implies (but does not explicitly say, to my knowledge) is, I think, extremely right and extremely important, namely that the habit of logicians, old and new, of basing logic as well as their philosophy of language on some kind of "ontology" -that is to say, on things, properties and values that "are there", potentially or actually, in some "domain" or other- this habit should give place to a semantics in terms of the *human activities* of seeking and finding.

Many people, however, including the present writer, have had difficulties in getting a firm grasp on the differences which Hintikka claims to see between Lorenzen's and Lorenz' "games" and his own "semantical games". Hintikka describes what he calls semantical games as "... games against a recalcitrant Nature who tries to frustrate my attempts" (below). This he offers in the place of "ontology", of whichever kind -Tarski's, Quine's, or Aristotle's. Hintikka here prefers to follow Kant, who held, Hintikka says, "that our ways of reasoning about existence, especially about interindividual existential inferences, must be grounded in the human activities through which we come to know the existence of individuals" (second paper below). "However Kant went astray in identifying the activities through which we in fact come to know the existence and non-existence of individuals...". Technically it seems of little importance whether one chooses to speak in terms of an ordered couple *(myself, Nature)* or in terms of an ordered couple *(the Proponent, the Opponent)*. It is philosophically important that both concepts (concept pairs) and both nomenclatures can be subsumed under a view of the structure of rationality that is based on the notion of *an ordered couple of logical roles*, the most general characterization of which would be $(Role_1, Role_2)$. Earlier logic and philosophy distinguished only one logical role, the role of the Thinker, also called *the Subject* of a process of ratiocination.

The new two-role conception should, I presume, be broadened to n-party games -dialogical or semantical- based on a distinction on n logical roles, for some n greater than 2 (see contribution by Leopold-Wildburger, this volume).

There is a difference as to background and scientific and philosophical interests and focus. Hintikka's interests are with epistemic logic (Hintikka 1962), contemporary linguistics and main-stream (American) philosophy of language. On the other hand, Naess, Lorenzen, and also Apostel, who is inspired by Perelman, are geared not toward linguistics but toward social and political problems and their involvement with questions of intersubjective human understanding. This leads them to see human interaction, verbal or other, as constituting the essence of semantics, whereas the human activities with which Hintikka replaces the usual ontology-based semantics are solitary games-against-Nature, capable of definition in terms of the strategies of a single human brain. All of them are, in some way or another, oriented toward activity of one kind or another, rather than toward ontology ("what there is"). Leopold Apostel has been active in the budding theory of argumentation for a long time. He is very well versed in the research done by Perelman and Olbrechts-Tyteca as well as in the more logic-oriented approaches represented here. This enables him to compare and to take a universal overview. This overview takes into account a number of publications and authors that are not otherwise represented here -except indirectly, by their influence on the authors of this volume. His own position is an intermediate one between the emphasis on empirical research into persuasive argumentation of the former school, and the formal analyses and suggestions for regimentation in studies that are rooted in an interest in questions of validity (or, as one often says, in the possibilities of a distinction between "rational" and "irrational" argumentation). -- In connection with Apostel's distinction of "global" versus "local" attributes of discussion, Jürgen Habermas might also be mentioned, as a much read author who is interested in certain global features of discussion (and, it seems to me, only in global features).

In Note 8 Apostel promises us a future synthesis of Lorenzen/ Lorenz' results and those of Hintikka. The paper contains a definition (p. 98) of a very general concept 'discussion', which should be compared with Günther's definition (p. 175 ff.), and with the various implicit definitions of concepts of discussion in this volume.

The short paper by Krabbe in this section formed the introduction to the conference. He suggests a number of working-rules and points of departure that may be helpful in structuring, or at least in clearing the ground before theoretical action takes place.

In the last paper in this group, Inhetveen shows how to take the mystery out of "possible-worlds" semantics so as to render this highly fruitful formalism conceptually accessible to students of argumentation.

It is to be hoped that the various academic networks to which our authors belong, and which until now have had little or no contact with one another, will be able to free themselves from their academic isolation to the benefit of normative studies of argumentation and of semantics based on human activities. The editors of this volume would like to think that the chronological bibliography offered here (p. 295 - 333 ) may be instrumental in this respect. This isolation is no doubt the outcome mainly of the diversity of the languages in which the various contributions were presented, which has prevented them from being known worldwide: English, French, German, Dutch, and, worst of all, Norwegian.

# A NECESSARY COMPONENT OF LOGIC: EMPIRICAL ARGUMENTATION ANALYSIS

Arne Naess

## *1. Logic has empirical components and needs empirical research*

The use in argumentation of the calculus of propositions, or of Alfred Tarski's theory of truth, or of any other formal logical instrument involving the terms 'true' and 'false', presupposes some sort of agreement or similarity between formal usage and common usage. This relation is an empirical relation not adequately revealed through intuition, but capable of being increasingly clarified through painstaking research, applying research instruments of contemporary social science.

What holds good of formal theories involving 'true' and 'false', holds good of the logical constants and the primitive terms of the so-called philosophical logics. In this talk I shall not elaborate upon the use of terms, but attack a broader subject, that of empirical components in argumentation analysis. In my view there is a startling difference in quality between the treatment of formal and empirical components of problems raised[1].

Empirical questions are largely 'solved' through appeal to intuitions of a low degree of testability. The terms 'true' and 'false' are used in argumentation, and one may try to single out their various usages by means of empirical research. In one analysis, I did not succeed in reducing the usages to less than 13 different kinds.

In what follows I shall mention some useful conceptualizations in argumentation research.

## 2. *'Argumentation analysis'*

This term may cover a large variety of approaches, but I shall confine myself to one kind of approach among the many. It is characterized primarily by a painstaking way of treating certain empirical questions that arise when one studies cases of explicit argumentation. Cases of explicit argumentation usually occur as parts of discussions and debates, sometimes of a rather polemical kind. In order to deal with these empirical questions scientifically, we must try to use history, psychology, sociology, political science, etc., as auxiliary disciplines, as well as common sense and what we experience in daily life. In empirical argumentation analysis, cases of argumentation are studied as acts or processes of communication between people and carefully recorded in observational journals. (Today televised debates furnish rich intersubjective material.)

The approach to argumentation analysis I shall talk about here specializes in investigating the superbly *open and deep* kind of argumentation. It should, in my opinion, characterize philosophical research. In philosophy the chain of arguments is never cut off for good where it is traditionally cut off, be it because nobody so far has asked further questions, or because practical people or scientists say it is pointless to continue.I am thinking here of chains, for instance, of the following kind: "Why do you hold that p?" --"Because q"; "Why do you hold that q?" --"Because r";... . The "Deep and Open" approach to argumentation legitimizes continuation of the chain as long as the questioner can clarify what it is that he asks us to answer. This characteristic sets the approach apart from psychological and sociological studies of communication, and also from most classical and modern studies of rhetorics and debate. Increased collaboration with other approaches is not only possible, however, but highly desirable.

The approach is different from, but of course not incompatible with those largely inspired by formal logic, such as that of Paul Lorenzen. An example of an argumentation rule of his approach: If a person says p & q, it is sufficient to refute p *or* q in order to refute him, but if he says p v q, one then has to refute *both* p and q. Empirical studies do not start with propositions, but with *utterances in concrete situations*. The functions of the utterances are normally complex, having relevant performative aspects, but careful analysis may result in 'destilling' p's and q's appropriate for formal treatment.

A pronounced empirical approach such as the one I am advocating does not exclude theory-construction. Botany is empirical yet contains, and also presupposes, theory-construction. Debates, perhaps even more than flowers, inspire deep reflection!

### 3. *Options in a clarification and assessment game*

One way of describing rules in use in discussion (here between two persons, A and B) that are intended *to clarify and to assess* arguments in terms of options, is as follows. ('T', 'U' stand for utterances in the form of declarative sentences.)

(1) A: T

(2) B: (2.a): Yes (2.b): No

(2.c): Please be more precise!

(2.d): Please be more understandable but within the framework of preciseness relations!

(2.e): Announce kind of claim. Three options: the sentence was meant:

1. Not entirely as a clarification-assess-

ment (but, e.g., as a somewhat performatory, persuasive, rhetorical, exclamatory, hortatory ... remark).

or: 2. As a theory-formulation; or as a factual, descriptive, observationally-true claim; or as a correctness claim; or as a theoretical acceptability claim; or ... .

or: 3. As a postulational contribution; as an invitation to accept a statement for the sake of the discussion.

(3) A: (3.a) as a reaction to (2.a): $T_1$
(a tentatively more precise formulation, put forward by A in order to test whether there is real agreement of some kind or other -- see Section 4).

(3.b) as a reaction to (2.b):

1. Pro-argument '$pro_1$'

or: 2. Tentative reformulation: U, where Syn(A, T, U) (i.e., U is synonymous with T for A)

or: 3. Tentative 'precization': $T_1$

⋮

(3.c) as a reaction to (2.c): $T_1$

...

From this kind of scheme it is clear that the options are many at each stage of a discussion. Furthermore, the number of 'correct' or constructible courses of discussion increases very rapidly with the number of stages. As early as stage (3), the number of possible discussion situations is perhaps of the same order as it would be in a game of chequers.

In the next section of this talk, I shall concentrate on the move "Please be more precise!", either as a move made by the receiver, or as a move by the speaker who makes his or her formulation more precise in order to test (i.e., confirm or disconfirm) an argument for agreement or disagreement.

## 4. *Analysis of agreement and pseudo-agreement*

Let us consider the following discussion, which is the shortest possible specimen of a class of very common discussions, to be called "discussions of type $D_1$" (with "$A_1$" and "$A_2$" used as values for the participant-variables "A" and "B"):

(1) $A_1$: The newspaper is thin today.

(2.a) $A_2$: Yes. (2.b) $A_2$: No.

(3) $A_1$: I mean, the newspaper has few pages today.

(4.a) $A_2$: I agree. I thought you meant that the newspaper contained little news.

(4.b) $A_2$: I disagree: the newspaper does *not* have few pages. I thought you meant that the newspaper contained little news.

Let me introduce three abbreviations:

$T_0$: The newspaper is thin today.
$T_1$: The newspaper has few pages today.
$T_2$: The newspaper contains little news today.

With "syn" for "is synonymous to", and "-T" for negation of T, the above discussion may be rendered as follows:

*Discussion, type $D_1$*

(1) $A_1$: $T_0$

(2.a) $A_2$: $T_0$ (2.b) $A_2$: $-T_0$

(3) $A_1$: $T_0$ syn $T_1$

(4.a) $A_2$: $T_1$, $T_0$ syn $T_2$ (4.b) $A_2$: $-T_1$, $T_0$ syn $T_2$

A person $A_1$ sends the declarative sentence $T_0$ to another person, the receiver $A_2$. $A_2$ sends back his utterance of agreement or disagreement with $T_0$. Concerning the verbal usages of $A_1$ and $A_2$, we know: For $A_1$, $T_0$ is synonymous with $T_1$, but not with $T_2$. For $A_2$, $T_0$ is synonymous with $T_2$, but not with $T_1$. It is reasonable to assume that, for each of them, $T_1$ as well as $T_2$ is more precise than $T_0$.

The following diagram is to be read horizontally, starting from above:

"If $A_1$ takes $T_1$ to be true (which he, as the sender, does in any case), and $A_2$ takes $T_1$ and $T_2$ to be true, then there is verbal agreement at (2.a) and real agreement at (4.a). If $A_2$ takes $T_1$ to be true and $T_2$ to be false, then there is verbal disagreement at (2.b) and real agreement at (4.a). Furthermore, there is verbal pseudo-disagreement at (2.b). If $A_2$ takes $T_1$ to be false and $T_2$ to be true, there is verbal agreement at (2.a) and real disagreement at (4.b). Furthermore, there is pseudo-agreement at (2.a). If $A_2$ ... "

| $A_1$ | $A_2$ | | Agreement-relation: | | |
|---|---|---|---|---|---|
| $T_1$ | $T_1$ | $T_2$ | verbal? | real? | pseudo? |
| t | t | t | a | a | |
| t | t | f | d | a | d |
| t | f | t | a | d | a |
| t | f | f | d | d | |

t - true
f - false
a - agreement
d - disagreement

Suppose this type-$D_1$ discussion has ended at step (4.a). Conclusion: There is real agreement between $A_1$ and $A_2$. *But only relative to step (4.a).* Let us suppose the discussion starts again, $A_1$ repeating $T_1$ as a step (5) and $A_2$ repeating $T_1$ as a step (6.a). After these moves, $A_1$ reveals a little more about what he means by $T_1$, and the discussion takes on the same color as before:

(7) $A_1$: $T_1$ syn $T_{11}$

(8.a) $A_2$: $T_{11}$, $T_1$ syn $T_{12}$ (8.b) $A_2$: $-T_{11}$, $T_1$ syn $T_{12}$

If this second instalment of the discussion ends at step (8.b), then it ends with real disagreement in relation to (8.b), and with pseudo-agreement in relation to steps (2.a) and (4.a).

*Example:*

(7) $A_1$: I mean, the newspaper *available here* today has few pages.

(8.b) $A_2$: I disagree. I thought you referred to the newspaper with today's *date* . (I got my copy in the city. It really has few pages.)

The diagrammatical representation is similar to the foregoing one:

| $A_1$ | $A_2$ | | Agreement-relation: | | |
|---|---|---|---|---|---|
| $T_{11}$ | $T_{11}$ | $T_{12}$ | verbal? | real? | pseudo? |
| t | t | t | a | a | |
| t | t | f | d | a | d |
| t | f | t | a | d | a |
| t | f | f | d | d | |

Discussions of type $D_1$ may continue indefinitely. As a consequence of the steps taken, agreements and disagreements will be realized, as follows:

| | |
|---|---|
| At the end of step (4.a), we may conclude: | there is real agreement between $A_1$ and $A_2$ about $T_0$. |
| At the end of step (8.b), we may conclude: | real disagreement about $T_0$; pseudo-agreement in relation to steps (2.a) and (4.a). |
| At the end of step (12.a), we may conclude: | real agreement about $T_0$; pseudo-disagreement in relation to step (8.b). |

At the end of step (16.b),
we may conclude: real disagreement about $T_0$; pseudo-agreement in relation to step (12.a).

At the end of every step (4i.a),
where i=1,3,5 ...,
we may conclude: real agreement about $T_0$.

At the end of every step (4j.b),
where j=2,4,6,...,
we may conclude: real disagreement about $T_0$.

From the above, we conclude that either 'real agreement' is to be understood as 'real agreement in relation to step x in an argumentation', or else real agreement is something unverifiable. *The 'relational real agreements' confirm an hypothesis about agreement; the 'relational real disagreements' disconfirm an hypothesis about agreement.* I.e., they yield confirming or disconfirming *instances* in relation to the working hypothesis. Analogously, 'pseudo-agreement' and 'pseudo-disagreement' are relational terms, too.

In so far as agreement is taken to be agreement about truth or falsity we may conclude: *The attribution of truth or falsity to something said in a discussion is in principle always ad hoc, preliminary, and tentative.*

If $A_2$ answers 'true' at steps (4.a) and (12.a) in our example, it does not preclude that he says 'false' at (8.b) and (16.b). A more vague, general conclusion is that verbal agreements and disagreements always remain essentially verbal. Agreement about *propositions* is never *reached* through argumentation, but remains a more or less well confirmed hypothesis.

## 5. *Degree of definiteness of intention (discrimination acuity) as a factor in argumentation*

The simplest way in which the *finite degree of the speaker's definiteness of intention* influences patterns of argumentation (e.g., with the $D_1$ pattern) runs as follows: At stage (2), participant B asks A whether by expression $T_0$ he means (the same as by expression) $T_1$ or (expression) $T_2$. At stage (3), A answers that he has not made, or that he does not make this distinction. B then stops the $D_1$-type discussion at stage (4), because if $T_1$ were meant his answer would be "Yes", whereas if $T_2$ were meant it would be "No". B may take the initiative in a new discussion: How would A justify not making the distinction?

In our example of a $D_1$-discussion (Section 4), $A_2$ may at step (4) say: "I did not think of the distinction between being physically thin and being journalistically thin!" $A_2$'s *degree of discrimination* stops short of a distinction between $T_1$ and $T_2$. $A_2$ may admit the relevance and validity of this distinction, and may take a stand on it. In that case the discussion may continue.

In many cases the instigator of a discussion *must* have thought about a certain distinction, we would say. Consider the following start of a discussion (not belonging to the class $D_1$):

| | | |
|---|---|---|
| (1) | The General: | Our glorious attack on the enemy starts tomorrow at 5 o'clock. |
| (2) | The Major : | Herr General, do you mean 5 o'clock in the morning or 5 o'clock in the evening? |
| (3a) | The General: | Alas, that distinction did not occur to me. |

The General's answer is clearly relevant for the communication intended by him. In other cases, the relevance of a question can be disputed; in still other cases, a question is clearly irrelevant. To give an example in which the relevance is disputable:

(3b) The General: Of course at 5 in the morning.
(4a) The Major : By "glorious", Herr General, do you mean...?
(5) The General: Irrelevant! (And irreverent?)

Here is a case of clear irrelevance:

(4b) The Major : Taking note of Einstein's rejection of absolute time, may I ask the General whether by "5 o'clock" he means ... ?
(5) The General: Irrelevant!

## 6. *The hermeneutical spiral as a factor in argumentation*

Suppose at step (2) B expresses disagreement with A, and that A then continues the debate, offering a first *pro-argument*. It sometimes happens that, in the light of that pro-argument, B changes his *interpretation* of the initial formulation, $T_0$, and now accepts it. The pro-argument then has a *retroactive effect*. Generally, every move of the participants may have retroactive effects.

In discussions of great and complex systems of thought, retroactive effects are indispensable and decisive. An all-embracing system of thought intends to color everything (including the very principles of argumentation). Starting from the sentence of the system that is offered as No. 1 (e.g., in a book), there is no way yet of explaining it adequately to the outsider. But going back to it again and again as one reads more of the text, one usually supposes that a (non-continuous) development of understanding will take place, which eventually will furnish a kind of understanding of the system as a whole (including sentence No.1). To illustrate that movement, a spiral serves us better than a circle.

Suppose a person starts reading the first three sentences of a text, namely T, U and V. He interprets them to mean $T_1$, $U_1$, $V_1$, and continues, now reading W. This makes him change his first interpretations of T, U and V into $T_2$, $U_2$, $V_2$:

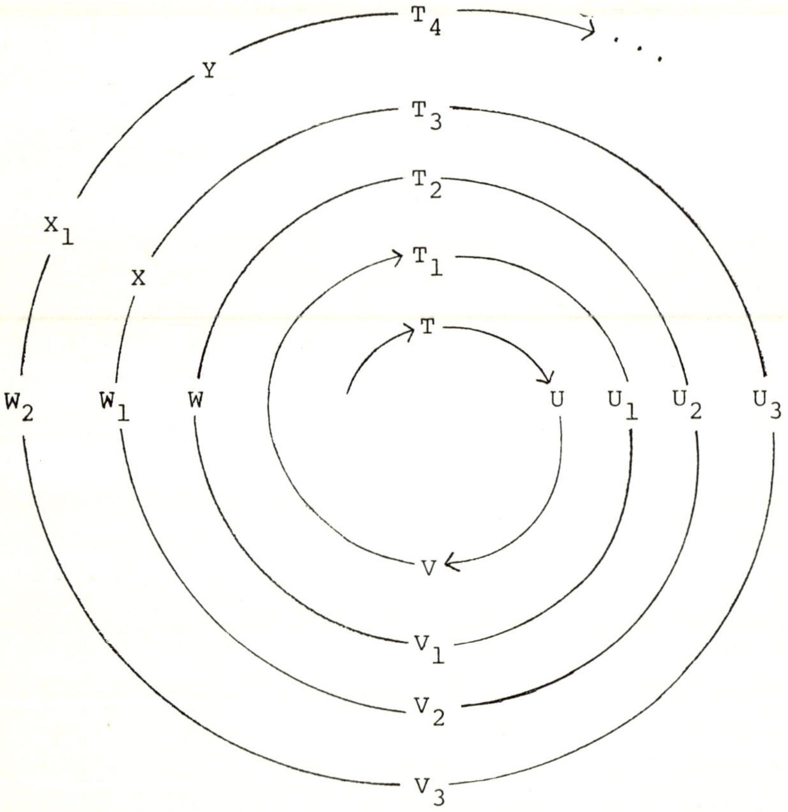


The new interpretations $T_2$, $U_2$, $V_2$, furnish a new context for W. Rereading this sentence, he now interprets it as synonymous to $W_1$. The next Sentence, X, may in turn occasion changes of interpretation, and so on.

In the case illustrated, the reader of the text always has to go all the way back to the beginning of the text after reading a new sentence. In such a case a spiral movement is created.

In the second part of my contribution to this volume (below p. 245), these principles are applied to a particular philosophical text, viz., that of Spinoza's *Ethics*.

## NOTES

(1) As an example of the neglect of empirical components in logic, let me recount an amusing incident that occurred at the congress of Unified Science convened by the logical empiricists at the Sorbonne in the thirties. As a central feature of that congress, the organizers had chosen the presentation of Alfred Tarski's Theory of Truth. This theory has an empirical component: the 'adequacy' of definitions in relation to common usage. While I had a large amount of material on that, only a small fraction of it could be said directly to confirm or corroborate the empirical pretensions of Tarski's paper. But the material was declared largely irrelevant because intuitive understanding was considered sufficient.

# DIE DIALOGISCHE BEGRÜNDUNG VON LOGIKKALKÜLEN

P. Lorenzen

## 1. *Drei Typen von Logikkalkülen*

Die modernen Logikkalküle gehen auf Frege zurück. Sie sind von Peano und Russell vereinfacht - und sie sind seit Hilbert Gegenstand einer mathematischen Disziplin, der Metamathematik. Da die Logik selbst aber bekanntlich aus der klassischen Antike stammt, möchte ich einleitend zu meinem Thema der dialogischen Begründung von Logikkalkülen auf die Entstehung der Logikkalküle aus der antiken Eristik über die Syllogistik und die Axiomatisierung der Geometrie eingehen.

Im Hauptteil werde ich kurz die drei Typen von Logikkalkülen, die von Hilbert, Gentzen und Beth vorgeschlagen worden sind, darstellen - und dann ausführlicher auf die dialogische Einführung logischer Partikeln und die Begründung allgemeiner Dialogregeln eingehen.

Die Erörterung der sog. semantischen Vollständigkeit von Logikkalkülen einschliesslich von Modalkalkülen wird den Schluss bilden.

Dieser Schluss soll in 45 Minuten erreicht werden - ich beginne daher schleunigst mit der historischen Einleitung, also mit dem 5. Jahrhundert ante, in Athen. Die redefreudigen Bürger dieser Stadt zahlten sogar Geld für Leute, die sich erboten, jeden, der bereit war, Fragen mit "ja" oder "nein" zu beantworten, zu widerlegen. Das waren Profis der eristischen Kunst.

Der Eristiker stellte eine Fangfrage A oder non-A. Der Antwortende durfte wählen. Hatte er gewählt, etwa $\neg A$, so musste er weitere Fragen dieser Art beantworten, bis der Eristiker eine Reihe von Antworten, etwa $B_1, \ldots, B_m$ zusammen hatte - und dann, unter dem Beifall des Publikums, feststellen konnte, dass wer $B_1, \ldots, B_m$ zugestimmt habe, nun auch A zustimmen *müsse*. Die Wahl von $\neg A$ war widerlegt.

Für uns stellt sich die Leistung des Eristikers so dar, dass er für Prämissen $B_1, \ldots, B_m$ Zustimmung gefunden hatte, aus denen A *logisch* folgt.

Es ist aber das Verdienst von Aristoteles gewesen, überhaupt zu bemerken, dass in dem Schlussakt dieser eristischen Dialoge, nämlich in dem scheinbar selbstverständlichen Zwang des Übergangs von $B_1, \ldots, B_m$ zu A, ein ganzes System von Regeln, die Syllogistik, steckte.

In moderner Zählung gibt es 21 syllogistische Regeln, die zwangsläufig von 2 Prämissen der Arten $S\,a\,P$, $S\,\tilde{a}\,P$, $S\,e\,P$, $S\,i\,P$ $S\,o\,P$, $S\,\tilde{o}\,P$ auf eine Konklusion dieser Art führen.

Die in der Stoa entwickelte Junktorenlogik ist uns nur in Bruchstücken erhalten - aber est steht fest, dass weder die aristotelische Syllogistik noch die stoische Junktorenlogik jemals ausreichend entwickelt waren, um die Beweise der geometrischen Lehrsätze aus den euklidischen Axiomen und Definitionen ernsthaft als rein logische Beweise zu führen.

Eine konsequente Axiomatisierung der Geometrie gibt es erst seit Pasch und Hilbert. Ihr liegt die Meinung zugrunde, dass ein Wirklichkeitsbereich, hier der Bereich der räumlichen Figuren, dadurch Gegenstand einer mathematischen Theorie würde, dass gewisse Grundbegriffe und Grundtheoreme über diesen Bereich auf nicht-mathematische Weise aufgestellt würden, z.B. durch die sog. Anschauung oder Erfahrung, alle weiteren Begriffe müssten dann aber explizit definiert, alle weiteren Theoreme logisch deduziert werden. Man nennt das die axiomatische Methode. Eine Kritik dieser Methode, vielmehr ihres Anspruchs, *die* Methode der mathematischen Erfassung von Wirklichkeitsbereichen zu sein, ist nicht Thema dieses Vortrags. Ich kann daher hier nur meinen tiefen Zweifel an der Vernunft dieses Anspruchs anmelden.

Die axiomatische Methode erfreut sich, wie Sie alle wissen, trotz solcher Zweifel von Konstruktivisten, allgemeiner Beliebtheit. Für die Logik ist wichtig, dass die axiomatische Methode die Logik als ein System von Deduktionsregeln voraussetzt: die Theoreme sollen ja aus den Axiomen nach *logischen* Regeln deduziert werden.

Nach der soweit durchaus zutreffenden Beobachtung von Th. Kuhn haben Wissenschaftler die Neigung, Methoden, die in einem Bereich als erfolgreich anerkannt sind, auch auf andere Bereiche zu übertragen. So ist auch die axiomatische Methode der Geometrie ein Paradigma geworden - und ist dabei sogar auf die Logik selbst übertragen worden. Das hat zur Formalisierung der Logik geführt, zu den Logikkalkülen.

Selbstverständlich wäre es sinnlos, die Theoreme der Logik aus gewissen Axiomen *logisch* deduzieren zu wollen. Das Paradigma wird daher so modifiziert, dass gewisse Theoreme der Logik als Axiome an den Anfang gestellt werden und alle übrigen daraus *formal* deduziert werden müssen. Der Ausdruck "formal" stammt zwar aus der Metaphysik, er meint hier aber nur, dass die Deduktionsregeln nicht auf die Bedeutung der Zeichen zurückgreifen dürfen: das Deduzieren soll ein blosses Operieren mit bedeutungslosen Schreibfiguren sein.

Was sind dabei die "Theoreme" der Logik? Das sind die "logischen Regeln", wie sie in den axiomatischen Theorien, z.B. der Geometrie, gebraucht werden. Die Logik hat die Aufgabe, diese Regeln in ein übersichtliches System zu bringen- *und* sie zu begründen. Die erste Aufgabe, die logischen Regeln in ein übersichtliches System zu bringen, wird durch die Aufstellung von Logikkalkülen gelöst. Die mathematische Logik beschränkt sich auf diese Aufgabe - sie überlässt das Begründungsproblem der sog. philosophischen Logik. Darauf werde ich, wie angekündigt, noch ausführlich eingehen. Zunächst muss ich kurz die drei wichtigsten Typen von Logikkalkülen - ich nenne sie nach Hilbert, Gentzen und Beth - vorführen.

Eine logische Regel regelt den Übergang von gewissen Aussagen zu einer weiteren Aussage: in der Eristik von den Prämissen $B_1$, ..., $B_m$ zu A.

Fassen wir die Prämissen konjunktiv zusammen: $B_1 \wedge B_2 \wedge \ldots \wedge B_m$, so haben wir einen Übergang von einer Aussage B zu einer Aussage A. Geschieht dieser Übergang nach einer logischen Regel, so sagt man: B impliziert A. Ich schreibe dafür $B \prec A$. Eine Aussage A, die auch ohne Prämissen logisch erschliessbar ist, heisst logisch wahr Mit $\gamma$ für eine leere Konjunktion, ist A also genau dann logisch wahr, wenn $\gamma \prec A$.

Hat man als logische Partikel den Subjunktor $\to$ zur Verfügung, so gilt $B \prec A$ genau dann, wenn $\gamma \prec B \to A$. Der Hilbertsche Typ von Logikkalkülen kapriziert sich darauf, die logisch wahren Aussagen als Theoreme eines Kalküls formal zu deduzieren.

Gewisse logisch-wahre Aussagen werden als "Axiome" an den Anfang gestellt und aus ihnen wird nur nach der modus-ponens-Regel deduziert: $B,, B \to A \Rightarrow A$. Für die Logik der Subjunktion allein lautet z.B. das Fregesche Axiomensystem

$$A \dot{\to} B \to A$$

$$C \to B \dddot{\to} C \dot{\to} B \to A \ddot{\to} C \to A$$

Es zeigt m.E. gerade durch seine Raffinesse am deutlichsten, dass der Hilbert-Typ keine sehr glückliche Lösung des Problems ist. Unter dem Schlagwort einer "natürlichen" Logik hat Gentzen vorgeschlagen, nicht die logisch-wahren Aussagen zu deduzieren, sondern die logischen Implikationen

$$B \prec A$$

Gentzen schreibt diese als *Sequenzen*, indem er teils B als Konjunktion darstellt

$$B_1 \wedge \ldots \wedge B_m \prec A,$$

teils zusätzlich A als Adjunktion darstellt

$$B_1 \wedge \ldots \wedge B_m \prec A_1 \vee \ldots \vee A_n$$

Gewisse Sequenzen werden als Axiome an den Anfang gestellt. Es genügt dafür z.B.

$$B \wedge c \prec c \vee A \text{ (mit Primaussagen c)}$$

Der Rest sind formale Deduktionsregeln, die von Sequenzen zu Sequenzen führen, z.B. für die Subjunktion

$$\frac{C \wedge B \prec A}{C \prec B \rightarrow A}$$

$$\frac{C \prec B \qquad C \wedge A \prec D}{C \dot{\wedge} B \rightarrow A \prec D}$$

Offen gestanden, kommt mir der Ausdruck "natürlich" gerade an dieser Stelle ziemlich gekünstelt vor. Die Pointe des Gentzenschen Typs von Logikkalkülen liegt aber darin, dass in ihren Regeln die Prämissen stets aus Teilformeln der in der Konklusion vorkommenden Formeln bestehen.

Diese Teilformeleigenschaft gilt nicht für die Schnittregel

$$\frac{C \prec B \qquad B \prec A}{C \prec A}$$

Der Gentzensche Hauptsatz besagt aber, dass diese Schnittregel zulässig ist, d.h. sie darf benutzt werden, *als ob* sie eine Kalkülregel wäre, sie gehört aber nicht zur Definition des Sequenzenkalküls.

Durch Beth ist es dann üblich geworden, diese Sequenzenkalküle zunächst upside-down zu lesen. Statt eine Ableitung zu suchen die oben von Axiomen ausgeht, und durch Deduktionsschritte nach unten schliesslich zu einer vorgegebenen Sequenz gelangt, geht man oben von der Sequenz aus und "entwickelt" nach unten bis man in allen Zweigen schliesslich zu Axiomen gelangt. Solche Entwicklungen lassen sich nach Beth bequemer als Tableaux schreiben. Statt von der Sequenz $B_1 \wedge \ldots \wedge B_m \prec A$ geht man in einem zweispaltigen Tableaux von der *Stellung*

$$\begin{array}{c||c} B_1 & \\ \vdots & \\ B_m & A \end{array}$$

aus. Jeder Entwicklungsschritt entwickelt dann nur *eine* dieser Formeln, die übrigen Formeln brauchen nicht wiederholt zu werden. Z.B. sind die Entwicklungsschritte für die Subjunktion jetzt

$$\begin{array}{c||c} \Gamma & B \to A \\ & \\ B & A \end{array}$$

wobei $\Gamma$ (statt C) für eine Spalte von Formeln steht und mit einer Verzweigung

$$\begin{array}{cc|c||c|c} \Gamma & (B \to A) & & D & \\ & & & & \\ & & A & B & \end{array}$$

$\Gamma\ (B \to A)$ steht hier für eine Spalte von Formeln, in der $B \to A$ vorkommt.

An die Stelle der Ableitbarkeit der Sequenz tritt jetzt die Abschliessbarkeit der Stellung: die Ausgangsstellung ist genau dann eine logische Implikation, wenn es *eine* Entwicklung gibt, die in *allen* Zweigen abgeschlossen ist. Ein Zweig heisst dabei abgeschlossen, wenn eine Primformel c sowohl links wie rechts von || auftritt. Das entspricht den "Axiomen"

$$B \wedge c \prec c \vee A$$

Für die Junktorenlogik erhält man durch diese Entwicklungskalküle bequeme Entscheidungsverfahren, für die Quantorenlogik einen bequemen Zugang zur sog. semantischen Vollständigkeit.

## 2. *Das Begründungsproblem*

Wie es in der mathematischen Logik üblich ist, kann man diese Typen von Logikkalkülen als bloss formale Varianten betrachten. Der Gentzensche Ausdruck "natürlich" beansprucht aber mehr. Im folgenden möchte ich zeigen, dass eine dialogische Begründung die Entwicklungskalküle tatsächlich auszeichnet - als "vernünftig", wie ich statt "natürlich" sagen möchte. Dazu muss als erstes gezeigt werden, wie man als "vernünftig" begründen kann, dass wir für die Formulierung von Aussagen (d.h. Sätzen, die als wahr behauptet werden können) überhaupt gewisse Partikel, eben die logischen Partikel, verwenden.

Klammert man sich an solche Wörter wie "vernünftig" und "begründen", so gibt es sofort tausend bildungssprachliche Argumente, dass man ohne Logik nichts "begründen" könne, dass man ohne Logik nichts als "vernünftig" auszeichnen könne.

Trotzdem erzeugen alle diese Argumente nur einen verbalen Nebel, der das Problem verschwinden lässt, nämlich das Problem eines schrittweise überprüfbaren Aufbaus unserer sprachlichen Mittel, mit denen wir - als Gebildete - so unermüdlich und beliebig (egal wofür, egal wogegen) argumentieren können.

Es gibt nur eine sprachfreie Basis, die als Ausgangspunkt eines solchen methodischen Aufbaus dienen kann: die Praxis unseres sprachfreien Handelns.

Im Handlungszusammenhängen kann jeder Normalsinnige lernen,

wie Elementarsätze, etwa der Form

$$N \pi P \quad \text{bzw.} \quad N \varepsilon Q$$

mit einem Eigennamen N, einem Tatwort P oder einem Dingwort Q und einer Kopula $\pi$ bzw. $\varepsilon$ (im Deutschen etwa: "tut" bzw. "ist") verwendet werden.

Diese Sätze werden exemplarisch mit den darin vorkommenden Wörtern gelernt. Es entsteht so eine Redepraxis, die aus dem Handlungszusammenhang "begründet" ist. Das nennt man nach Bühler eine *empraktische* Begründung. Nur durch Teilnahme an den Handlungen erwirbt man sich die dazu "passenden" Reden. Man lernt durch Übung was es heisst, solche Aussagen zu behaupten oder zu bestreiten, ihnen zuzustimmen oder sie abzulehnen (etwa durch Kopfnicken oder Kopfschütteln). Man führt einen Negator $\neg$ ein, um das Bestreiten einer Aussage a als Behauptung von $\neg$ a ausdrücken zu können.Dieser bis dahin bloss empraktisch eingeübte Gebrauch von Elementaraussagen wird ersichtlich von Person zu Person stark schwanken. Es empfiehlt sich daher, ihn zu normieren. Z.B. behauptet der eine dass ein Ding N eine "Fliege" sei, ein anderer "nennt" das einen "Käfer".

Viele Allsätze, die als Beispiele in der Syllogistik auftreten, lassen sich als Normierungen für solchen schwankenden Sprachgebrauch begründen. "Fliegen sind keine Käfer" hat die Form S e P, und ist zu lesen als das *Verbot*, einem Satz N $\varepsilon$ P zuzustimmen, wenn vorher dem Satz N $\varepsilon$ S zugestimmt wurde.

Entsprechend sind gewisse Allsätze der Form S a P begründbar als das *Verbot*, einen Satz N $\varepsilon$ P zu bestreiten, wenn vorher der Satz N $\varepsilon$ S behauptet wurde.

Anders ausgedrückt: die Übergangsregel N $\varepsilon$ S $\Rightarrow$ N $\varepsilon$ P führt zu einer unbestreitbaren Konklusion, *wenn* der Prämisse zugestimmt wurde. Solche Übergangsregeln, deren Konklusionen man zustimmen "muss", wenn man den Prämissen zugestimmt hat, sind noch keine logischen Regeln. Sie sind *vor*logisch, sie liefern aber eine Redepraxis, die - in etwas komplizierten Fällen - die Einführung von eigens für diese Redepraxis erfundenen Partikeln, den logischen Partikeln, rechtfertigt.

Die elementare Rechenpraxis liefert einen zweiten Bereich mit solchen Ubergangsregeln. In der einfachsten Notation I, II, III, .... der Zahlen geschieht das Addieren z.B. nach den folgenden Regeln

$$\frac{m + |}{m|}$$

$$\frac{m + n}{p} \Rightarrow \frac{m + n|}{p|}$$

Schon hier wird man kaum ohne Logik zurechtkommen, wenn man sich kritisch selber davon überzeugen will, dass für jedes nach diesen Regeln errechnete Resultat

$\vdash \frac{m + n}{p}$ (d.h. dass $\frac{m + n}{p}$ ableitbar ist)

stets auch $\vdash \frac{n + m}{p}$ gilt.

Schon zur Formulierung der *Zulässigkeit* der Regel

$$\frac{m + n}{p} \Rightarrow \frac{n + m}{p}$$

empfiehlt sich als erste logische Partikel ein Subjunktor $\rightarrow$. Die Behauptung $\vdash \frac{m + n}{p} \rightarrow \frac{n + m}{p}$ soll so verwendet werden, dass jedem Herausforderer (Opponenten), der $\vdash \frac{m + n}{p}$ beweisen kann, vom

Behauptenden (Proponenten) dann $\vdash \frac{n+m}{p}$ bewiesen werden soll.

### 3. *Empraktische Einführung der Verwendungsregeln*

Durch Allquantoren $\wedge$ lässt sich noch explizit machen, dass hier dem Opponenten die Wahl der Zahlen m, n, p erlaubt ist. Diese zunächst durch deontische Sätze der deutschen Sprache formulierten Verwendungsregeln für $\rightarrow$ und $\wedge$ sind aber selbstverständlich in einer einzuübenden Redepraxis unabhängig davon, ob man Deutsch versteht - und ob man insbesondere deontische Modalitäten versteht Man kann Redepraxis wie jedes sinnvolle Handeln allein durch Übung lernen: empraktisch.

Ublich ist an dieser Stelle der Hinweis darauf, dass Kinder Spielregeln, etwa für Halma, lernen können ohne schon deontische Sätze gelernt zu haben. Dieser Hinweis ist zwar richtig, aber insofern irreführend, weil er dazu verführt, die logischen Dialogregeln als blosse Spielregeln misszuverstehen. Logische Dialoge sind aber eine vernünftige Redepraxis - nur in den Schulen, einschliesslich der Hochschulen, werden daraus "Dialogspiele". Hat man es mit den (generellen) Subjunktionen zu den ersten logisch zusammengesetzten Aussagen gebracht - über die blosse Negation von Elementarsätzen hinaus - dann ist die Einführung der Konjunktionen und Adjunktionen leicht zu begründen. Liegen mehrere Subjunktionen mit gleichem Antecedens vor

$$B \rightarrow A_1$$
$$\vdots$$
$$B \rightarrow A_n$$

dann wäre es ersichtlich denkökonomisch, dafür

$$B \rightarrow A_1 \wedge \ldots \wedge A_n$$

schreiben zu können. Das erreicht man dadurch, dass die Konjunktion so eingeführt wird, dass der Proponent einer Konjunktion

$A_1 \wedge A_2$ nach Wahl des Opponenten sowohl $A_1$ als auch $A_2$ behaupten muss. Entsprechend lassen sich mehrere Subjunktionen mit gleichem Sukzedens $B_1 \rightarrow A, \ldots, B_m \rightarrow A$ durch Einführung des Adjunktors v zusammenfassen zu $B_1 \vee \ldots \vee B_m \rightarrow A$. Für v sieht die definierende Verwendungsregel so aus

| O | P | |
|---|---|---|
| | $B_1 \vee B_2$ | |
| ? | $B_i$ | $(i = 1, 2)$ |

mit einem i nach Wahl des Proponenten P. In dieser Notation schreiben sich die dialogischen Definitionen $\wedge$ bzw. $\rightarrow$ folgendermassen

| | | | |
|---|---|---|---|
| | | $A_1 \wedge A_2$ | |
| $?_1$ | $?_2$ | $A_1$ | $A_2$ |

mit einer Verzweigung durch die Wahlerlaubnis des Opponenten bzw.

| | |
|---|---|
| | $B \rightarrow A$ |
| B ? | A |

Die Negation beliebiger Aussagen wird dialogisch definiert durch:

| | |
|---|---|
| | $\neg A$ |
| A ? | |

Schliesslich werden - bei Benutzung von Variablen - die Quantoren dialogisch durch

| | | | | | |
|---|---|---|---|---|---|
| | | | $\bigwedge_x A(x)$ | | |
| 1 ? | 2 ? | .... | A (1) | A (2) | .... |

mit evtl. unendlicher Verzweigung

und durch

| | | |
|---|---|---|
| | $\bigvee_x B(n)$ | |
| ? | $B(n)$ | $(n = 1, 2, \ldots)$ |

mit einem n nach Wahl des Proponenten definiert.

Die dialogische Definition der 3 Junktoren, der 2 Quantoren und des Negators geschieht stets durch je *eine* Verwendungsregel. Diese 6 Regeln lassen sich aus jeder Redepraxis begründen, die überhaupt Übergangsregeln benutzt - solche Redepraxen wiederum werden aus sprachfreien Handlungszusammenhängen begründet.

Es fällt demgegenüber auf, dass der Sequenzenkalkül für jede logische Partikel genau 2 Kalkülregeln hat. Diese Verdoppelung tritt dadurch ein, dass bei mehrfach zusammengesetzten Aussagen der Dialog nicht durch eine Zeile zu Ende kommt. Durch Subjunktion und Negation werden dann auch vom Opponenten zusammengesetzte Aussagen behauptet. Der Opponent wird also die Rolle des Proponenten übernehmen - dadurch entsteht für jede Partikel eine zweite dialogische Verwendung, wenn wir notieren, wie der *Proponent* zur Verteidigung seiner Behauptung ziehen muss.

Ich nehme den Fall der Negation als den einfacheren voraus, weil dann, wenn der Opponent nur aufgrund von Negationen seinerseits Behauptungen übernimmt, der Proponent nicht zugleich eine neue Behauptung - wie bei der Subjunktion - übernimmt. Ohne Subjunktionen findet durch Negationen ein reiner Rollentausch statt. Der Dialog sieht daher nach einer negierten These des Proponenten so aus

$$\begin{array}{r||l} A_1 \wedge A_2 & ?_i \\ A_i & \end{array} \qquad\qquad (i = 1, 2)$$

bzw.

$$\begin{array}{c||c} B_1 \vee B_2 & ? \\ B_1 \mid B_2 & \mid \end{array}$$

mit einer Verzweigung.

Für die Quantoren als "grosse" Konjunktoren bzw. Adjunktoren erhalten wir entsprechend

$$\begin{array}{c|c} \bigwedge_x A(x) & ?\, n \\ A(n) & \end{array} \qquad (n = 1, 2, \ldots)$$

bzw.

$$\begin{array}{c|c} \bigvee_x B(x) & ? \\ B(1) \mid B(2) \mid \ldots. & \mid \quad \mid \ldots. \end{array}$$

mit evtl. unendlicher Verzweigung.
Für eine Negation links von || ensteht

$$\begin{array}{c|c} \neg A & A\ ? \end{array}$$

Der Dialog für beliebig zusammengesetzte Aussagen - vorausgesetzt, dass keine Subjunktionen vorkommen - ist durch diese Entwicklungsschritte vollständig geregelt.

Nach K. Lorenz heissen diese Dialoge "streng". Eine These heisst streng-wahr, wenn sie in einem strengen Dialog so verteidigt werden kann, dass sie schliesslich in allen Zweigen zu wahren Primaussagen rechts von || oder falschen Primaussagen links von || führt.

## 4. *Materiale Dialoge. Semantik*

Von *formaler* Logik ist hier für die Einführung der logischen Partikeln noch nicht die Rede. Wir haben es zunächst mit *materialen* Dialogen um logisch zusammengesetzte Aussagen zu tun. Die Primaussagen kommen aus einer vorlogischen Redepraxis.

Die strengen Dialoge reformulieren in einem pragmatischen Kontext das, was in den üblichen Lehrbüchern als "Semantik" auftritt, nämlich dass z.B. für die Konjunktionen

$A_1 \wedge A_2$ genau dann wahr ist, wenn $A_1$ *und* $A_2$ wahr ist
$A_1 \wedge A_2$ genau dann falsch ist, wenn $A_1$ *oder* $A_2$ falsch ist

Während diese Semantik aber voraussetzt, dass man metasprachlich schon "und" und "oder" zur Verfügung hat, entfällt der zirkelhafte Vorgriff auf eine Metasprache bei den dialogischen Definitionen - die dialogische Praxis ist demgegenüber eine neue, durch Übung erwerbbare Praxis, die zur Redepraxis der Elementaraussagen hinzukommt. Wie ich hoffe, vorhin überzeugend nachgewiesen zu haben, ist der erste Schritt, durch den eine elementare Redepraxis sinnvoll erweitert wird, die Hinzunahme von Übergangsregeln überhaupt. In einem zweiten Schritt begründen solche Regeln dann die Einführung des Subjunktors als erster logischer Partikel nach dem Negator. Die kleinen und grossen Konjunktoren und Adjunktoren sind demgegenüber sekundär.

## 5. *Erweiterungen der strengen Dialoge. Liberalisierungen*

Deshalb müssen die strengen Dialoge um die Subjunktion erweitert werden. Definiert man, wie in der klassischen Logik üblich $B \rightarrow A$ durch $\neg B \vee A$, so verschwindet diese Aufgabe zwar, sie wird aber nicht gelöst.In der klassischen Semantik tritt dieses Problem nicht auf, weil man zu ihr stets das tertium non datur als Dogma hinzufügt: Die Behauptung, dass für jede materiale Aussage entweder A oder $\neg$ A streng-wahr sei, ist ersichtlich nichts als ein Dogma. Bei bloss junktorenlogischer Zusammensetzung ist das tertium non datur zwar beweisbar, wenn man sich - was durchaus vernünftig ist - auf entscheidbare Primaussagen beschränkt. Mit Quantifizierungen über unendliche Variabilitätsbereiche bricht dieser Beweis aber, wie zuerst Brouwer 1907 gesehen hat, zusammen.

Diese Kritik am tertium non datur lässt schon erwarten, dass die Hinzunahme des Subjunktors zu den strengen Dialogen auf die Kontroverse zwischen effektiver (intuitionistischer) und klassischer Logik führen wird.

Für die strengen Dialoge, wie sie hier definiert sind, gibt es keine Stellungen $B \,||\, A$

in denen links *und* rechts von || Formeln stehen. Daher wird die dialogische Definition des Subjunktors:

| | | |
|---|---|---|
| | \|\| | $B \rightarrow A$ |
| B ? | \|\| | A |

erst dann anwendbar, wenn geregelt wird, wie solche Dialoge fortgeführt werden sollen.

In dem kürzlich erschienenen Buch "Dialogische Logik" ist dokumentiert, wie K. Lorenz und ich uns etwa 15 Jahre darum bemüht haben, eine "vernünftige" allgemeine Dialogregel zu finden.

Rückblickend kann ich sagen, dass wir dabei viele Wege versucht haben, die sich als Holzwege herausgestellt haben - aber dass sich schliesslich ein Weg gezeigt hat, der, jedenfalls nach unserer Meinung, für jeden gangbar ist.

Der Grundgedanke ist jetzt sogar ganz einfach zu formulieren: weil die strengen Dialoge so streng sind, dass in ihnen noch nicht einmal Subjunktionen zu verwenden sind, muss eine allgemeine Dialogregel den bisherigen strengen (zu strengen) Dialogverlauf *liberalisieren*.

Im strengen Dialog antwortet jeder Zug immer auf den unmittelbar vorgehenden Zug des Dialogpartners, sei es als Angriff (mit einem Fragezeichen) oder als Verteidigung auf einen Angriff. Diese Bindung an den unmittelbar vorgehenden Zug soll liberalisiert werden.

Diese Forderung ist ersichtlich sehr unbestimmt. Um eine Auswahl unter den Liberalisierungen treffen zu können, scheinen mir folgende Zusatzforderungen "vernünftig" zu sein:

1. Die Liberalisierung soll *konservativ* sein, d.h. alle Aussagen, die streng-wahr sind, sollen verteidigbar bleiben

2. Die Liberalisierung soll *konsistent* sein, d.h. für keine Aussage soll zugleich A und $\neg$A verteidigbar werden.

Es sei hierzu bemerkt, dass die strenge Dialogregel trivialerweise in diesem Sinne konsistent ist: Ist A verteidigbar, so ist $\neg$A nicht verteidigbar, denn der Opponent braucht ja nur die Verteidigung von A zu übernehmen.Hier wird der Symmetrie der strengen Dialoge für Proponent und Opponent benutzt. Diese Symmetrie beruht darauf, dass subjunktionsfreie Thesen des Proponenten immer nur zu weiteren Thesen (für den Proponenten oder Opponenten) führen. Schon die eristische Ausgangsituation von Dialogen war aber die, dass der Opponent gewissen Sätzen als *Hypothesen* zustimmt - die Regeln für die logischen Partikeln dienen dann dazu, von den Hypothesen auf eine These zu schliessen (im eristischen Fall: auf die Negation der vom Antwortenden gewählten These). Die strenge Dialogregel regelt nicht, wie Dialoge, die von Stellungen mit Hypothesen und einer These ausgehen

$$\begin{array}{c||c} B_1 & \\ \vdots & \\ B_m & A \end{array}$$

sich entwickeln sollen.

Für den Opponenten bleibt es dabei, dass er nur auf eine These zu antworten hat. Für den Proponenten muss man dagegen die Dialogregel so liberalisieren, dass er auch vorgehende Züge des Opponenten angreifen darf.

Das legt nahe, für den Opponenten die strenge Regel beizubehalten, dass er nur auf den unmittelbar vorhergehenden Zug des Proponenten (durch Angriff oder Verteidigung) antworten darf.

Diese Regelung liegt nicht nur nahe, sie hat darüber hinaus den Vorteil, dass dadurch die Forderung der Konservativität sofort erfüllt ist: liberalisiert man die Dialogregel nur für den Proponenten (d.h. erlaubt man nur ihm *mehr* Züge als im strengen Dialog), dann kann er jede These, die er streng verteidigen könnte, a fortiori auch bei einer liberalen Regelung verteidigen.

## 6. *Die effektive Dialogregel*

Die einfachste Liberalisierung, die dem Proponenten Rückgriffe gestattet, ist nun diejenige, die ihm *beliebige* Rückgriffe gestattet. Diese allgemeine Dialogregel, die dem Proponenten bei jedem Zug gestattet, eine beliebige vorhergehende Aussage des Opponenten *anzugreifen*, sei die *effektive* Dialogregel genannt. Es wird sich herausstellen, dass die effektiven Dialoge genau zur intuitionistischen Logik führen - ich vermeide den Ausdruck "intuitionistisch" nur deshalb, weil ich zur Begründung dieser Dialogregel *nicht* auf die Gründe zurückgreife, die Brouwer und Heyting für die intuitionistische Logik benutzt haben.

In effektiven Dialogen ist eine Subjunktion folgendermassen zu behandeln. Tritt sie als These auf,so haben wir als dialogische Definition von $\rightarrow$

| | |
|---|---|
| $\neg$ | $B \rightarrow A$ |
| $B$ ? | $A$ |

Tritt sie als Hypothese auf

| | |
|---|---|
| $\ulcorner (B \rightarrow A)$ | $D$ |

so darf der Opponent nach dem Angriff des Proponenten (B ?) wählen, ob er A behaupten will oder B angreifen. Das führt zu der Verzweigung

| | | | |
|---|---|---|---|
| $\ulcorner (B \rightarrow A)$ | | | $D$ |
| | $A$ | $B$ ? | |

also genau zu der Bethschen Form der Regel des "natürlichen" Sequenzenkalküls für $\rightarrow$.

## 7. *Das Problem der Konsistenz. Schnittregel*

Für die dialogische Begründung fehlt aber noch der entscheidende Schritt. Da nämlich die Symmetrie zwischen Proponent und Opponent aufgehoben ist, ist die Konsistenz nicht mehr trivial. Es muss jetzt erst bewiesen werden, dass für eine effektiv-verteidigbare These A niemals zugleich $\neg$ A effektiv-verteidigbar ist. Dies ergibt sich nicht mehr daraus, dass der Opponent für die Hypothese A einfach die Verteidigungsstrategie des Proponenten für die These A übernehmen könnte - der Opponent hat ja nicht die Freiheiten der Angriffswiederholung, die der Proponent im effektiven Dialog hat.

Im Gegensatz zum Intuitionismus muss in der dialogischen Begründung die Konsistenz der effektiven Dialogregel bewiesen werden Das geschieht durch eine Variante des Gentzenschen Hauptsatzes: die Regel

$$\Gamma \,\|\, B,\ \Gamma_B \,\|\, A \Rightarrow \Gamma \,\|\, A$$

ist für die materialen effektiven Dialoge zulässig. Diese Schnitt-regel enthält für das leere System $\Gamma$ und fur $\lambda$ (falsum) statt A den Spezialfall

$$\|\, B \ ,\quad B \,\|\, \lambda \Rightarrow \ \|\, \lambda$$

d.h. wären B und $\neg$ B effektiv-verteidigbar, dann auch jede Elementaraussage. Also sind niemals B und $\neg$ B zugleich effektiv- wahr.

Auf den Beweis dieses Schnittsatzes möchte ich hier nicht eingehen, er benötigt in BI 700 zwei Seiten. Es scheint mir wichtiger zu sein, den Versuch zu machen, den Streit zwischen Intuitionisten und Klassikern dadurch zu beenden, dass ich nach dieser dialogischen Begründung der effektiven Dialoge *auch* für eine klassische Dialogregelung plädiere.

Durch die Zulassung von Subjunktionen treten Hypothesen auf der Seite des Opponenten auf, während gleichzeitig auch eine neue

These auftritt. Die Angriffserlaubnis auf diese Hypothesen vor Verteidigung der These gehört - so kann man sagen - zum Sinn der Subjunktion. Dass die effektive Dialogregel zusätzlich beliebige Wiederholungen dieser Angriffe erlaubt, folgt nicht zwingend - ist m.E. aber dadurch gerechtfertigt, dass sich die Konsistenz auch für diese einfachste Liberalisierung der Angriffserlaubnis beweisen lässt. Das Faktum, dass die effektive Logik schon als "intuitionistische" ohne diese dialogische Begründung entstanden war, scheint mir auch ein Hinweis auf die Vernünftigkeit dieser Dialogregel zu sein.

## 8. *Die klassische Dialogregel*

Nichtsdestotrotz ist nichts gegen die Frage einzuwenden, warum man sich denn bei der Liberalisierung des Proponenten auf die Erlaubnis von *Angriffs*wiederholungen beschränke, man könne doch dem Proponenten die Wiederholung beliebiger Antworten, also von Angriffen *und* Verteidigungen, erlauben - falls diese stärkere Liberalisierung auch noch konsistent ist.

Das ist in der Tat so - eine allgemeine Dialogregel, die dem Proponenten jederzeit erlaubt, nicht nur frühere Aussagen des Opponenten anzugreifen, sondern sich auch gegen frühere Angriffe zu verteidigen, eine solche Dialogregel ist ebenfalls konsistent. Diese Dialogregel heisse die klassische Dialogregel, weil sie - wie sich herausgestellt hat - genau die klassische Logik liefert. Der Konsistenzbeweis kann wieder durch einen Schnittsatz geliefert werden.

Über die strenge Wahrheit (Verteidigbarkeit) hinaus, haben wir damit zwei weitere Wahrheitsbegriffe (Verteidigbarkeiten) für logisch-zusammengesetzte Aussagen begründet: die effektive und die klassische Wahrheit (Verteidigbarkeit).
Die effektive ist die fundamentalere: Was effektiv-wahr ist, ist auch klassisch-wahr - die Umkehrung gilt nicht.

Die klassischen Verteidigungen benutzen eine zusätzliche Liberalisierung der allgemeinen Dialogregel. Diese zusätzliche Liberalisierung lässt sich bei Beibehaltung der effektiven Dialogregel auch dadurch erreichen, dass man zusätzliche Hypothesen erlaubt. Hierüber gilt der einfache Satz, dass eine Stellung

$$\ulcorner \;\Big\| \; A$$

genau dann klassisch-verteidigbar ist, wenn der *effektive* Dialog, der zu jeder These des Proponenten, angefangen mit A, eine entsprechende Stabilitätshypothese $\neg\neg A \rightarrow A$ hinzunimmt, gewinnbar ist.

Ist nämlich im effektiven Dialog eine Stellung

$$\begin{array}{c|c} \ulcorner & A \\ & \vdots \\ & B \end{array}$$

erreicht, und möchte der Proponent nach *klassischer* Erlaubnis seine These A wiederholen (damit er dann anschliessend eine Verteidigung von A wiederholen kann), so darf er dies *effektiv* tun, wenn die Stabilitätshypothese $\neg\neg A \rightarrow A$ hinzugefügt wird

$$\begin{array}{c|c} \ulcorner & \\ \neg\neg A \rightarrow A & A \end{array}$$

Der *effektive* Dialog spielt sich dann so ab

$$\begin{array}{rl||ll} & \ulcorner & & \\ \neg\neg A \rightarrow A & & & A \\ & \multicolumn{1}{|l||}{A} & \neg\neg A & \multicolumn{1}{|l}{} \\ \neg A & \multicolumn{1}{|l||}{} & A & \multicolumn{1}{|l}{} \\ & \multicolumn{1}{|l||}{} & \vdots & \multicolumn{1}{|l}{} \\ & \multicolumn{1}{|l||}{} & B & \multicolumn{1}{|l}{} \end{array}$$

Der rechte Zweig ist trivialerweise abgeschlossen, der linke Zweig kann vom Proponenten jetzt mit A fortgesetzt werden, weil A als Angriff auf $\neg$ A *effektiv* erlaubt ist.

Mir scheint es berechtigt zu sein, dass man aufgrund dieses einfachen Zusammenhangs sagt, dass die klassischen Dialoge nur eine - gelegentlich zweckmässige - Variante der effektiven Dialoge sind. Insbesondere ist die klassische Dialogregel stets dann zweckmässig, wenn alle vorkommenden Aussagen stabil sind, d.h. wenn $\neg \neg A \rightarrow A$ effektiv-wahr ist.

Wie man schon seit den Zeiten weiss, als Gödel seine berühmten Beweise führte, sind alle logisch-zusammengesetzten Aussagen stabil, wenn sie logisch aus stabilen Primaussagen *ohne* Adjunktionen zusammengesetzt sind. Eine einfache Uminterpretation (statt $B_1 \vee B_2$ liest man $\neg . \neg B_1 \wedge \neg B_2 .$, statt $\bigvee_x B(x)$ liest man $\neg \bigwedge_x \neg B(x)$ ) genügt also schon, um jede klassisch-wahre Aussage zu einer effektiv-wahren Aussage zu machen.

Von Gödel wurde diese Uminterpretation dazu benutzt, um zu zeigen, dass die Konsistenz der effektiven (intuitionistischen) Logik genau so "unbewiesen" (bedenklich, zweifelhaft - oder wie immer man sich ausdrückte) sei, wie die der klassischen. Jetzt aber liefert diese Uminterpretation einen trivialen Konsistenzbeweis der klassischen Dialoge, indem man sich auf den Konsistenzbeweis (via Schnittsatz) der effektiven Dialoge stützt.

## 9. *Die Beziehung materialer Dialoge zu Logikkalkülen*

Es bleibt nach dieser Begründung allgemeiner Dialogregeln daher nur eines zu klären: in welcher Beziehung stehen die hier betrachteten materialen Dialoge zu den Logikkalkülen, also zur formalen Logik.

Zu den strengen Dialogen gibt es keine zugehörigen "strengen" Logikkalküle - das wird sofort einsichtig, wenn wir uns vergegenwärtigen, wie man von den effektiven Dialogen zu einer (effektiven) formalen Logik kommt. Das muss - so will mir scheinen - schon

Aristoteles gesehen haben, obwohl sich das aus den Texten kaum zwingend herauslesen lassen wird. Aber er hat doch gesehen, dass ein als Opponent Antwortender, der Sa M und Ma P zugestimmt hatte, auch Sa P zustimmen "musste", ganz gleichgültig, welche Terme S und P das nun waren - und obwohl er zu Anfang des Streites die These ¬ S a P, also S o P, aufgestellt haben mochte. Dieser Zwang ist dialogisch leicht zu begründen.

Abgesehen von einem Allquantor hat S a P die Form einer Subjunktion. Schreiben wir s bzw. p für x ε S bzw. x ε P, so haben wir die folgende Dialogstellung (mit m für x ε M)

$$\begin{array}{c||c} s \to m & \\ m \to p & s \to p \end{array}$$

und dazu die folgende effektive Entwicklung

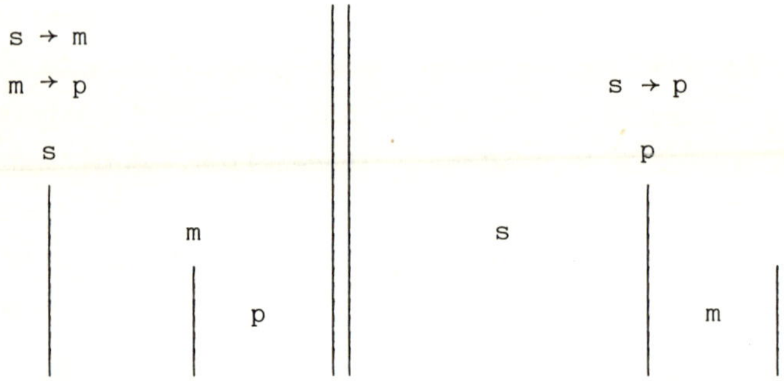

In allen drei Zweigen haben wir dabei eine Stellung

$$\begin{array}{c||c} \ulcorner & \\ c & c \end{array}$$

erreicht, in der links und rechts *dieselbe* Primaussage auftritt. Eine solche Stellung heisse formal-abgeschlossen.

Was Aristoteles gesehen haben wird, ist nun dieses: eine formal-abgeschlossene Stellung ist immer gewonnen. Denn ob c nun wahr oder falsch ist, in beiden Fällen steht entweder rechts von || eine wahre Formel oder links von || eine falsche.

Bei Dialogstellungen, die so verteidigt werden können, dass sie schliesslich in *allen* Zweigen formal-abgeschlossen sind, sagen wir daher, dass die Hypothesen (als Prämissen) die These (als Konklusion) *logisch* implizieren. Das ist die dialogische Definition der logischen Implikation.

Ist eine These ohne Hypothesen formal-abschliessbar,so heisst sie logisch-wahr.

Da wir zunächst effektive Dialoge betrachten, haben wir genauer die effektive logische Implikation und die effektive logische Wahrheit definiert. Diese Definition ist auf strenge Dialoge nicht anwendbar. Aristoteles hat auch schon gesehen, dass die Untersuchung der logischen Implikation und der logischen Wahrheit jetzt zweckmässigerweise mit Formeln - statt mit materialen Aussagen - weitergeführt wird.

Wir nehmen a, b, c ... daher jetzt als Primformeln. Aus ihnen werden weitere Formeln A, B, ... mit den logischen Partikeln zusammengesetzt. Von der materialen Wahrheit oder Falschheit wird nicht mehr geredet - es genügt, die formale Abgeschlossenheit in allen Zweigen zu erreichen.

Z.B. können wir jetzt beweisen, dass ¬ ¬ a → a *nicht* effektiv-logisch wahr ist (sondern nur klassisch-logisch wahr)

| | |
|---|---|
| | ¬ ¬ a → a |
| ¬ ¬ a | a |
| | ¬ a |
| a | λ |

Damit ist die Stellung

| | |
|---|---|
| ¬ ¬ a | |
| a | λ |

erreicht, die keineswegs formal-abgeschlossen ist.

Nur wenn – wie klassisch erlaubt ist – das a der zweiten Zeile wiederholt werden darf, entsteht eine formal-abgeschlossene Stellung.

Beim Auftreten von Quantoren in den materialen Dialogen müssen für den Übergang zur formalen Logik auch noch die Konstanten (z.B. in der Arithmetik die Zahlzeichen) durch Variable ersetzt werden. Im materialen Dialog lautet die Entwicklung für einen Allsatz als These

$$\ulcorner \quad \left\| \begin{array}{l|l|l} \bigwedge_x \; A(x) & & \\ A(1) & A(2) & \ldots . \end{array} \right.$$

mit einer evtl. unendlichen Verzweigung.

Statt der Konstanten benutzen wir freie Variable. Lässt sich die Dialogstellung

$$\ulcorner \, \| \; A(y)$$

mit einer Variablen y, die weder in $\ulcorner$ noch in $\bigwedge_x A(x)$ auftritt – die also "neu" ist, wie man sagt – in allen Zweigen formal abschliessen, dann lassen sich auch die evtl. unendlichen vielen Zweige im materialen Dialog formal abschliessen: man braucht nur y sukzessive durch alle Konstanten zu ersetzen. An der formalen Abgeschlossenheit ändert sich durch diese Ersetzung nichts, weil diese Ersetzung weder $\ulcorner$ noch $\bigwedge_x A(x)$ verändert – 'y' ist ja neu.

Seit Gödel wissen wir auch, dass dieser Zusammenhang nicht umkehrbar ist. Ist $\ulcorner \, \| \; A(n)$ für alle n abschliessbar, so braucht $\ulcorner \, \| \; A(y)$ mit einer freien Variable y deshalb nicht abschliessbar zu sein. Das hätte man eigentlich auch nicht erwarten sollen – aber faktisch kam die Gödelsche ω-Unvollständigkeit 1931 sehr überraschend.

Erst durch die Ersetzung der materialen Quantorenschritte durch formale Quantorenschritte (mit Variablen statt Konstanten) entstehen Logikkalküle. Es gibt nur noch uninterpretierte Primformeln a, b, ...

a x, b y, ...

a x y, ...

...

*und* es gibt keine unendlichen Verzweigungen mehr.

Die Entwicklung einer Stellung bis zur formalen Abgeschlossenheit in allen Zweigen ist, wenn überhaupt, in endlich vielen Schritten erreichbar.

Wir haben jetzt genau den effektiven (intuitionistischen) Beth-Kalkül vor uns, der - upside down gelesen - ein Gentzenscher Kalkül wird. Die Hilbert-Kalküle sind dann nur unzweckmässige Varianten dieses Sequenzenkalküls.

Der Ubergang von den materialen klassischen Dialogen zu klassischen Logikkalkülen geht genau entsprechend vor sich. Alle Kalküle sind in dieser dialogischen Begründung durch den Schnittsatz als konsistent bewiesen. Die Konsistenz ist dabei definiert als materiale Konsistenz: eine logische Implikation führt bei jeder Interpretation der Formeln stets von material-wahren Aussgane zu material-wahren Aussagen. Eine logische Wahrheit ist bei jeder Interpretation stets eine material wahre Aussage. Diese Konsistenz (Korrektheit oder soundness) gilt sowohl für die effektiven wie für die klassischen Dialoge. Die Konsistenz stützt sich nicht auf Intuitionen oder Plausibilitäten, sondern auf die dialogischen Definitionen der logischen Partikel. Für die allgemeine Dialogregel wird die Konsistenz durch einen Schnittsatz bewiesen. Der Ubergang zur formalen Logik benutzt dann nur die Trivialitäten, dass (1) die formal-abgeschlossenen Stellungen stets material-abgeschlossen sind und dass (2) die formale Abschliessbarkeit mit formalen Quantorenschritten stets die formale Abschliessbarkeit mit materialen Quantorenschritten ergibt.

## 10. *Zur Frage der sog. Vollständigkeit*

Es bleibt nur übrig, die seit Gödel übliche Umkehrung zu untersuchen, die sog. Vollständigkeit. Wenn eine Formel bei jeder Interpretation z.B. effektiv-wahr ist, wird sie dann auch effektiv-logisch wahr sein? Das ist eine merkwürdige Frage.

Die Entstehung dieser Frage ist trotzdem leicht verständlich, wenn man von Logikkalkülen des Hilbert-Typs ausgeht (und das war bei Gödel noch der Fall). Man ist dann, z.B. für die effektive Logik nur intuitiv davon überzeugt, dass die aufgestellten "Axiome" des Logikkalküls material konsistent (korrekt) sind. Im Falle der klassischen Junktorenlogik kann man diese materiale Konsistenz allerdings durch die Interpretation mit Wahrheitswerten beweisen. Für die klassische Quantorenlogik beruft man sich aber schon wieder auf Intuition, auf die klassische Intuition - man benutzt nämlich die klassische Quantorenlogik auf der Metastufe.

Nun ja, wie auch immer man zu der Meinung kommt, die Axiome seien "korrekt" (sound) - es bleibt die selbstverständliche Frage, ob man auch hinreichend viele Axiome aufgestellt habe, so dass *alle* logischen Wahrheiten nach der Schlussregel des modus ponens aus den Axiomen deduzierbar seien. Hat man vielleicht ein oder gar mehrere Axiome vergessen? Das ist der Ursprung der Frage nach der Vollständigkeit.

Mit der dialogischen Begründung der Logikkalküle wird diese Frage aber obsolet. Jede logische Partikel wird ja durch eine dialogische Definition eingeführt - und nach Begründung der materialen allgemeinen Dialogregeln werden formale Dialoge mit ihrer formalen Abgeschlossenheit als zweckmässige Instrumente für die Untersuchung materialer Dialoge definiert.

Logisch-wahre Formeln sind per definitionem diejenigen, die im Beth-Kalkül abschliessbar sind. Dass man etwas von der materialen Wahrheit verliert, wenn man zur bloss formalen Wahrheit über-geht, das zeigt die Unvollständigkeit in der Arithmetik.

Die sogenannte semantische Frage nach der Vollständigkeit, ob nämlich - jetzt etwa für den klassischen Fall - eine Formel, die bei *jeder* Interpretation klassisch wahr ist, auch klassisch logisch-wahr ist, diese Frage bleibt merkwürdig. Wie will man denn je wissen, dass eine Formel bei jeder Interpretation wahr ist? Selbst wenn man sich bei Interpretationen auf arithmetische Aussagen als den materialen Aussagen beschränkt, dieser Bereich "aller" arithmetischen Aussagen ist indefinit, keine Konstruktion eines definiten Aussagenbereichs kann ihn erschöpfen. Wie will man also etwas über ihn beweisen? Nun, man beweist eine Behauptung über "alle" Aussagen genau dadurch, dass man die Behauptung als logisch-wahr beweist. Die formale Logik wird ja nur deshalb eingeführt, weil man damit etwas über den indefiniten Bereich *aller* Aussagen beweisen kann.

Folgt man der dialogischen Begründung, so wird tatsächlich das Vollständigkeitsproblem obsolet. Sequenzenkalküle sind Beth-Kalküle upside-down gelesen und Logikkalküle des Hilbert-Typs werden einfach dadurch als "vollständig" nachgewiesen, dass man zeigt, dass in ihnen alle Formeln $B \rightarrow A$ ableitbar sind, für die $B \prec A$ im Sequenzenkalkül ableitbar sind. Nach der Pragmatik der dialogischen Begründung der Beth-Kalküle besteht für eine sog. Semantik kein Bedarf mehr.

An dieser Stelle darf ich wohl vermuten, dass diejenigen, die nicht an die Dialogpraxis als Basis aller Logik gewöhnt sind, jetzt dadurch verwirrt sind, dass es doch den Gödelschen Vollständigkeitsbeweis der klassischen Quantorenlogik gibt - und dass in den letzten 20 Jahren seit Kripke semantische Vollständigkeitsbeweise der Modallogik und der intuitionistischen Logik geradezu Mode geworden sind.

## 11. *Vollständigkeit ohne Semantik*

In der noch verbleibenden Zeit möchte ich versuchen zu zeigen, wie diese Vollständigkeitsbeweise zu verstehen sind, auch dann, wenn man sich keinerlei Illusionen mehr über Semantik macht.

Der Gödelsche Beweis liefert, unvoreingenommen betrachtet, nichts über "alle" arithmetischen Aussagen, sondern er geht von der Nicht-Ableitbarkeit einer Formel aus. Im Beth-Kalkül ist das die Nicht-Abschliessbarkeit einer Stellung

$$B \parallel A$$

Die Frage, ob abschliessbar oder nicht-abschliessbar, ist im allgemeinen nicht entscheidbar. Aber man kann leicht sog. spezielle Entwicklungen so definieren, dass stets dann, wenn die Stellung überhaupt abschliessbar ist, eine Abschliessung auch in einer speziellen Entwicklung erreicht wird.

In einigen Fällen, in denen man nach endlich vielen Schritten keine Entscheidung erreicht hat, wird man beweisen können, dass ein Zweig auch bei unendlicher Verlängerung unabgeschlossen bleibt. Die klassische Metamathematik benutzt das Königsche Lemma, um hier die "Existenz" eines unendlichen Zweiges zu beweisen - dadurch ändert sich aber nichts daran, dass man nur in einigen Fällen einen solchen Zweig wird konstruieren können.

Hat man einen solchen Zweig, dann ist es fast trivial, dass er ein Gegenmodell der Ausgangsstellung liefert: man nimmt die Primformeln, die im Zweig links von || stehen, als "wahre" Primaussagen, die Primformeln, die im Zweig rechts von || stehen, als "falsche" Primaussagen. Die im Zweig auftretenden freien Variablen nimmt man dabei als Konstanten. Die Entwicklungsregeln (man beschränke sich der Einfachheit halber auf subjunktionsfreie Aussagen) sind dann gerade so, dass bei dieser Interpretation der im Zweig vorkommenden Formeln alle Formeln links von || streng-wahr werden, alle Formeln rechts von || streng-falsch werden. Also wird insbesondere B streng-falsch und A streng-wahr. Nun ja, das kann man "Semantik" nennen. Das ist aber dann nur ein Wort.

Zu jeder klassisch nicht-abschliessbaren Stellung existiert (im klassischen Sinne) ein strenges Gegenmodell. Das ist,was Gödel wirklich bewiesen hat. Ersetzt man hier den metamathematischen Einsquantor V durch $\neg \bigwedge \neg$ , so wird ein effektiv-wahrer Satz daraus. Nützlich daran ist, dass ein spezielles Entwicklungsverfahren angegeben wird, das stets zu einer Abschliessung führt, wenn die Ausgangsstellung überhaupt abschliessbar ist. Es ist nun m.E. das Verdienst von Kripke, dieses Entwicklungsverfahren der klassischen Quantorenlogik für die klassische Modallogik verallgemeinert zu haben. Durch eine modallogische Interpretation der effektiven Quantorenlogik hat das dann auch zu speziellen Entwicklungsverfahren für diese geführt - und man kann dann stets versuchen, die Nicht-Abschliessbarkeit einer Stellung durch Konstruktion eines Gegenmodells zu beweisen.

Wenn man in der üblichen klassischen Naivität von der strengen Dialogik als Semantik ausgeht, und dann in zirkelhafter Weise die materiale (semantische) Konsistenz klassischer Kalküle dadurch beweist, dass man die klassische Logik auf der Metastufe anwendet - so hat der Gödelsche Vollständigkeitssatz doch wenigstens insofern Sinn, als er die Gegenmodelle wieder aus der strengen Dialogik entnimmt.

Bei Kripke gibt es dagegen keine Semantik *von* den Modalkalkülen, sondern es wird eine Definition modallogischer Wahrheit nur deshalb gewählt, weil sie zu den Modalkalkülen passt.

In der Tradition von Lewis benutzt man als Modalkalküle zumeist noch Kalküle vom Hilbert-Typ. Zum modus ponens als Schlussregel wird zwar eine weitere Schlussregel, zumeist

$$A \Rightarrow \Delta A$$

(mit $\Delta$ für die sog. Notwendigkeit)

hinzugenommen, der Rest sind aber weitere Axiome, insbesondere

$$(*) \qquad \Delta A \rightarrow A$$

und das Lewis-Axiom

$$(L) \qquad \Delta A \rightarrow \Delta \Delta A$$

Die Interpretation ist der freien Intuition überlassen - nur so ist es wohl verständlich, dass die Kripkesche Modelltheorie als "Semantik" akzeptiert wurde.

Die Tatsache, dass schon Aristoteles eine modale Syllogistik detailliert ausgearbeitet hat, sollte uns allerdings skeptisch gegen moderne Phantasieinterpretationen machen. Aristoteles hat - so wird man vermuten dürfen - viel Einfacheres im Sinn gehabt, wenn er von der Ananke als logischer Notwendigkeit sprach.

Ausgehend von der Eristik gibt es folgenden einfachen Weg, der zu einer Modallogik führt. Man unterstellt, dass der Opponent in jedem Dialog stets ein gewisses Minimalsystem von Sätzen anerkennen wird: ein Minimalsystem $\Sigma$ des allgemein anerkannten Wissens ein apriorisches Wissen - oder wie immer man es nennen will.

Relativ zu einem solchen Wissen $\Sigma$ lässt sich dann die "relative Notwendigkeit" $\Delta_\Sigma$ von Aussagen definieren durch

$$\Delta_\Sigma A \leftrightharpoons \Sigma \prec A$$

Diese Definition allein führt zu keiner Modallogik. Aber Aristoteles hat schon bemerkt, dass man leicht zu Implikationen zwischen diesen relativen Notwendigkeiten gelangen kann, die *gleichmässig* für all $\Sigma$ gelten. Dadurch erhält man eine *Modallogik*, weil diese Implikationen auf der Metastufe *unabhängig* von der Auszeichnung eines bestimmten $\Sigma$ sind.

Es findet sich sogar bei Aristoteles (jedenfalls lese ich dies aus I, 8 der Ersten Analytik heraus) die Einsicht, dass eine Implikation der Form

$$\Delta B_1 \wedge \ldots \wedge \Delta B_n \prec \Delta A$$

genau dann (gleichmässig für alle Σ) gilt, wenn gilt

$$B_1 \wedge \ldots \wedge B_n \prec A$$

Der Einfachheit halber ist hier Δ statt $\Delta_\Sigma$ geschrieben. Dieser triviale metalogische Satz begründet ersichtlich den folgenden Modalkalkül: man nimmt Δ als logischen Operator (wie den Negator) zur Quantorenlogik hinzu. Eine Stellung aus Modalformeln

$$\Gamma \parallel A$$

wird quantorenlogisch so lange entwickelt, bis man zu einer Stellung

$$\Gamma(\Delta B_1, \ldots, \Delta B_n) \parallel \Delta A$$

kommt. Als Δ-Schritt erlaubt man dann die folgende Entwicklung

| $\Gamma(\Delta B_1, \ldots, \Delta B_n)$ | $\Delta A$ |
|---|---|
| $B_1$ | |
| . | |
| . | |
| $B_n$ | $A$ |

Der Querstrich zeigt an, dass für die weiteren Entwicklungen alle Formeln oberhalb des Querstriches *nicht* mehr benutzt werden dürfen. Mit dieser Begründung eines Modalkalküls entfällt jeder Grund, noch nach einer Semantik zu suchen.

Das Axiom (*) ist trivial, weil ja Σ als wahr vorausgesetzt wurde - das Lewissche Axiom braucht dagegen nur als ein Mittel untersucht zu werden, bei Zulassung iterierter Modalitäten in konsistenter Weise eine formale Vereinfachung zu erreichen.

Das ist alles nicht schwierig und - wie Kripke gezeigt hat - lässt sich das spezielle Entwicklungsverfahren des Gödelschen Vollständigkeitsbeweises auf die Modalkalküle ausdehnen. Ist eine modallogische Stellung

$$B \parallel A$$

nicht abschliessbar, so versucht man einen nicht abgeschlossenen Zweig zu konstruieren. Und anschliessend *nennt* man die Mengen von Primformeln, die in diesem Zweig auftreten (wegen des Δ-Schrittes treten sie hierarchisch geordnet auf) ein Gegenmodell.

Für eine *Begründung* der Modalkalküle liefert die Existenz solcher Modelle nichts, weil nur die Modalkalküle die Definition gewisser Hierarchien von Primformelmengen als "Modelle" rechtfertigen. Ohne Rückgriff auf eine dialogische Interpretation sind dagegen der Spekulation über eine Semantik möglicher Welten augenscheinlich keine Grenzen gesetzt.

Dass dann noch über eine solche Semantik der klassischen Modallogik die effektive Quantorenlogik "begründet" werden soll, scheint mir geradezu aberwitzig. Formal ist das aber nicht schwierig, weil nur eine einfache Abbildung der effektiven Formeln A auf modale Formeln $\overline{A}$ benötigt wird:

$$\overline{p} \leftrightharpoons \Delta\, p \text{ für Primformeln}$$
$$\overline{\neg A} \leftrightharpoons \Delta \neg \overline{A}$$
$$\overline{B \to A} \leftrightharpoons \Delta\, (\overline{B} \to \overline{A})$$
$$\overline{{}_x A(x)} \leftrightharpoons \Delta \bigwedge_x \overline{A(x)}$$

Dann folgt schon, dass A genau dann effektiv-logisch wahr ist, wenn $\overline{A}$ klassisch-modallogisch wahr ist (mit den Axiomen (∗) und (L)). Für das Begründungsproblem ist diese Abbildung irrelevant, weil die dialogische Begründung nach der Definition der logischen Partikeln als erste formale Logik ja den Kalkül der effektiven Quantorenlogik liefert - alles andere ist danach von dieser Basis aus zu begründen.

## SHERLOCK HOLMES CONFRONTS MODERN LOGIC: TOWARD A THEORY OF INFORMATION-SEEKING THROUGH QUESTIONING

Jaakko Hintikka and Merrill B. Hintikka

### 1. *Sherlock Holmes vs. philosophers on deduction*

If one looks at intelligent laymen's ideas about such concepts as deduction, inference, and logic, we find a curious contrast to the prevailing philosophical views. There used to be--and to some extent still is--a strong current of popular thinking which assigns to logic and logical inference an important role in gaining new information about virtually any subject matter. In contrast to such an opinion, Wittgenstein claimed in the *Tractatus* that all logical truths are tautological, and most philosophers have agreed with him. Even when some heretic philosopher has subsequently voiced doubts about Wittgenstein's conception, these verbal disagreements have seldom led to any serious attempts to spell out the precise sense in which deduction is supposed to yield new information. And even those happy few of us who have ventured further and have in fact defined concepts of deductive information have admitted that logical inference does not in some other valid sense increase our knowledge of empirical reality. What is more important, such recent theories of deductive information do not assign to it anything like the importance which the other line of thought ascribes to logic as a tool of obtaining nontrivial new information. Moreover, Wittgenstein's claim had little novelty about it. He was merely giving a deeper foundation to similar claims that had been made by his compatriots Ernst Mach and Moritz Schlick. And they were in turn part of a longer tradition which goes back at least to Descartes' criticisms of the value of syllogistic reasoning. It is hence correct to say that there is a veritable mainstream of philosophers of logic who have denied the informativeness of logic and logical inference.

In contrast to their doctrine of the tautological nature of deductive reasoning there is the other type of view which was mentioned earlier and which we shall refer to as the Sherlock Holmes view on logic, deduction, and inference. Not surprisingly, the best description of these ideas of the great detective comes partly from that inimitable chronicler of the exploits of Sherlock Holmes, Dr. Watson, and partly from the great detective himself. It is indeed to Dr. Watson that we owe a summary of Sherlock's own article on his method, which is claimed to rest precisely on those reputedly useless procedures, deduction and inference.

"...it attempted to show how much an observant man might learn by an accurate and systematic examination of all that came his way. ... The reasoning was close and intense, but the deduction appeared..to be far fetched...Deceit, according to him, was an impossibility in the case of one trained to observation and analysis. His conclusions were as infallible as so many propositions of Euclid. So startling would his results appear to the uninitiated that until they learned the processes by which he had arrived at them they might well consider him a necromancer. 'From a drop of water,' said the writer [i.e., Sherlock Holmes], 'a logician could infer the possibility of an Atlantic or a Niagara without having seen or heard of one or the other. ...All life is a great chain, the nature of which is known when even we are shown a single link of it. Like all other arts, the Science of Deduction and Analysis is one which can only be acquired by long and patient study...'."

This illustrates a widespread view according with deduction and logic are most useful in gaining substantial knowledge concerning the world and can indeed produce, in the mind of a one trained in "the Science of Deduction and Analysis", completely unexpected results. Indeed, a little later Sherlock Holmes claims that "those rules of deduction laid down in that article of mine ...are invaluable to me in practical work." Similar testimony are easily forthcoming from the likes of Hercule Poirot and Nero Wolfe. It represents an extreme form the idea of the value of logic in all information-gathering.

It seems to us that philosophers have far too casually dismissed the deductions of detectives as being either illegitimately so-called or else mere enthymemes, inferences from premises which have been only partially formulated. It is indeed true, we believe, that there is nothing in Holmes' "Science of Deduction and Analysis" which is in the last analysis incompatible with philosophers' thesis that in one perfectly good sense of the word logical inferences are tautological. However, saying that leaves untouched the task of explaining those uses of logic--or is it "logic"?--which apparently yield new information. Collingwood was wrong in claiming the methods of a clever detective for his idealistic methodology of history and philosophy. But even apart from Collingwood, the Sherlock Holmes conception of deduction and logic presents an important challenge to philosophical logicians. Not only do we have the task of reconciling somehow the surprising-looking inferences of an acute detective with philosophers' thesis of the tautological character of all logical deduction. Not only do we have in the arguments of Sherlock Holmes and his ilk an amusing and pedagogically handy source of application and illustrations. We believe that the very structure of "deduction" and "inference" in the sense of Sherlock Holmes presents an important new task for philosophical logic. We cannot just take the familiar tools of contemporary philosophical logic and apply them to a new area. In order to understand the methods of a Sherlock Holmes and to discuss and to evaluate them rationally we need new conceptualizations. It is our purpose in this study to indicate what some of the relevant new concepts and results are that will enable us to do this. We believe that the resulting new theory in philosophical logic will soon have an abundance of other applications both in philosophy and outside of it that will look weightier than our perhaps somewhat frivolous-looking references to Conan Doyle. Later, we shall try to indicate what some of these intra- and interdisciplinary applications might be.

## 2. *Making tacit information explicit through questioning*

The first observation we need here is pretty obvious, even though it later turns out to need major qualifications. What Sherlock is doing in his so-called deductions is not so much to draw explicit inferences from explicit premises. Often he is eliciting from an enormous mass of undigested background information the suitable additional premises, over and above what has perhaps been announced as such, from which the apparently suprising conclusion can be drawn by our familiar commonplace deductive logic. The schematic picture of the enterprise is therefore not this familiar proof-tree figure, where $p_1, p_2, \ldots, p_k$ are the requisite explicit premises and $c_1, \ldots, c_1$ the successive conclusions:

(1) 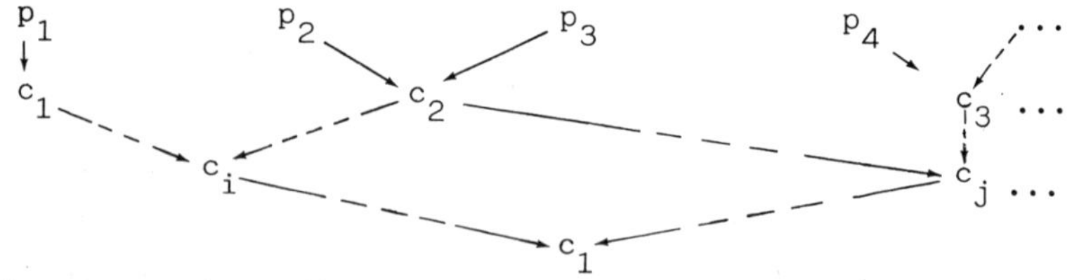


How are we to refine this schematic picture? The crucial part of the task of a Holmesian "logician", we are suggesting, is not so much to carry out logical deductions as *to elicit or to make explicit tacit information*. This task is left unacknowledged in virtually all philosophical expositions of logical reasoning, of deductive heuristics, and of the methodology of logic and mathematics. For this neglect the excuse is sometimes offered that such processes of elucidation and explication cannot be systematized and subjected to rules. It may indeed be true that we are dealing here with problems which belong as much to heuristics as to logic or epistemology and also true that we cannot usually give effective rules for heuristic processes. It does not follow, however, that they cannot be rationally discussed and evaluated, given a suitable conceptual framework. It is the main purpose of this paper to sketch such a framework.

The key idea on which the framework is based is the notion of *question*. We shall consider the newly explicit (previously unacknowledged) premises as being answers to questions addressed to the tacit knower. The previously unacknowledged item of information is prompted to actuality by the question whose answer it is. In this sense, *the process of activating tacit knowledge is controlled by the questions which serve to elicit this information to actuality*. By studying these questions and the way they limit their answers we can in effect study the Holmesian "Science of Deduction". For example, one question can be better than another one in the sense that answers to the former will be more informative than answers to the latter. Our task of examining the actualization of tacit predeductive knowledge therefore becomes a part of a larger task of studying questions, answers, and their interrelations.

To put the same point in other words, we can already see why a sharp theory of the question-answer relationship is absolutely vital for our enterprise. Our leading idea is to study certain types of information-gathering by thinking of the information as being obtained as answers to questions. The process can be controlled by choosing the questions appropriately. One cannot understand this control, however, without understanding how it is that a question determines its (full) answers, that is to say, without understanding the question-answer relationship.

## 3. *The structure of question - inference complexes*

Thus we have to refine the schema (1) by letting the premises $p_1$, $p_2$,...to come about as answers to questions, answers which may be thought of as being based on tacit background information. However, this is not enough. It is not enough merely to think of each of the premises $p_m$ as an answer to some question based on some tacit deeper premises $m_i$, $m_{i+1}$ ..., somewhat like this:

(2)
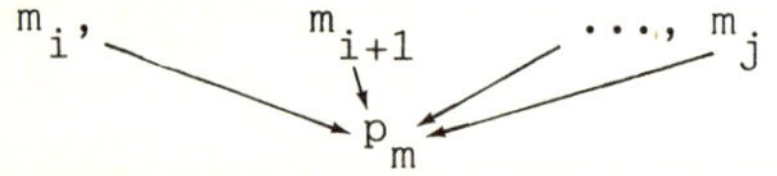


For one thing, the background information on the basis of which the relevant questions are answered may be impossible to capture by any finite (or countable) set of sentences of the language we are using. The content of one's information is specified by a set of sample-space points ("possible worlds"). There is no necessity that such a set is the set of models of any finite or countable set of sentences in a given language.

This already shows an advantage of the questioning model of information-gathering as compared with an inferential (deductive *or* inductive) model. An inference must be an inference from explicit sentences to an explicitly formulated conclusion, and they must all be formulated in some fixed language. There is no need that a question is answered on the basis of information that is specifiable in some given language even when both the question and its answer are formulated in that a language. This gives the questioning model extra flexibility. It also shows that (2) is not the right way of making the schema (1) more comprehensive in the way we want.

What we can explicitly indicate in our schema are only the different questions which prompt the appropriate premises as their answers. These answers are in the first place the premises $p_1$, $p_2$, ... Hence the schema (1) has to be replaced by something like this:

(3)

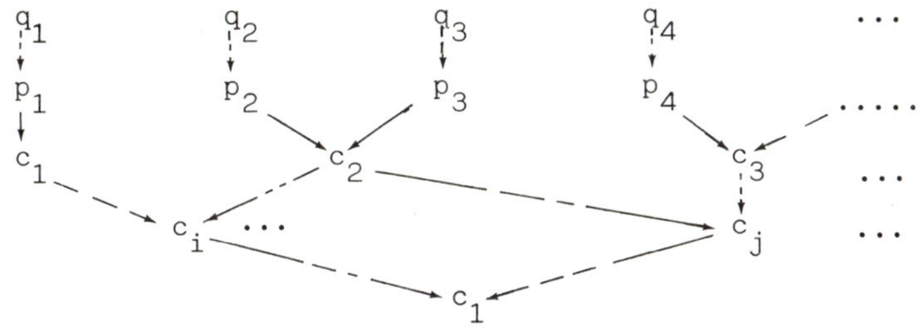


Here dotted lines indicate answers and solid lines inferences.

This is not yet a fully realistic picture. In (3), all questions are thought of as being answered on the sole basis of tacit background information. This is not realistic. The answers may be partly based on the inferential conclusions $c_i$. Hence any one part of (3) might have to be replaced by something like this:

(4)

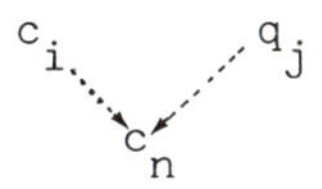


In other words, answers to questions do not always precede (temporally or logically) deductive inferences.

All these observations concerning the interplay of questions and inferences must of course be given a more explicit formulation later, in the same way as the rules of inference one is using must be formulated explicitly.

Several different points can meanwhile be raised by reference to our tentative schematic framework. One interesting conceptual link which we can now discuss within our framework is the connection between *memory* and *intelligence*. Eliciting tacit information by questioning can be viewed as one possible recall procedure. At the same time, it can be generalized so as to become a common model of several different kinds of information-gathering activities, deductive as well as inductive. This partially shared model for recall and intelligent inquiry may perhaps serve as an explication of a link between memory and intelligence.

For another thing, our general idea should not surprise any Sherlock Holmes fan. The *denouement* of almost every successful story or novel in the Sherlock Holmes tradition can be paraphrased in the form of real or imaginary questions Holmes addressed to himself (or to the reader). In some cases, the great detective has to carry out an observation or even an experiment to answer the question. More frequently, all he has to do is to perform an *anamnesis* and recall certain items of information which he already had been given and which typically had been recorded in the story or novel for the use of the readers, too, or which are so elementary that any intelligent reader can be expected to know them. Take, for instance, the well-known incident of the dog in the night. The famous race horse *Silver Blaze* had been stolen and his trainer had been found killed in the heath. Several suspects had cropped up, and all sorts of sundry information about the events of the fateful night had been recorded by the invaluable Dr. Watson. The import of Sherlock Holmes' famous comment on the "remarkable incident of the dog in the night" can be brought out by two questions: Did the trainer's watchdog in the stable bark when the horse was taken out by whoever stole it? The answer is known to be negative. ("But the dog did not bark!" "*That* is the remarkable incident of the dog in the night.") Who is the only person a trained watchdog is likely not to bark at? His master, of course. Hence Sherlock Holmes' "deduction" of the role of the trainer.

Thus the role we have assigned to questioning in information-gathering is not unnatural in the context we have chosen to discuss it. Philosophers may nevertheless prefer to use as their paradigm the Socratic method of questioning or the process of scientific investigation, especially in a clinical context. We believe that these will be found to exhibit the same structural features as we are trying to discover in the Sherlock Holmes' "Science of Deduction".

### 4. *On the principle of total evidence. Bayesianism*

We can now also see one factor which has misled earlier analysts of human information-seeking, deductive as well as inductive. In the philosophy of empirical sciences this misleading assumption has been known as *the principle of total evidence.* Its role and its relative justification is seen best in theories which deal with scientific inferences in probabilistic terms as a series of steps of conditionalization. Such theories are sometimes called (somewhat inaccurately) Bayesian theories of scientific inference. Suppose we are given a prior probability distribution P(x), and suppose that we have some background information $e_o$. Suppose we then obtain some new evidence $e_1$. What is the probability distribution which now represents our epistemic state? Clearly it is no longer P(x) or even $P(x/e_1)$. It is $P(x/e_o \& e_1)$. And here $e_o$ must really be thought of as codifying literally *all* one's pertinent information. Otherwise our probabilistic treatment leads to paradoxes and mistakes, as can easily be shown.

This may be all right for small-scale applications, but it clearly tends to make Bayesian theories somewhat unrealistic models of actual large-scale scientific procedures. For in real-life applications it is very often literally impossible to contemplate actually or to write down *all* the potentially relevant information. There is in general no guarantee that this information can be codified any one sentence (our "$e_o$") or a countable set of sentences of any one given language. Hence the need of imposing the requirement of total evidence is fairly generally acknowledged to be a weak point in Bayes-type probabilistic approaches to scientific inference.

This problem has been noted in the philosophy of science and has been discussed there to some extent. In our opinion, it is one of the most serious problems affecting Bayesian views of scientific inference. It has not been pointed out, as far as we know, that there is a precisely analogous problem in the philosophy of deductive sciences. There, too, it has been assumed in studying inferential processes that all the relevant information has in some sense been already brought in and made instantly available. This is one of the oversimplifications involved in conceptualizing the situation depicted in (3)-(4) as if it were (1) or (2). It is a deductivist's version of the problem of total evidence. It is at least as desirable to develop means of dispensing with the deductivistic version of the principle of total evidence as it is to overcome its inductivistic version--which in the last analysis probably cannot be disentangled from each other. Even more importantly, we want to find means of discussing rationally and theorizing about those processes which serve to make our incomplete evidence (premises) more and more total. It seems to us that their study has been badly neglected by philosophers of logic, science, and knowledge.

## 5. *The role of observations*

In the spirit of these remarks, we can already see one important direction into which our observations can be extended beyond philosophical logic and philosophy of language. (This is one of the kinds of applications foreshadowed in my earlier remarks.) Not all of the items of background information need be thought of as having been there in the back of one's mind prior to our exercise. In other words, not all the questions that lead to the premises $p_i$ need be thought of as being addressed to oneself (i.e. to the logician in question). Some of the premises $p_i$ and some of the intermediate conclusions $c_n$ as depicted in figure 4 may be uncovered by suitable *observations* instead of having been part of one's background knowledge. However, the interesting thing is that *this does not change the picture* essentially. For we can still think of the premises $p_i$ as having been elicited from a mass of merely potential knowledge by means of suitable questions. Only now some of them are questions put to nature in the form of pertinent observations. The different items of this potential knowledge need not be hidden somewhere in one's unconscious. They may simply be observable but so far unobserved facts. But this does not change the basic logical and methodological situation. We can still think of the new information (especially the premises $p_i$) as being obtained as answers to suitable questions. Observations actually made have to be chosen from a great many possible observations quite as much as actually used premises are selected from a wealth of collateral information. We can try to understand this choice of observations and the rest of their role in establishing certain conlusions by thinking of them as answers to questions put to nature. Then the relative virtues of different questions of this kind can be studied and assessed in the same way as the merits and demerits of questions which are calculated to tease out tacit information. It is in this way that the theory of information-seeking through questioning we are trying to develop becomes applicable beyond its first range of applications, viz. beyond the explication of tacit knowledge. Even though we cannot push the new applications very far in this paper, a few remarks are in order.

First, the Kantian metaphor of "putting questions to nature" receives in this way a less metaphoric explication, at least in one of its possible applications. The application we are giving to it is not merely metaphoric, either, in that we can make many of the same concepts apply to observations as are applicable to questions and their answers. They include methodological concepts governing the choice of questions (including the choice observations or experiments), informational comparisons, etc.

Secondly, the dependence of observations on their theoretical background can now be discussed in a sharper manner than before. For instance, we have in recent years heard a lot of the theory-ladenness of observations. One can now see, however, that there is perhaps a sense in which we have a stronger reason to speak of the problem-ladenness or question-ladenness of observations. In our methodological model or perspective, an observation is always an answer to a question. This question-ladenness of course implies concept-ladenness. For an answer to a question normally has to be formulated in terms of the same concepts as the question was formulated in.

One can say more than this, however. Often, the correct way of expressing the content of one's observation is in the form of a conclusion which the imaginary bare observation allows us to draw, a conclusion which goes beyond the mere registration of one's sense-impression. This is precisely the kind of situation depicted in figure 4. The imaginary bare observation we can think of as one of the $m_i$'s in the misleading figure (2), whereas the correct conceptualization of the actual observation is what we find in schema (4). What in (4) looks like an intermediate conclusion $c_n$ in fact depends both on the question $q_j$ to which it is an answer and on the interim conlusion $c_i$ to which this question can be thought of as being conditional on.

One main reason for saying this is that the would-be chain of reasoning from the background information to the premises $p_i$ and to the intermediate conclusions $c_j$ can be completely unconscious. Again we can have classical illustrations among the most famous instance of Sherlockianisms.

"'Dr. Watson, Mr. Sherlock Holmes,' said Stamford, introducing us.

'How are you?' he said cordially,.... 'You have been in Afganistan, I perceive.'

'How on earth did you know that' I asked in astonishment.'

Later, Sherlock answers the question.

"'You appeared to be surprised when I told you, on our first meeting, that you had come from Afganistan.'

'You were told, no doubt.'

'Nothing of the sort. I *knew* you came from Afganistan. From long habit the train of thought ran so swiftly through my mind that I arrived at the conclusion without being conscious of intermediate steps. There were such steps, however. The train of reasoning ran, "Here is a gentleman of a medical type, but with the air of a military man. Clearly an army doctor, then. He has just come from the tropics, for his face is dark, and that is not the natural tint of his skin, for his wrists are fair. He has undergone hardship and sickness, as his haggard face says clearly. His left arm has been injured. He holds it in a stiff and unnatural manner. Where in the tropics could an English army doctor have seen much hardship and got his arm wounded? Clearly in Afganistan." The whole train of thought did not occupy a second. ... .'

'It is simple enough as you explain it,' I said, smiling."

Several comments are in order here. First, one of the intermediate steps in Sherlock Holmes' rational reconstruction of his line of thought is literally obtained as an answer to the appropriate question. (Cf. "Where in the tropics...?")

Secondly, contemporary psychology of perception confirms the appropriateness of calling the "conclusion" $n_j$ an *observation*. The question is whether the allegedly unconscious steps of reasoning are merely traversed so quickly as to e cape active attention or whether they are sometimes truly inaccessible to conscious reflexion and built right into one's unedited sense impressions. The answer we obtain from such psychologists as J.J. Gibson and David Katz affirms the latter alternative. Perception, they tell us, means pickup of information, not pickup of unstructured sense-impressions, just as I have claimed.

This also vindicated Sherlock's habit of formulating his unconsciously reached conclusions as *perceiving that* statements, sometimes offered as equivalents to conclusions of deductions. For instance, concerning a deduction he had performed Sherlock Holmes asks the faithful Dr. Watson:

> "So you actually were not able to *see* that that man was a sargeant of Marines?" (Our italics.)

These observations already show something of the subtle interplay of observation and deduction which is characteristic of our model of information-seeking through questioning. In particular, they lead us to suspect that our figure (2) is oversimplified in still another important respect. There may not be any fundamental layer of starting-points $m_i$ at all. What happens in actually epistemic situations is double movement: downwards to ever richer conclusions and upwards towards more and more primitive data. There is no more reason to expect that the latter movement ever comes to a natural end than there is in the case of the former process.

In scientific contexts, too, the same structure is found. In an observational situation, much of the largely tacit background knowledge is taken for granted. This background knowledge corresponds to the $m_i$'s of our schema (2). What is actually registered as an observational statement is in our structure an intermediate conclusion $c_n$ somewhere between the background information and the end-product conclusion, somewhat as in (4).

Along somewhat different and more general lines, we can now also understand the role of observations in the Holmesian conception of logic and deduction. In our introductory quote above, perhaps the most interesting and most puzzling feature that may strike the reader is the strange coexistence of the notions of, on the one hand, observation and, on the other hand, reasoning, deduction, analysis, inference, and logic. Sherlock Holmes' compleat logycien appears at times as the perfect observer who notes the most minute revealing features of the world around him. Holmes "claimed by a momentary expression, a twitch of a mouth or a glance of an eye, to fathom a man's innermost thoughts." At other times, we seem to be presented with a complete reasoner who can in his mind run so swiftly through a long series of intermediate steps, following all the rules of deduction, that he himself need not be immediately conscious of them.

## 6. *Question-answer sequences as games against Nature*

From the perspective we have reached, one can now see what the connecting link between the two conceptions is. The missing link is questioning. Both the teasing out of previously unattended-to premises, which is what Sherlock Holmes calls deduction, and observation can be conceptualized as question-answer processes. Later, we will see that this similarity between observation and deduction can be pushed still further.

How precisely are we to study the uses of questions and answers for the (Sherlock Holmesian) purposes we are here interested in? The first and foremost problem confronting a logician here is to spell out the question-answer relationship. Somewhat surprisingly, we do not find a satisfactory answer in the earlier literature on the logic, semantics, grammar, or pragmatics of questions. (This surprise can be lessened somewhat by realizing what is involved in such an answer to the question of answerhood, viz. to spell out the logical and semantical relation of utterances made by two different speakers with different collateral information. This background knowledge has to be brought in, which logicians and linguists alike have refused to do.) Jaakko Hintikka has analyzed the question-answer relationship in a number of earlier works.[1] Here we shall simply take the results of those earlier analyses for granted, including the crucial distinction between full and partial answers (replies) to a given question. Likewise, the important notion of presupposition is explained in those earlier writings of mine.

How is the process of information-gathering through questioning and deduction to be conceptualized? We shall present a formalization which looks somewhat different from the one sketched above but which nevertheless embodies the ideas presented earlier. We can think of the process as a game against nature, who may alternately be thought of as the store of my own tacit information. The reason for using the concepts of game theory is that this theory is the best existing framework for studying any questions of strategy. In the present case, the relevant strategies would involve both strategies of questioning and interconnected with them strategies of deduction.

The game in question can be explained as follows.

There are two players, myself and nature. Speaking intuitively and tentatively, my aim is to prove a certain conclusion $C_o$. Initially, I have at my disposal an initial premise $C_1$ (which may be vacuous). The different sentences which come up during the game may be thought of as being expressed in some fixed first-order language which is extended only so that questions can be asked in the extended language. (Some extensions will be explained later.) The course of the game can be described by reference to a scorekeeping device which is not unlike Beth's semantical *tableau*. The differences will be explained later. At this point all that needs to be noted is that we shall call this scoresheet a *tableau* and that we can use about them the same terminology as about Beth *tableaux*. In particular, we shall use the notion of closure, the notions of the left column and the right column, and the notion of *subtableau* in the same way as Beth. The different *subtableaux* of a given tableau are related in the same way as in Beth, that is disjunctively. They all have to be closed for the *tableau* itself to be closed.

Our use of Beth *tableaux* is in keeping with the best traditions of Sherlock Holmes, who speaks in connection with his "Science of Deduction" of *analysis*. As Beth pointed out in his very first paper on the subject, the *tableau* method is an excellent reconstruction of the old idea of analytical method. Beth's reconstruction of the traditional method is applicable only in the realm of deduction, however. What we are doing here can be thought of as an extension of Beth's "Science of Deduction and Analysis" beyond its narrowly deductive applications.

Initially, the *tableau* contains $C_o$ in its right column and $C_1$ in its left column.

There are moves of three different kinds:

(1) deductive moves;

(2) interrogative moves;

(3) definitory moves;

(1) The rules for making deductive moves are the same as in any usual formulation of the *tableau* method.

As Jaakko Hintikka has argued elsewhere,[2] there nevertheless are reasons to modify all the *tableau* rules in the same way as some of them are modified in the transition from classical to intuitionistic logic and to allow only one sentence at any one time in the right column of any one *subtableau*.

The instantiation rules of *tableau* construction can extend our initially given language by introducing dummy names (indefinite individuals). We assume that this is possible only when an existential sentence is instantiated in the left column or a universally quantified sentence in instantiated in the right column of a *subtableau*.

(2) An interrogative move is relative to a *subtableau* $\sigma_j$. It consists of a question addressed by me to nature. The presupposition of the question must occur in the left column of the *subtableau*. Nature must provide a full answer. Let this answer be $A_i$. Then $A_i$ is added to the left column of $\sigma_j$.

For simplicity, we shall assume that a full answer can always be given, in the sense of a substitution-instance of the matrix of the question which together with certain supplementary information provided by the answerer is a full answer. This supplementary information will be introduced into the left column of $\sigma_j$ together with the rest of the answer.

Substituting terms must be individual constants (in the case of wh-questions).

The fullness of nature's reply is to be judged in the basis of my background knowledge plus the assumption that I know the truth of all the sentences in the left column of $\sigma_j$. (This is what makes the question relative to $\sigma_j$.)

(3) A definitory move is also relative to a *subtableau* $\sigma_j$. It consists in the introduction of a new predicate symbol, say P(x). It is introduced by means of an explicit definition, that is, by adding to the left column of $\sigma_j$ either.

$(x) \quad (P(x) \leftrightarrow S(x))$

or

$(x) \quad (P(x) \leftrightarrow (x=a_1 \vee x=a_2 \vee \ldots \vee x=a_k))$

where S is an expression in the vocabulary that has been used in $\sigma_j$ and has one free variable, and where $a_1, a_2, \ldots, a_k$ are individual constants.

## 7. *Payoffs and strategies*

As the case usually is in game theory, players' strategic

considerations are determined essentially by the payoffs. We shall not try to specify them fully here. The following general principles are nevertheless important.

(1) An interrogative move involving a wh-question is the more expensive the more layers of quantifiers there are in the question, including the quantifiers masquerading as wh-words (with the exception of the outmost layer of such quantifiers). We can tentatively think of the "price" of a question being equal to the same number of units as there are layers of quantifiers in the question.

Here quantifiers occurring outside the question proper do not count.

(2) A definitory move is the more expensive the more layers of quantifiers there are in the definiens S. Again, each additional layer can be thought of as costing a unit.

(3) Of deductive moves, each of those introducing new dummy names costs a unit.

What these principles amount to in intuitive terms is that a move is the more expensive the more it complicates the configurations of individuals one is considering in the deduction (in the sense of introducing new individuals into the argument). This "cost" of adding new individuals to our deductive argument (whether they are actual individuals or "arbitrary individuals" represented by dummy names) reflects the importance of such moves for successful deduction. The selection of the new individuals to be introduced is the crucial strategic consideration in our games.

This is again reflected by what we find in actual Sherlock Holmes type arguments. Take the example closest at hand: the curious episode of the dog in the night. What happens in it is that three individuals are for the first time related to each other by Holmes: the unknown thief, the dog, and the trainer. (We may perhaps say that the dog is introduced into the argument and the other two are related to each other by its means.) The surprise of Holmes' "deduction" is not in the relation of the three individuals (two of which turn out to be identical) but in asking for the first time what their relation is. And this was made possible by the introduction of one of them.

## 8. *Deductions sometimes replaceable by questions and answers*

The closer examination of the payoffs and different strategies would take us too far. Suffice it to mention here one interesting fact. Most of the deductive moves--including some of the most interesting ones--can be repplaced by a suitable question, assuming that an answer to it is forthcoming.

For instance, assume that $(F_1 \vee F_2)$ occurs in the left column of some *subtableau* $\sigma_j$. A deductive move might involve splitting $\sigma_j$ in two, with $F_1$ and $F_2$, respectively, added to their left columns. However, instead of doing so one could ask "Is it the case that $F_1$ or is it the case that $F_2$?" This can be done because the presupposition of this question is $(F_1 \vee F_2)$. Whichever the answer is, one is saved the trouble of continuing the construction of one of the two *subtableaux* into which the deductive move would have split $\sigma_j$.

Likewise, suppose that (Ex) F(x) occurs in the left column of $\sigma_j$. Then a deductive move might involve the introduction of a new dummy name "$\alpha$" whereupon "F($\alpha$)" is inserted into the left column of $\sigma_j$. Instead of doing this, one might ask: "Who or what (call that individual x) is such that F(x)?" One can do so because the presupposition of this question is (Ex) F(x). If the answer is "b", then one can insert "F(b)" into the left column of $\sigma_j$ instead of "F($\alpha$)". Since "b" is a real name, dealing with it can only facilitate the deduction as compared with the deductive move. (Notice that we presupposed here the existential-quantifier reading of the desideratum of the question.)

Furthermore, a definitory move can often be replaced likewise by a question-answer move. For instance, a definitory move might involve the introduction of the sentence

(*) $(x)\,(P(x) \Leftrightarrow S(x))$

into the left column of some *subtableau* $\sigma_j$. Instead of this, one might ask: "Who or what (call one of them x) are such that S(x)?", presupposing the universal-quantifier reading of the desideratum. The answer will then be a sentence of the same form, except that the new primitive predicate "P" is replaced by some previously used predicate. Once again, the deductive task can only be enhanced by the change.

This extensive interchangeability of deductive and interrogative moves (as well as definitory and interrogative moves) can be taken to be a vindication of the idea that the art of deduction is essentially tantamount to the art of asking questions. This idea is perhaps the most central ingredient in the Sherlock Holmes conception of logic, deduction, and inference.

## NOTES

1. They are mostly summed up in Jaakko Hintikka, The Semantics of Questions and the Questions of Semantics (Acta Philosophica Fennica, vol. 28, no. 4). North-Holland, Amsterdam, 1976.

2. Jaakko Hintikka and Esa Saarinen, "Information-seeking Dialogues: Some of Their Logical Properties," Studia Logica, vol. 32 (1979), pp. 355-363.

# SEMANTICAL GAMES AND TRANSCENDENTAL ARGUMENTS

Jaakko Hintikka

## 1. *Kant on the logic of existence*

Kant had the right idea in his theory of mathematics, but he was mislead by an antiquated philosophical dogma.[1] Following his general transcendental vantage point, he maintained that our ways of reasoning about existence, especially about interindividual existential inferences, must be grounded in the human activities through which we come to know the existence of individuals. This idea is an eminently interesting one, and the fact that Kant identified the types of reasoning in question with mathematical rather than logical ones marks only a difference in terminology between Kant and contemporary philosophers of logic. For us, what Kant was dealing with is unmistakably such logical reasoning as is codified in the modern logic of quantification theory, not anything we would any longer consider distinctively mathematical reasoning.

However, Kant went astray in identifying the activities through which we in fact come to know the existence and nonexistence of individuals. He located these "activities" in sense-perception. In doing so, he was following a long tradition which ultimately goes back to Aristotle. This is nevertheless a false tradition. Only in rare cases can we wait till the relevant individuals kindly prove their existence by showing up in our passive sense-perception. Normally, we have to get up and look for (search for) them. Hence the true basis of the logic of existence and universality lies in the language-games of seeking and finding, not in the structure of our faculty of sense-perception, as Kant mistakenly claimed.

## 2. *Seeking and finding, and game-theoretical semantics*

Nothwithstanding this mistake, Kant's interesting arguments allow for analogous conclusions as applied *mutatis mutandis* to modern logic. Even though logical and mathematical inferences do not reflect the structure of our outer and inner sense, they reflect the structure of our language-games of seeking and finding. The right approach to the contemporary philosophy of logic and logical semantics is therefore through a study of the rule-governed activities of seeking and finding. These activities, conceived of as games against nature, are precisely my semantical games.[2] Game-theoretical semantics thus admits of a transcendental deduction in precisely the same sense as Kant's transcendental arguments for his theory of space, time, sense-perception, and the mathematical method. Game-theoretical semantics is the true Kantian approach to language, I am thus led to say, even though I must qualify it as a neo-Kantian or, more accurate still, meta-Kantian approach to language, I am thus led to say, even though idea but correcting his crucial mistake.[3] This basic idea is to focus on the activities through which we come to know the relevant propositions, that is, the propositions whose logical form is determined by the concepts of existence and non-existence of individuals (plus propositional connectives). These propositions are the ones which are studied in modern first-order logic (quantification theory), and the activities in question are our processes of attempted verification of such propositions. In game-theoretical semantics, these verification processes are conceptualized as games against a recalcitrant Nature who tries to frustrate my attempts. These games are thus two-person games. (We can call the players "myself" and "Nature.") Their usefulness is largely due to the fact that they are games in the strict sense of the mathematical theory of games.

### 3. *A transcendental refutation of certain related views*

This insight into the close kinship between game-theoretical semantics and Kant's philosophy shows that my game-theoretical semantics is not without interesting philosophical antecedents, even apart from the connection with Wittgenstein's concept of language-game, which I have discussed elsewhere.[4] The same observation also suggests further consequences. It helps to put into a perspective certain similar approaches to the philosophy of logic and semantics. We can usefully discuss them by reference to the question whether they allow for analogous "transcendental deductions."

Indeed, at first sight it might look as if several recent approaches to logical semantics are very much along the same meta-Kantian lines as game-theoretical semantics. Both Michael Dummett and Dag Prawitz have proposed treating the theory of meaning, not by means of static truth-conditions, but in terms of the actual processes through which we come to know the propositions whose logic we are dealing with.[5] For instance, Dummett characterizes his theory of meaning as one "which takes verification and falsification as its central notions in place of those of truth and falsity" (Evans and McDowell, note 5 above, p. 115). Likewise, Prawitz emphasizes that "the meaning of a sentence cannot be treated in isolation from the question of how the truth of the sentence may be established." I could not agree more, nor on my interpretation could Kant.

However, both Dummett and Prawitz give their approach what

I cannot help considering an unfortunate turn. They both use mathematical language as their paradigm case, and interpret the relevant methods of verification as methods of proof. This may be fine as a theory of mathematical truth (though even such a claim would be highly controversial in its own right). However, it seems to me perfectly hopeless as a step towards general theory of meaning. When we move outside purely mathematical languages, the truth of a proposition can seldom be established by means of formal proof procedures. Leibniz notwithstanding, we cannot establish the truth or falsity of empirical propositions by calculation. Hence the kind of theory Dummett and Prawitz envisage cannot serve as a general theory of meaning.

## 4. *A test-case: branching quantifiers*

This general argument can be buttressed by more specific ones It seems to me that there are several semantical phenomena both in natural languages and in formal ones which cannot be satisfactorily accounted for on the basis of the Dummett-Prawitz approach. Here I shall mention only one of them. It is constituted by the semantical behavior of branching (more generally, partly ordered) quantifiers.[6] The simplest nontrivial example of a branching-quantifier proposition is a sentence of the following form:

$$(1) \qquad \begin{matrix} (x)\ (\exists y) \\ (z)\ (\exists u) \end{matrix} \Big> M(x, y, z, u)$$

Here $M$ can be assumed not to contain any quantifiers. It may contain propositional connectives.

The meaning of (1) is immediately obvious in game-theoretical semantics. In this semantics an existential quantifier represents my move (in a game against Nature): I select an individual from the given domain (universe of discourse) whose name is to be substituted for the quantified variable. Likewise a universal quantifier represents a similar choice of an individual by Nature. (Of course, not any random choice will do if a player wants to win. A player must try to find the right kind of individual; which is what makes semantical games games of seeking and finding.)

All that is needed in game-theoretical semantics to handle branching quantifiers is to recall one of the most important general concepts of game theory, the concept of information, with its associated notions of informational dependence and independence of different moves, codified in the notion of information set.[7] The information set of the move connected with a quantifier $q_1$ is the set of moves connected with those quantifiers $q_2$ which bear the partly ordering relation to $q_1$, i.e., which intuitively speaking are "to the left of" $q_1$ in the same branch. For instance, in (1) the value of "$y$" is chosen independently of the choice of values of "$z$" and "$u$" but not independently of the choice of the value of "x".

The truth of a propositions means in game-theoretical semantics the existence of a winning strategy for myself. This existence can be expressed by a second-order proposition, which in the case of (1) is clearly

(2) $$(\exists f)\ (\exists g)\ (x)\ (z)\ M(x, f(x), z, g(z))$$

In comparison, we may note that for the linear quantifier sentences

(3) $$(x)\ (\exists y)\ (z)\ (\exists u)\ M(x,y,z,u)$$

and

(4) $$(x)\ (z)\ (\exists y)\ (\exists u)\ M(x,y,z,u)$$

the analogous "translations" will be

(5) $$(\exists f)(\exists g)(x)(z)\, M(x,f(x),z,g(z,x))$$

and

(6) $$(\exists f)(\exists g)(x)(z)\, M(x,f(x,z),z,g(z,x))$$

respectively.

Thus technically game-theoretical semantics yields a translation both of first-order logic and of the theory of partly ordered quantifiers into fragments of second-order logic. The enormous strength of second-order logic (with standard semantics in Henkin's sense)[8] prompts the question: How strong is the fragment which serves as the translation of the theory of partly ordered quantifiers? In other words, how strong is this theory? An interesting answer is in fact forthcoming. I have shown that the theory of partly ordered quantifiers is as strong as the whole second-order logic in the sense of having an equally difficult decision problem.[9] Hence it cannot be axiomatized, and hence the semantics of partly ordered quantifiers cannot be captured by any considerations that pertain to actual means of proving (showing the logical truth of) sentences containing partly ordered quantifiers. Hence the Dummett-Prawitz program is doomed to remain incapable of handling branching quantifier sentences.

Such sentences are not formal curiosities, either. I have shown[10] that branching quantifiers are indispensable for the semantical representation of a large number of natural-language sentences. I have even argued that *all* irreducible forms of partly ordered quantifier structures are needed for the purpose. Hence one cannot dismiss this semantical phenomenon as being merely a marginal one.

One may of course try to get around this conclusion. I believe that such attempts are all ultimately going to be defeated by the naturalness of the game-theoretical semantics of sentences containing partly ordered quantifiers.

For instance, why cannot one use the same idea of informational independence in the formal "games" of theorem proving as was used in semantical games to give branching quantifier sentences their meaning? The answer is that there cannot be incomplete information in games of formal proof and disproof. A logician may forget or overlook earlier steps in his or her argument, but such failures are mistakes, and cannot be subject to semantical rules.

Likewise, in the formal rule of existential instantiation it does not even make sense to ask what the substituting term depends on, for any singular constant not previously used will do. Hence the notion informational dependence or independence does not apply to the formal games of theorem-proving.

### 5. *Material vs. logical truth, formal argumentation, and semantics*

I suspect that mistakes in this general direction have been encouraged by a false analogy between ordinary material truth (truth *simpliciter*) and philosophers' artificial notion of "logical truth." The two are of course related to each other, but they are not analogous. Logical truth is not truth in some particular Platonic domain of logical entities (or in some mind-created domain, either). It is much more appropriately characterized as truth *simpliciter* in each possible world. It follows that the activities through which we establish logical truths are not special cases of the activities for establishing ordinary (material) truth. Yet the false analogy between the two "kinds of truth" still seems to mislead many philosophers. Activities which can lead to our knowing certain logical truths are because of the false analogy assumed to be representative also of how material truths are established.

Apart from such detailed criticisms, the analogy with Kant enable us to locate the overall shortcoming of these competing approaches. In a sense, they go wrong in exactly the same place as Kant, but in a different direction. In the "transcendental argument" adumbrated above, I located Kant's mistake in a wrong answer to the question: What are the activities by means of which we come to know the truth of the proposition we are dealing with? Kant's answer was (for propositions whose logic is essentially that of quantification theory) seen to be perception rather than the activities of seeking and finding. In the approaches I am criticizing, a yet different answer is in effect given to the same question. It amounts to identifying formal argumentation as the relevant kind of knowledge-acquiring activity. This is in my opinion quite as fatal a mistake as Kant's, and in some ways it is a much less plausible answer than the Kantian one.

Yet mistakes in this general direction are surprisingly persistent. It is almost a dogma among many philosophers of logic that the "language games" which constitute the "logical home" (to use Wittgenstein's metaphor) of our basic logic notions, for instance of quantifiers, are those of argumentation or consequence-drawing. This view is for instance unmistakably present in P.F. Strawson's *Introduction to Logical Theory* and occurs in a slightly different form in his later idea of communication as a semantically important activity.[11] Another version of the same general type of view is Lorenzen's idea[12] that the rules of certain competitive dialogues are constitutive of the rules of our logic. The ultimate hopelessness of dialogues as the foundation of logic and semantics should nevertheless be obvious. Dialogues are intra-linguistic activities. They cannot create or maintain the links between language and reality which lend our language its significance. On the contrary, they already presuppose these links. Theory of argumentation cannot serve as the foundation of logic and semantics. The real dependencies obtain in the opposite direction.

This helps us to understand the relation of game-theoretical semantics to other current approaches.[13] It is of course not the whole story. For instance, within the Lorenzen-Lorenz theory of dialogical logics there are recently developed conceptualizations which can serve some of the same purposes as my semantical games.[14] It is nevertheless highly misleading philosophically to speak of such games as dialogical games. "Hide-and-seek" is not a variety of conversation, as little as football is a variant of chess. One of the virtues of the Kantian analogy is that it serves to bring out the reasons of the infelicity of trying to associate semantical games of seeking and finding to dialogical games.

Thus it may look as if the Kantian analogy has given me a conclusive argument in favor of game-theoretical semantics and against its competitors as philosophical theories. Whatever the merits of Prawitz, Dummett, and Lorenzen may be as mathematical logicians, their theories cannot have the philosophical significance they ascribe to their respective views. Theory of inference or theory of argumentation cannot serve as the basis of semantics or philosophy of logic in the way it has been claimed to serve.

## 6. *From semantical games to dialogical ones*

Our observations do in fact show, it seems to me, that the philosophical foundations of the competitors of game-theoretical semantics are in need of much closer scrutiny than they have been given so far. Unfortunately, the matter is not quite as clear-cut as I have made it out to be. As so often in philosophy, there are further ways of looking upon our problems. Once again the Kantian (transcendental) vantage point proves its mettle by suggesting a further line of thought. It is true that the activities through which we come to know the truth of quantificational propositions are more aptly construed as those of seeking and finding rather than as activities of formal argumentation. However, it does not follow that there is not some more general description of the relevant activities of verification and falsification which enable to relate them to the language-games of argumentation. After all, it is clear that the rules of proof are not unrelated to the semantical games of seeking and finding on my own account.[15] Instead of denigrating the language activities of formal proof, I should instead show their connection with semantical games. Dummett, Prawitz, and Lorenzen were seen to be wrong in their unqualified philosophical claims. However, it does not follow that the language-games they have actually studied are uninteresting or unimportant. The constructive task here is to put these language-games into perspective by means of a closer analysis of their structure. An important step in so doing is to spell out explicitly the epistemic element which is implicit in the idea of verification and in the idea of defending a proposition in a dialogical game. It seems to me that this is one of the many instances in which the resources of epistemic logic have been neglected by logicians to the detriment of the clarity of their arguments.

These tasks largely remain to be done. We can find clues as to how they can be accomplished, however. One thing we can do is to try to conceptualize the activities of verification and falsification as special cases of sequences of questions put to Nature.[16] This is in keeping with the Kantian viewpoint. As it happens, the idea of information acquisition by means of questions put to Nature is even in a literal agreement with what Kant says.[17]

By construing the processes of coming to know the truth or falsity of the relevant propositions as a series of questions put to Nature, we can subsume the study of the activities of verification and falsification --at least in some of its aspects-- to the more general study of information-seeking dialogues consisting of questions and answers. These games can then be related --we may hope-- also to the dialogical games of Lorenzen and to the verification and falsification methods of Dummett and Prawitz.

In both respects, most of the work remains to be carried out.

It is not even known what precisely will happen when this program is pursued seriously. A beginning is being made, however. Dialogical games of information-gathering are what is dealt with in my (joint) paper "Sherlock Holmes Confronts Modern Logic" (this volume). The deserve a much more detailed study than they have so far received, both in their own right and in their relation to the games of seeking and finding. Furthermore, it remains to relate these interrogative games to Lorenzen's dialogical games and to the Dummett-Prawitz proof procedures. In particular, it remains to be seen how many of the claims of these philosophers can be vindicated in this way. There are in any case indications that not everything can be saved. For instance, all the three logicians just mentioned have claimed that the natural logic resulting from their respective approaches is an intuitionistic one. I have put forward an argument which appears to show that the natural "logic" --in a sense that evolves from my dialogical games-- is neither a classical nor an intuitionistic one.[18]

Moreover, these questioning logics, whether intuitionistic or not, are not the rock bottom of logic in the way several philosophers have thought. On the more fundamental level of the games of seeking and finding, game-theoretical semantics also suggests non-classical logics (incidentally *ipso facto* assigning to them also a viable pragmatics). This logic is not an intuitionistic one, however, but of the nature of a functional interpretation (in Gödel's sense).[19] In general, as an important but so far neglected application of game-theoretical semantics we could show how various functional interpretations of logic and arithmetic can be given an eminently natural "transcendental deduction" from my general vantage point.[20]

The most important task here is nevertheless a deeper analysis of the information-acquiring interrogative games themselves. It is here that our paper "Sherlock Holmes Confronts Modern Logic" is calculated to make a beginning. It has also become clear that suitable dialogical games which generalize ours have extremely interesting applications to problems (including important linguistic problems) quite apart from their relation to competing approaches.[21] Lauri Carlson's unpublished work is an impressive demonstration of the success of such applications.[22] It may be that such concrete applications are a better index of the merits of my approach than philosophical arguments.

## NOTES

1. The interpretation summarized here of Kant's theories of mathematical reasoning, space, time, and perception is presented in my books, Logic, Language-Games, and Information, Clarendon Press, Oxford, 1973, chapters 5-9, and Knowledge and the Known, D. Reidel, Dordrecht, 1974, chapters 6-8. (See especially the former, chapter 5, "Logic, Language-Games, and Transcendental Arguments.")

2. See Logic, Language-Games, and Information (note 1 above), ch. 3, "Language-Games for Quantifiers." Many of my subsequent contributions to the detailed development of game-theoretical semantics are collected in Esa Saarinen, editor, Game-Theoretical Semantics, D. Reidel, Dordrecht, 1979.

3. Several of the philosophical implications of game-theoretical semantics were spelled out in my Logic, Language-Games, and Information (note 1 above) already prior to its main applications to linguistic and logical semantics.

4. See my paper, "Language-Games" in Saarinen, editor (note 2 above), originally in Jaakko Hintikka et al., editors, Essays on Wittgenstein in Honour of G.H. von Wright (Acta Philosophica Fennica, vol. 28, nos. 1-3), North-Holland, Amsterdam, 1976, pp. 105-125.

5. For Michael Dummett, see "What Is a Theory of Meaning? I," in Samuel Guttenplan, editor, Mind and Language, Clarendon Press, Oxford, 1975, pp. 99-138; ibid. II, in Gareth Evans and John McDowell, editors, Truth and Meaning, Clarendon Press, Oxford, 1976, pp. 67-137; "The Justification of Deduction," Proceedings of the British Academy, vol. 59 (1973), pp. 1-34; Elements of Intuitionism, Clarendon Press, Oxford, 1977; "The Philosophical Basis of Intuitionistic logic," in H.E. Rose et al., editors, Logic Colloquium '73, North-Holland, Amsterdam, 1975, pp. 5-40. For Dag Prawitz, see "Meaning and Proofs: On the Conflict Between Classical and Intuitionistic Logic," Theoria, vol. 43 (1977), pp. 1-40; "On the Idea of a General Proof Theory," Synthese, vol. 27 (1974), pp. 63-77; "Intuitionistic Logic: A Philosophical Provocation," in the Entretiens de Düsseldorf of Institut International de Philosophie 1978 (unpublished); "Proofs and the Meaning and Completeness of the Logical Constants," in Jaakko Hintikka et al., editors, Essays on Mathematical and Philosophical Logic, D. Reidel, Dordrecht, 1978, pp. 25-40; "Ideas and Results From Proof Theory," in J.E. Fenstad, editor, Proceedings of the Second Scandinavian Logic Symposium, North-Holland, Amsterdam, 1975, pp. 235-250.

6. See here my papers "Quantifiers vs. Quantification Theory" and "Quantifiers in Natural Languages: Some Logical Problems" in Saarinen, editor, note 2 above, pp. 49-79 and 81-117, respectively.

7. The information set of a move m by a player p is the set of those moves whose outcome is known by p at m. See also R. Duncan Luce and Howard Raiffa, Games and Decisions, John Wiley, New York, 1957, p. 43.

NOTES

8. Leon Henkin, "Completeness in the Theory of Types," Journal of Symbolic Logic, vol. 15 (1950), pp. 81-91, and cf. Jaakko Hintikka, "Standard vs. Nonstandard Logic: Higher-Order, Modal, and First-Order Logics," in E. Agazzi, editor, Modern Logic, D. Reidel, Dordrecht, 1980.

9. See "Quantifiers vs. Quantification Theory" in Saarinen, editor, note 2 above. (Originally published in Linguistic Inquiry, vol. 5 (1974), pp. 153-177.)

10. Op. cit. (note 9 above).

11. P.F. Strawson, Introduction to Logical Theory, Methuen, London, 1952; "Meaning and Truth," in Logico-Linguistic Papers, Methuen, London, 1971.

12. The basic writings of the Lorenzen school are conveniently available in Paul Lorenzen and Kuno Lorenz, editors, Dialogische Logik, Wissenschaftliche Buchgesellschaft, Darmstadt, 1978 (with further references to the literature). See also Wolfgang Stegmüller, "Remarks on the Completeness of Logical Systems Relative to the Validity-Concepts of P. Lorenzen and K. Lorenz," Notre Dame Journal of Formal Logic, vol. 5 (1964), pp. 81-112.

13. Frequently game-theoretical semantics enables us to deepen the insights obtained in the competing approaches. For instance, the verificationists have pointed out repeatedly that in their view there is no valid general reason to believe in the law of bivalence (according to which each proposition p is true or false). In game-theoretical semantics, the truth of p means that there is a winning strategy for myself in the correlated semantical game G(p), and the falsity of p means that Nature has a winning strategy in G(p). Not only is it immediately clear on the basis of these definitions that there is in general no reason to expect p to be either true or false; in the game-theoretical approach we see at once what the law of bivalence amounts to. It amounts to the assumption of determinateness of semantical games, that is, to the assumption that one of the two players has a winning strategy. Now it is known from game theory and its applications to logic that determinateness postulates are often especially strong and especially interesting assumptions. Indeed, there exists a flourishing branch of foundational studies examining the consequences of different determinateness assumptions. (See J. Mycielski and H. Steinhaus, "A Mathematical Axiom Contradicting the Axiom of Choice," Bulletin de l'Academie Polonaise des Sciences, Ser. III, vol. 10, 1962, pp. 1-3; J. Mycielski, "On the Axiom of Determinateness," Fundamenta Mathematicae, vol. 53, 1964, pp. 205-224; Jens Erik Fenstad, "The axiom of Determinateness," in Jens Erik Fensted, editor, Proceedings of the Second Scandinavian Logic Symposium, North-Holland, Amsterdam, 1971, pp. 41-61 (with further references to the literature).

14. I am referring to what Lorenzen and Lorenz call material games. The introduction of these games has not led the architects of this approach to change the label "dialogical," however.

NOTES

15. One way of looking at the activity of attempting to prove _p_ as an enterprise of trying to construct a counter-example to _p_, i.e., to construct a domain in which I don't have a winning strategy in G(_p_).

16. See here especially my joint paper with Merrill B. Hintikka "Sherlock Holmes Confronts Modern Logic" (this volume) to which the present note serves as an introduction and background material. Cf. also "Sherlock Holmes Formalized," in L. Geldsetzer, editor, _Festschrift_ for A. Diemer, forthcoming, and "Towards an Interrogative Model of Scientific Inquiry," in W. Callebaut _et al._, editors, _Theory of Knowledge and Science Policy_, Communication & Cognition, Ghent, 1979, pp. 208-220.

17. _Critique of Pure Reason_, B xiii.

18. Jaakko Hintikka and Esa Saarinen, "Information-Seeking Dialogues: Some of Their Logical Properties," _Studia Logica_, vol. 32 (1979),pp. 355-363.

19. See Kurt Gödel, "Über eine bisher noch nicht benützte Erweiterung des finiten Standpunktes," in _Logica: Studia Paul Bernays dedicata_ (no editor given), Editions Griffon, Neuchatel, 1959, pp. 76-83. Note here how the translation into second-order logic exemplified by (2) and (5)-(6) above is of the nature of a functional interpretation. It can be varied further in different ways, e.g., by limiting the values of function variables (including those of a higher type) to recursive functions.

20. As was first pointed out by Dana Scott (unpublished), we can for instance in this way obtain an eminently natural motivation for Gödel's interpretation of elementary arithmetic (see the preceding note). For other uses of functional interpretations, cf. Jaakko Hintikka and Lauri Carlson, "Conditionals, Generic Quantifiers, and Other Applications of Subgames," in Saarinen, editor (note 2 above), pp. 179-214. Cf. also Jean-Yves Girard, "Functional Interpretation and Kripke Models," in Robert Butts and Jaakko Hintikka, editors, _Logic, Foundations of Mathematics, and Computability Theory_ (Part One of the Proceedings of the Fifth International Congress of Logic, Methodology, and Philosophy of Science), D. Reidel, Dordrecht, 1977, pp. 33-57.

21. Cf. e.g. the papers mentioned in notes 6, 16, and 20 above.

22. Lauri Carlson, _Dialogue Games: An Approach to the Theory of Text_ (forthcoming).

# TOWARDS A GENERAL THEORY OF ARGUMENTATION

L. Apostel

## 1. *Logic and rhetorics, heuristics, proof theory*

The fact that many divergent algebras are named "logics", has intensified the need for their legitimation or justification. No formal system is "a logic" if it is only given syntactically by a set of restrictions about sequences of signs allowed and about their modes of transformation. Only algebras that have specific relations to human thought have the right to be called "logics". No agreement however exists about these relations.

It is widely accepted that "logic" should at least contain rules determining the evaluation of debates, disputes, arguments. Logic should at least contain a theory about "rational (whatever that word may mean) discussions". We agree with this point of view, but we stress the fact (not as widely accepted, so we believe) that it constitutes only a necessary but not a sufficient condition for some algebra to be called a "logic". It is certainly true that the final product of a thought process can be neglected, if it does not find expression in an exposition that may be argued about, accepted or rejected. But this does not mean that thought processes are reducible to their social end products. Thought is also search, attempt to find solutions for problems. If *rhetorics* is to be one part of logic, *heuristics* is to be another part. Moreover, the theory of the consolidation of the results of heuristic search, the theory of "justification", sometimes called *"the theory of proof"*, is neither reducible to *rhetorics* nor to *heuristics*. We wanted to mention this point at the beginning of this paper; we shall not be concerned with heuristics or proof in the sequel. But the need for a general theory of argumentation should not make us forget the other dimensions of logic. The overevaluation (after centuries of neglect) of Aristotelean and Medieval Rhetorics could be as harmful in the future as the over-evaluation of syntax and semantics has been in the last fifty years. These words of warning should not prevent us however from recognizing the social value of general rhetorics. In actual practice, logic should help us to participate more critically and more fruitfully in concrete disputes. Its social value depends upon its performing this crucial pedagogical function.

## 2. *Theory of discussion*

Recognizing the value of rhetorics for logic, we should be careful not to limit its scope too much. The theory of discussion has many aspects.

a. *Discussions actually occur and can be studied as empirical phenomena*. The observation of these discussions and the theoretical explanation of their types, development and interacting features, gives us the empirical theory of argumentation; social psychologists have done much work on this topic in recent years[1]. Different from this empirical study is the normative theory of discussions; even this normative study can be pursued in many ways. A normative study of discussions can be closely related to empirical inquiry (for instance, the study of efficient methods of deliberation in schools of management and the study of persuasive communication in speech departments have practical purposes; they are of a normative nature but are developed in close interaction with the empirical study of discussions). On the other hand the a-priori study of rules for rational discourse as found in Lorenzen, Lorenz, Hintikka, Naess, Hamblin, Barth and Krabbe[2] is an exercise in "formal dialectics". In between these two poles a theory of argumentation as developed by Perelman[3] is an empirical effort (based on text studies, not on live social interactions), refraining from actual evaluation, but studying as a matter of fact the various types of evaluation that are applied to and in actual discussions.

b. Both normative and descriptive studies of discussions can concentrate on the *externally observed* utterances exchanged, or on the *interactions of intentions and beliefs* that constitute the driving forces of these observable exchanges. Perelman defines rhetorics as the study of attempts to increase the degree of conviction in certain beliefs (using epistemic terms without formalisation) while Barth and Hamblin stress that the theory of argumentation is concerned with externally expressed *commitments* subscribing to certain theses.

c. Discussions can be studied globally or locally. If I call a discussion "balanced" because all speakers intervene with comparable frequency and because all positions are equally well defended, I express a global attribute of this discussion. If on the other hand I describe the rules by means of which "or" statements (disjunctions) can be introduced into discussions, then I describe a local step in the development that occurs.

Looking at the existing literature we observe that a tendency exists (a) to separate as strongly as possible the *descriptive* theory of argumentation from the *normative* theory of argumentation, (b) to separate also the *intensional-epistemic* from the *external* theory of argumentation and (c) to separate the *global* from the *local* theory of argumentation. These tendencies are, according to the point of view of the present article, counterproductive.

We present some arguments against these separations. Both from the point of view of the producer of arguments and from the point of view of the persons who listen to and evaluate the arguments produced, a discussion functions as a whole. *The norms introduced to regulate local interactions should be justified from the point of view of norms introduced to regulate global interactions;* if not, the atomisation of the theory of argumentation leads to the disappearance of the object of this discipline.

Moreover, as we indicated already, the commitments expressed, the questions asked and the answers given are caused by epistemic states and by preferences. Both the external and the internal dynamics should be taken into account; *from the formal point of view this entails that the theory of assertions, the theory of speech acts, the theory of beliefs and the theory of preferences should be presupposed and used by the development of the theory of argumentation.*[4]

Finally, we defend the unpopular but essential point of view that *the norms regulating an activity should be derived from the nature of the activity itself.* This would imply that the normative theory of discourse should be derived from the descriptive theory of argumentation. This point of view, using facts to establish values and starting from reality to establish norms, contradicts existing practice. It has as logical consequence: *the inductive support on observational bases of deontic statements concerning norms regulating argumentative actions becomes the basic theory of logic in general* (as far as it is based on dialectics or rhetorics). Yet we recognise that this deontic part of logic is one of the least developed regions of our discipline (especially in its interaction with inductive support)[5]. But this difficult position has to be defended if we do not want to lose the most important contribution a theory of argumentation can make. We introduced the theory of argumentation as a basis for logic because we wanted to overcome the arbitrariness of formalism. The theory of logical rules based on a theory of argumentation should thus be derived from reality. Either this entails that rules should be derived from observed reality (as we propose) or this entails to the contrary that they should be derived from a priori synthetic insight about discussions and arguments. If neither justification is forthcoming then the theory of argumentation lacks normative foundation (and thus is unable to legitimate a logic) or its normative foundation is once more purely conventional (and thus in no way superior to Gentzen type laws for logical connectives). In as far as we do not believe in synthetic a priori insights in rules for debates, we are compelled to subscribe to the difficult position we have just sketched. In the present paper, limitations of space will not allow us to use empirical facts about discussions, combined with deontic logic and inductive rules, to establish a general theory of argumentation. We think it feasible to derive from observation some very general features of discussions, and believe that these features can lead us to the justification of some rules, both global ones and local ones. This type of reasoning remains provisional, however. It should be supplemented and, at the limit, superseded by the coming together of the empirical and formal theories of debate, a synthesis that, for opposite reasons, is absent from the work of Perelman and the psycho-sociologists on the one side, and from the work of Lorenzen-Lorenz and Hintikka on the other side.

Our point of view towards argumentation theory is, moreover, justified from the practical point of view: from the perspective of the receiver, trying to remain critical, a theory of fallacies is his main weapon of defence against rhetorics, and from the point of view of the producer a theory of efficient persuasion is the main weapon to be used in the construction of useful discourse. Both users of the theory of argumentation need the continuous interplay of norms and facts, of global and local, as much as of internal and external insights.

## 3. *What are discussions?*

Let us ask what the essential features of a discussion are! A discussion is the interaction between n participants. Monologues, dialogues and polylogues may all constitute discussions. Discussions occur in time; we do not lose essential information if we suppose this time to be discrete and state that the discussion occupies m moments. The time during which a discussion goes on is not necessarily continuous; a discussion may be interrupted and resumed. At any given moment of the time during which the discussion takes place, a participant functions either as a listener, receiving an argument, or as a speaker, who is presenting an argument (as a reader or speaker); these two roles can be taken up simultaneously in stead of successively.

At any given moment (during any given time-interval) of the continuation of the discussion some participants (in general one; but they can be several) utter a sequence of sentences (of diverse types) that we call texts (propositions, commands and questions are only atomic parts of texts).

At any given moment the internal states of the participants are characterised by the beliefs they hold at that moment, the commitments they hitherto have made and also the aims they pursue at that moment. Among these aims some refer to the belief systems of other participants (the aims they wish to pursue in so far as they are concerned with confirming or changing beliefs, commitments and aims of other participants).

In order for a discussion to take place at least one pair of incompatible statements must be held by participants (in general more) and at least some participants must aim to modify the beliefs of others. Pursuing different aims is as important however as holding different views; and asking different questions leads to an equally deep divergence. We think that for a discussion to take place, we should generalise the conditions concerning the difference and connectedness of views, and ask that certain subsets of participants have different beliefs, aims or questions; that they know about each other that these differences exist; that they are interested in changing this state of affairs *because they have to execute common actions that are incompatible with the existence of these divergences (the seeking of a consensus is only a special case).* We stress the fact that while they are *necessary*, divergences are not enough to produce discussions; the *insight* into their existence and the *common interest in their decrease* are as essential. Moreover, nobody will engage in a discussion if he or she cannot believe that there is at least a *chance to modify* the state of affairs. Finally the disputants must use languages that, even if they are not identical, should be close enough to make communication possible. For this reason we may simplify our exposition by stating that all participants use the same language.

Summarizing these remarks, a discussion is represented by the following ordered sequence:

1. The set P of n participants. 2. The discontinuous and ordered sequence T of moments t during which the discussion takes place. 3. The texts Ti,(k-n) produced by participant i during the time interval lying between tk and tn. i is a variable ranging over the names of the participants in a discussion, k-n is a pair of ordinal numbers. The ordinal numbers in question correspond to beginnings and ends of texts. For example: T2(6-9) is the text produced by the second participant during the interval ranging from the 6th to the 9th time period of the discussion. The discussion is considered to be subdivided into a finite number of exact time intervals, described by their first and last moment. 4. The statements S(i',tj) and H(i',tj) stating that the partici-

pant i' is either speaker or hearer at a given moment tj. i' is a name for a participant in the discussion (and thus a constant designating an object belonging to the set over which the variable i ranges).

5. The sets Bi'tjr of beliefs held by participant i', at moment tj with intensity r. B is the constant name of a set of beliefs; i' is -as mentioned before- the name of a discussion participant; tj is a moment (indicated by its ordinal number) during which the discussion takes place; r is an ordinal number measuring the strenght of a belief.

6. The set Pa'i'tjs: the set of aims pursued by participant i' at moment tj with intensity s. i' is as before, tj is as before; s is an ordinal number measuring the strenght (or intensity) of commitment of an actor to a purpose. a' is the end state aimed at by the commitment of the participant i'. One participant can thus aim, at one moment, to realise more than one end state but his commitment to them can be of different intensity. 7. The languages Li used by the participants i to perform the speech acts that, taken together, make up the discussion. 8. Among the beliefs of the participants there exist beliefs about the beliefs of other participants, and also beliefs about the relations between the beliefs of the different participants. (The belief about incompatibilities that is one of the more frequently quoted ones is not to be defined by logical means but as a belief in the impossibility to defend or to act in accordance with two different statements at the same time). This can be expressed symbolically as follows Bi'tjr (Bi''tj's): the beliefs current for i' at tj with intensity r, about the beliefs current for i'' at moment tj' with intensity s. 9. Among the aims of the participants we find aims as to the beliefs or aims participant i' at tj wants with intensity r, to be held by i'' at tm with intensity s. 10. Necessary also is a sequence Ar of rules for argumentation,

(1) stating the types of texts that are either obligatory or forbidden in the type of discussion present, (2) stating how the texts, the beliefs and aims have to depend upon earlier texts, beliefs or aims of the same or other participants. 11. A global evaluation function V defined over the set of all discussions and a local evaluation function v defined over the sequences of beliefs, aims and texts of one participant in one discussion indicate the degree with which the discussions reach their aims and, locally, the degree with which the discussion reaches the aim of the given participants.

This very natural and yet complicated concept can in consequence be represented in an abbreviated way by the sequence (P, T, S, H, B, Pr, L, BB and BPr, PrB and PrPr, AR, V and v). P is the name of the set of participants in the discussion D; T is the name of the set of time points during which the discussion takes place; S is the name of the set of speakers active in this discussion; H is the name of the set of hearers; B is the name of the set of beliefs held by the participants during the discussion D; Pr is the name of the set of aims pursued by the participants during the discussion D; L is the name of the language used by the participants in D; BB and BPr are the names of the sets of beliefs held by participants in D referring to the beliefs of other participants in D and to the aims of other participants in D; PrB and PrPr are the names of the sets of aims pursued during D by its participants concerning the beliefs of other participants in D and the aims of other participants in D; AR is the name of the set of rules according to which the D-process is to be explained; V is the evaluation function evaluating the set of discussions of which D is a member; v is the evaluation function evaluating the intervention of particular participants i in discussions D belonging to this same set.

We claim that this sequence "characterizes" a discussion in the following sense: only if we can give concrete values for all the variables in this sequence of 14 entities can we characterize a discussion in such a way that it can be encompassed by a theory of discussion.

We hope that this idea is at the same time specific and general enough to encompass the various concepts of discussion present in literature. Some particular features deserve to be pointed out. (i) Times, purposes, texts, beliefs, intensities of purposes and beliefs play crucial roles in this definition. We have the impression that elsewhere these features have not yet received the attention needed. (ii) We define evaluation functions over discussions as wholes and over partial interventions; but we do not introduce the simple opposition "winning or losing a discussion". We have no doubts about its utility, but we think this limiting case of a zero sum antagonistic discussion game is too specific. (iii) We can express some very general and trivial properties of the ideas introduced: the set P must be neither empty nor infinite (and this requirement holds for all the other sets introduced). All hearers must be speakers at some time, and conversely (this requirement of involvement does not hold for other interesting situations but the present concept imposes it). Some B and Pr sets of some participants are transformed during the discussion (stronger but less general requirements would be: all of them are transformed, or all of them are equally transformed). The AR do not change except if the discussion is interrupted by a metadiscussion about the AR. The AR are present in the B's of all participants (completely, or to a sufficient, or to an equal extent). The B and Pr sets of all participants are not identical. The V and v functions define orders that may be complete or incomplete. We could continue; this list of properties is by no means complete.

(iv) Our discussions are defined for polylogues in general and not only for dialogues. We have our reasons for this complication:

even if dialogues are used, many other persons co-participate in the minds of the disputants, and if - as might seem natural - the most important discussions are discussions among two or more human participants with nature as a metaphorical participant, then the basic dialogues involve at least three participants.

### 4. *Reduction to the theory of (inter-)action*

Our short presentation of discussions in 3. has a very important consequence: *the theory of discussion must be a part of the theory of goaldirected or purposeful interaction (1), and the theory of interaction must be a part of the theory of action (2).* It is one of our main theses that action theory has to be developed and, within action theory, interaction theory if argumentation theory has to take its proper place.

A small number of action logics has been presented (von Wright, Chisholm, Nowakowska, Aquist, Apostel)[6]. We consider these attempts to be useful, but they suffer from a serious drawback. All of them have been trying to understand actions by means of the introduction of classical logical operations defined on actions. This strategy was certainly correct: one should see to what extent tools already at our disposal can help us in performing new tasks. But the hesitant proposals as to suitable axioms for the combination of action-concepts with classical logical concepts show that the operations are not the most natural ones to be used in the development of action-theory.

This article is not the place to present another action-theory. But we have to convince the reader that action-theory is possible as a formal discipline. If not, no useful purpose would be served by the *reduction of the theory of argumentation to the theory of action.* The foundation would be too weak to lead us towards a useful logic. Without performing the more general and preliminary task, let us at least indicate how it could be done. Our proposal is to characterise actions by means of axioms stating properties of concepts specific to actions as such.

An action is a transformation of nature in order to realise a purpose. This entails that specific for action as such are (1) the degree of realisation of the purpose by the transformation, (2) the degree of anticipation of the transformation by the actor, (3) the degree of transformation of the actor, of his instruments and of the external world by the transformation. Let us suppose these degrees to be ordered. A definition of the action-concept by means of axioms about the consequences of increasing or decreasing these degrees, and by means of axioms about the interaction of these increases and decreases, yields a description of actions in terms of their intrinsic properties and avoids the artificialities of action-theory as it has been developed until now. We cannot here execute the plan we have just proposed. Let us only use this remark to show the reader that action-theory is not compelled to remain in its present unsatisfactory state.

### 5. *"Proponent", "Opponent", "defence" and "attack"*

Some actions are only preparing for other ones. An action is a preparatory action with respect to another one if a) it creates the conditions for the execution of the other one b) while its own product is not as such a purpose for its actor. An internal preparation (a problem solving process or a practical deliberation) is also preparation; planification is a type of internal preparation.

Some actions are interactions: actors coordinate their actions purposefully in such a way that the joint results at given moments will allow them to reach purposes they want to realise without being able to realise them alone.

*A discussion is a collective action (rather: an interaction) bringing together preparatory actions of different actors with the purpose to make possible later collective or individual actions.*

The preparing of a collective or individual action by means of an interaction of preparatory actions is, so we think, one of the main features characterising all discussions.

We want to show the usefulness of this praxeological description of discussions by making clear that four basic concepts of formal dialogue theory are definable in this context. The concepts are the following ones: "proponent", "opponent", "defence" and "attack". They have been used by Lorenzen-Lorenz in a creative way: the main result of dialogical logic until now due to these authors, is that different well known logical systems are the results of allowing the participants only one or to the contrary different means of attacking and defending statements[7]. This result is remarkable. It can, however, be considered as giving a non-arbitrary foundation for logic only if it can be proved, by an analysis of the discussion situation as such, that to optimalise the latter we have to impose on the proponents or the opponents different rights as to defence and attack. Friedrich Kambartel (in his paper "Überlegungen zum Pragmatischen und Argumentativen Fundament der Logik", *Konstruktionen versus Positionen*, Band I, pp. 216-228) has already pointed out that the different argumentation rules leading to different logics need to be justified in the context of a more general action-theory. We want to take some steps in the direction he has indicated and this is the reason why it is useful to carry out a derivation of some of the rules of attack and defence from our description of discussion as interactional preparatory action.

Let a proponent be an actor who introduces a given transformation of natural or verbal reality in order to prepare the future action. Let the opponent be an actor who attempts to eliminate the transformation introduced by the first in order to prepare the common action purpose in another way. The proponent takes the initiative; the opponent as opponent tries only to eliminate the effects of an initiative.

An attack against a position is an action attempting to eliminate that position; the actor who performs an attack is thus a local opponent. The defence of a position is an action attempting to consolidate a position; this can occur either by adducing new material for its defence or to the contrary by attacking an attack. The defending actor may thus be a local proponent (in the first case) or a local opponent (in the second case). Taking into account these two remarks the opponents and proponents are global roles; attack and defence are local performances.

We should certainly realise that these four concepts overstress the antagonistic character of discussions. Other performances are equally important in general discussions: questions, suggestions, doubts, specification, modifications, conditionalisation. In social cooperation not only he who counteracts initiative or helps it, is important; we have also persons who neither help nor counteract, but relate, or modify, or give qualified help or perform a conditional attack. But these more complex moves and roles will be analysable in action-theory if we can relate the simpler quadruplet (opponent, proponent, attack, defence) to general action-theory.

All actions aiming at certain ends have to aim at specificity, security and economy. The end should be reached as exactly as possible, as certainly as possible, and with minimal cost. These criteria of evaluation are multidimensional; they can not be maximalised simultaneously. For instance (in order to get as soon as possible to the context that is of interest to us): if a discussion is optimal if we reach as soon as possible agreement (if agreement can be reached) or the certainty that disagreement can not be overcome (if such is the case), then we should impose the following rule: any position can only be once attacked and once defended and the attack and defence should be concerned with the last position reached in the game. Commitments once made should never be withdrawn. Positions not immediately attacked should become general commitments. The memory needed to play the discussion game is then minimal. If to the contrary we allow multiple attacks and multiple defences we obviously are optimalising another feature of discussion: the stability of its results. The more attacks and defences have been allowed before reaching a result the stronger is our guarantee not to be compelled to abandon it in the future.

If the opponent, in virtue of the argumentation rules, receives the right to attack or defend in more ways than the proponent, the rules favour initiative over prudence; if the opposite case is realised, prudence is favoured above initiative. The same remark will hold when many defences are allowed but only one attack (initiative dominates) or when many attacks are allowed and only one defence (prudence dominates). If symmetrical roles are given to opponent and proponent, and symmetrical rights to defence and attack, neither initiative nor prudence are favoured. If however, the opponent gets more rights than the proponent, while on the other hand the attack gets more rights than the defence, then we have a mixture of two divergent asymmetries and this mixture cannot easily be understood from the point of view of action-theory.

The few remarks that have been made show however that differences in argumentation rules that, according to Lorenzen-Lorenz's discovery lead on the one side to intuitionistic logic and on the other side to classical logic, can only be understood in a non-arbitrary way if we relate the different argumentation rules to general dimensions of action.

We are of the opinion that this constitutes a strong argument in favour of the insertion of argumentation-theory into action-theory.

The fact that deliberations and discussions are actions of a preparatory kind did not yet enter the discussion. Should in this specific action-context special optimalisation conditions prevail? Preparatory action is not as costly as executive action; irreversible processes are not predominant. But we should try to have as complete an overview of the pro's and con's as possible (if the function of preparation is to be executed). This leads us to argumentation rules that allow the withdrawal of commitment; that allow repeated attacks and defences, but that give more rights to the critical opponent than to the creative proponent. We are not certain that this is the only attitude that can be defended but at least we see here some reasons to have a mixture of divergent asymmetries.

## 6. *Systematic connections between the theory of games and some theories discussed at this conference*

Having presented our first defence of an insertion of argumentation-theory into action-theory, we want to strengthen our case a) by studying the relation between game-theory and theory of argumentation, b) by commenting upon the relations between Hintikka's type of game theoretical logic and Lorenzen-Lorenz's type[8] c) by showing the relation between Hamblin's theory of formal dialectics and the theory of action.

These three arguments once presented will enable us moreover to show that the local dialogical logics need to be derived (as we stated earlier) from the global dialogical logics.

Both Lorenzen-Lorenz and Hintikka quoting at various places either Luce and Raiffa's important overview "Games and Decisions" or Claude Berge's "General Theory of Games" [9], understand dialogical logic as a special case of zero sum two person games. This proposal is important because it brings logic in close relation to a precise version of a theory that has been proposed as a schematisation of a theory of competitive social interactions. In earlier papers we did applaud this idea, however already regretting that no attempt was made to bring the theory of argumentation into contact with a non zero sum n-person game (the reader will be aware of the fact that our description of discussions makes this comparison imperative). At present we want to borrow from Anatole Rappoport an even more fundamental objection[10]. In his book "Fights, Games and Debates" he makes a fundamental distinction between *a fight*, the purpose of which is to destroy the will to resist of the adversary (even if some rules of fighting are observed and if the purpose is not to annihilate by all possible means the adversary, the aim remains not only to win, but fundamentally to transform the enemy), *a debate* in which the purpose is to modify the beliefs and the preferences of the adversary, and *a game* in which the purpose is (without any possibility to change the preferences or beliefs of the adversary and in principle without any animosity against him) to engage in a rule-regulated interaction having as its aim winning or losing. Rappoport has brought forward many other strong objections against the *descriptive* ambitions of the theory of games (that he accepts as a perfectly respectable mathematical discipline). The theory of argumentation must recognise the fact that some discussions (the ones called "eristic" by Chaim Perelman) come closer to fights than to games because their purpose is to beat the adversary, while other discussions (discussions intended to discover and enlighten their participants) need to be considered as analogous to the "cooperative games" studied by Schelling and his followers[10] but never mentioned either by Lorenzen-Lorenz or Hintikka. We wish to add that *metagames* and *dynamical games*[11] (having as their object other games or leading to the modification of the rules of the game) have to be used as partial models of the theory of argumentation. In particular, the theory of argumentation presented by Jaakko Hintikka as an outdoor game "against nature" where nature is taken, as it has been in statistical decision theory since Abraham Wald, as the absolute adversary, uses a formal model of "searching and finding" reducing these non-argumentative actions to forms of argumentation (the other participant being nature). This approach presupposes the classical zero-sum two person game as its only tool when it seems yet desirable to us to make a more complete use of the tools put at our disposal by game theory as such, and by Rappoport's more general theory of fight[12].

Such a theory of fight or of conflict can only be developed (as can also a theory of cooperation) as part of a general theory of interaction, belonging to the theory of action. A *conflict* exists between two actors if among the purposes of each is to be found the non realisation of some of the purposes of the others. The concept of conflict can be defined if we have at our disposal a general theory of purposeful action. This theory does not need to presuppose the general machinery of rational preferences, utilities and maximisation of expected utilities or minimisation of maximal risks (a technology that determines the features of the theory of games). It is understandable however that the logician wishing to get fast results has immediately taken over the best developed tool (a general theory of cooperation is only recently being developed by Thomas Marschak and Roy Radner in their "Theory of Teams"[13] and a general theory of conflicting action as a part of a theory of action is as undeveloped as the theory of action itself). We see no reason however to limit ourselves to beautiful tools, even if they are inadequate, when already more adequate instruments are beginning to be at our disposal.

### 7. *Hamblin's theory. What is an argument?*

In the best recent book about fallacies (published by C. Hamblin)[14] this author recognises that only within a general theory of argumentation the better known fallacies can find their places (as Chaim Perelman has stated long ago, without being quoted by Hamblin). It is, e.g., impossible to describe what the "fallacy of begging the question" is without introducing the theory of argumentation, because this fallacy consists in defending a conclusion by means of a premise that is no more accepted by the other participants than the conclusion was (in more general praxeological terms: trying to construct a product by means of tools that can only be constructed themselves when the product is already available). In order to construct such a theory of argumentation, Hamblin has to answer the question "what is an argument" and he comes to the following definition (that points immediately to a general theory of action): an argument (p. 245)[15] is an attempt to defend a conclusion in such a way (1) that the statements used for the defence are either completely accepted by the participants, or at least as well accepted as the other statements accepted by the participants (2) that the relation between the means of defence and the position defended are such that the participants commonly use them themselves (3) that the means of defence presupposed and not stated are also functioning as such in the common practice of the participants and (4) that the conclusion defended by means of the argument would be less accepted, if the argument were not used, than if it were used. In fact Hamblin gives a less relativistic description of argument than the one we reproduce here. (1') He wants the premises (entities more restricted than the more general "means of defence" introduced by us) to be "accepted" (not simply "as accepted as the other statements used by the other participants"), (2') he wants the "passage from premises to conclusions to be of an accepted kind" (we replace "of an accepted kind" by "a commonly used kind"), (3') he wants the unstated premises to be "omissible" (we want them to be "of a commonly unmentioned but used type"), (4') he wants the conclusion as "unaccepted in absence of the argument" (we simply want it to be less accepted in the absence of the argument). This definition of "argument" given by Hamblin and relativized even more strongly by us is only the third one occurring in his chapter about this topic: the first one uses *semantical* concepts ("accepted" being replaced by "true" or "valid"); the second one uses *epistemic* concepts ("accepted" being replaced by "believed" or "known"). We mention this to make our reader realise that even those authors who are willing to construct a "general theory of argumentation"[16] have a long way to go to develop it in sufficient independence so that it could, without *presupposing* a logic, be used itself as a foundation *for* such a logic.

The reason for our presentation of this definition of "argument" is the following one: requirements imposed on "arguments" are simply requirements imposed on all constructive actions. A task is executable for a given actor if the following conditions are satisfied (a) if the materials and the instrument of the task are at his disposal (b) if the combinations of instruments and materials needed can be realised by him (c) if needed processes, not explicitly provoked, are provoked as unintended side-effects (d) if without his performing the task the result would not come into existence.

These requirements correspond very closely to the ones imposed earlier on the various steps of an argument. An argument is thus simply a task performed by linguistic means in a cooperating group (in which conflict and resistance are neither necessarily absent or present).

If rules of logic are derivable from the rules defining a "good discussion" or a "good argumentation" (necessarily occurring itself as part of a "good discussion") then they must not in the first place occur as statements that can be defended against all strategies of the opponent, but to the contrary as conditions for the organisation of a normatively correct discussion.

This point of view is rather different, at first sight, from the one defended by Lorenzen-Lorenz and Hintikka. Yet the two modes of approach can be brought together even if they can never be identified.

If a discussion is a collective preparation of a common or individual action, then the following conditions must be realised (i) the various participants must have at their disposal different materials and instruments, all of which are necessary to execute the action described but none of which are sufficient to execute it (ii) the various participants must be able and willing to combine collectively to each other the various materials and instruments that together make the action asked for possible (iii) the various participants must be willing to discard provisionally the materials and instruments also at their disposal but not needed for the task planned (iv) the various participants must not only be willing and able to adapt their own possessions to the common task but also to make the possessions of the other adequate for the common task (v) if not all necessary prerequisites are present, they must be able and willing to enlarge their group, or to construct by means of their present belongings the tools and materials that are lacking (vi) while preparing the given task, even if other tasks are undertaken, they may not be such that they prevent the execution of the task whose preparation is planned (more specifically: no cyclical moves, by definition superfluous, are allowed). These norms can be derived from the definition of "preparation of a task" and as such are a priori. That preparations occur, and that collective preparations are needed, however are synthetic facts about our world. The typology of tasks and the specific rules adequate for specific tasks are of an empirical nature and can only be found by empirical research.

We want to attract the attention of the reader to the fact that these normative requirements applied to "adequate preparations" can be translated immediately into requirements for "good" discussions.

(i) A good discussion must bring together participants defending different positions. Optimal discussions will bring together participants whose participation to the exchange of views will be equal quantitatively and qualitatively; in consequence they will regularly change their roles as speakers and hearers; the distribution of points of view over the group will be such that the points of view are equally represented; the number of different points of view will neither be too large nor too small; the points of view will be such that they have maximal interaction with each other in such a way that they are partially compatible and partially incompatible and that the necessary adjustments needed to come to a consensus entail enrichments for all concerned. But a "good" discussion is not necessarily an "optimal" discussion.

(ii) Furthermore, in a good discussion the participants must be willing and able to take each others views into account; they must be willing to change their own views (if necessary) and be capable of changing them, (iii) the participants must be willing to eliminate from the discussion statements rejected by others as irrelevant, if they cannot after reasonable attempts show their relevance, (iv) the participants must be capable and willing to defend their own positions, (v) if some data or statements necessary to a synthesis that contains contributions from all concerned are lacking the various participants must be willing to seek and accept outside information or internal deductions completing the picture, (vi) the various participants if they engage in new discussions arising from earlier ones must either have completed these earlier ones or must be able to advance the earlier ones by means of the later ones (or conversely).

The reader will see that the requirements for "good" discussions correspond in detail to the requirements for "good" (or efficient) preparations for action.

## 8. *Decomposition of argumentative texts. Sub-games*

Both these sets of requirements are macro-requirements. If we want to perform the task we have set for ourselves, we must show that these macro-requirements entail micro-requirements.

In order to achieve this we must necessarily decompose either the texts, produced as arguments by participants, or the discussions themselves. In fact, the critic, evaluating the quality of discussions and of contributions to discussions, must necessarily formulate criteria of quality depending on (a) earlier or later discussions of the same disputants about the same or different topics (b) earlier or later discussions of other persons about the same or different topics (c) earlier or later interactions of the same persons with other persons in other discussion groups. The study of sets and of sequences of discussions, taken as wholes, and of sets and sequences of contributions to discussions must prepare the study of natural decompositions of arguments. This study must necessarily be a part of the study of sets and sequences of groups engaging in collective action and in the preparation of collective or individual actions, and of sequences and sets of interventions of actors in collective action and its preparation. This topic is still largely unexplored but should be the natural framework on which the theory of argumentation must be developed.

We can not do this systematically here, however. Let us try to perform our task in a less ambitious way. In general an argumentative intervention will not be undecomposable. We must thus consider sub-interventions. In their game theoretical simulation of discussions, Hintikka and Carlson[17] have made interesting use of sub-games. As interventions have to be decomposed in sub-interventions, actions have to be decomposed in sub-actions. In order to be efficient, sub-actions have to be connected to those preceding them and to those succeding them. If two different participants using the products of the same intervention of a third one execute two different moves, it must be possible (in order to bring these two divergent developments together again) to draw a simple or complex common conclusion from both to be used in the later development of the discussion. This means that we need an operation "and" applied not to simple statements only but to texts. The relation of "incompatibility" must also be applicable to interventions because this relation (understood, we repeat this, as a relation, deontic or modal in nature, between the performance or success of two actions) occurs in the definition itself of a "good" discussion. If it is to be possible to simplify the discussion by eliminating one of two interventions by showing that the same end product can be obtained by using only one of them, the connective "or" must be definable on the set of pairs of texts (or, more generally, on the set of relatively complete and autonomous discussion interventions). We do not claim that we have performed the task of deriving specific logical rules from criteria for "good" discussions. But we have at least shown that the presence of incompatibility relations, of possible synthetisation of divergent interventions, of simplification of the discussion lead us to define operations on discussion interventions, that, without being identical to the classically known logical operations, have some of their properties. Finally a discussion being a historical, temporal and purposive event, we need to have the possibility to plan future moves and to summarise past moves. As these moves are processes from starting points to final points we need antisymmetrical relations that will have some of the properties of "entailments". However, these operations we have just introduced are very deeply intensional in the following sense: they refer to the past and the future of the arguments and of the discussion. They are not at all invariant under time; they should have different properties for different discussion types and they depend strongly on context and purpose. In fact, *any logic that depends essentially, and not only formally, on a theory of argumentation, should by its very nature be content and context dependent* (we consider this not to be in contradiction with the formal character of logic because rules, the application of which depends upon the content of the argument and its context, are not by the same token *completely* dependent on content and context; they can still be the same for large classes of contexts and contents even if they are not purely formal).

### 9. *Equivocation and use of metaphors*

Before finishing, however, we wish to point out that in our definition of argument we have included the language L. The formal dialogues of Lorenzen-Lorenz and of Hintikka do not take equivocation and vagueness into account; the theories of argumentation of Arne Naess, C. Hamblin and C. Perelman attach great importance to this feature. We cannot do it justice here but we think that one remark is in order: a language is not a static entity. In fact arguing means constantly changing our language in various ways. One of the main tools for regulated language change, with conscious purpose, is the use of metaphoric language. In another paper [18] we tried to show that most of the forms of argument, collected by Perelman-Olbrechts in their "Traité de l'Argumentation" can be considered as uses of metaphors regulated by conversational postulates. In this same paper we have sketched the beginning of a formal account of metaphors. This formal account of the principal tool of regulated language-change, added to the technology of making utterances more precise, as developed by Arne Naess, and added to the analysis of equivocation performed by Hamblin, should be added to the "rules for good discussions" that according to us should constitute the foundation of argumentative logic in the logic (or theory) of action. This allows us, once again, to build a bridge between formal dialectics and informal theory of argumentation, an undertaking that is not only subsidiary but essential prerequisite to a nonarbitrary logic (as it is sometimes called: the reconciliation of Socrates and Frege) [19].

These are the points we have wanted to make in this paper. It is largely but not completely programmatic in nature. It hopes to prepare future work and it hopes to show that between the formal dialogues of Lorenzen-Lorenz and the completely informal rhetorics of Perelman an intermediary territory can be found that will in fact be necessary if theory of argumentation is to be able to overcome the formalist attitude of recent logic and bring this essential discipline back to its primary task: the analysis and evaluation of efficient argument. This intermediary territory- in fact the only chance for the future fertility of discussion-logic- can only be discovered however - so we think - when theory of discussion is seen as a sub-part of theory of interaction and of action.

NOTES

(1) For an exposition that brings empirical theories of argument in contact with logical theories, see L. Apostel, "Rhétorique, psycho-sociologie et logique" (Logique et Analyse, Nouvelle Série, 6e année, Décembre 1963, n 21-24-pp 236-314).

(2) Paul Lorenzen-Kuno Lorenz, Dialogische Logik, Wissenschaftliche Buchgesellschaft. Darmstadt -1978.

Jaakko Hintikka, Logic, Language-Games and Information, Oxford Clarendon Press -1973; chapter III "Language-Games for Quantifiers" and chapter V "Quantifiers, Language-Games and Transcendental Arguments".

Esa Saarinen (editor), Game Theoretical Semantics, Reidel -1979.

C.L.Hamblin, Fallacies, Methuen and Co -1970.

Arne Naess, Elementaire Argumentatieleer, Basisboeken-Ambo-Baarn -1978; dutch translation of En del elementaere logiske emner, Universitetsforlaget Oslo -1974.

E.M.Barth, "Formal Dialectics: Language Invariant Systems of Rules for Conflict Resolution Pertaining to Conflicting Propositional Attitudes" (prepublication).

Since 1974 at the University of Neuchâtel the "Travaux du Centre de Recherches Sémiologiques" appear in prepublication. This group of linguists, psychologists and logicians, under the guidance of Jean-Blaise Grize attack the same problems, combining text-analysis and logic. Their work deserves to be more widely known.

(3) C. Perelman, Traité de l'Argumentation, Presses Universitaires de France -1958.

Le Champ de l'Argumentation, Bruxelles, Editions de l'Université de Bruxelles -1970.

(4) In N.Rescher, Topics in Philosophical Logic, Reidel -1968; the reader can consult chapter V "Epistemic Modality", ch XIV "Assertion Logic" and ch XV "The Logic of Preference" to find clear introductions to the original works on these topics. An attempt to show the relevance of assertion logic to the theory of argumentation is to be found in "Assertion Logic an Theory of Argumentation" (Philosophy an Rhetoric, vol.4, no 2, 1971 - pp. 92-110 by L.Apostel). A combination of epistemic logic and preference logic is used in L.Apostel, "Logique inductive, modalités épistémiques et logique de la préférence" (Revue Internationale de Philosophie, 25e année, no 95-96, fasc 1-2, Bruxelles 1971, pp. 78-100). An attempt to show the relevance of action logic to the theory of speech acts as a foundation for linguistics is the core of the monograph Communication et Action (Communication and Cognition Press -1979- Gent, by L. Apostel).

(5) In Rescher (op.cit.) ch XVI "Deontic Logic" gives an overview of this topic. The best general reader on the topic is Risto Hilpinen's Deontic Logic, Reidel - 1972.

(6) For these works consult the references in our Communication et Action (see note 4).

(7) We cannot resist the desire to acquaint the reader with the major result of dialogical logic. He has only to compare p 63 of "Dialogische Logik" with p 68 of the same work. Def 10 states "The effective game rule is the following one (1)A propositional schema A of an opponent line in round n(n larger or equal to 0)may be attacked once in any later round (2)A propositional schema A of a proponent line in round n may be attacked as many times as desired in later rounds (3) A propositional schema A may only be defended once against an attack z in round n(n larger or equal to 1), when all later rounds have been closed." Def 13 states to the contrary: "The classical game rule is: (1) identical to 1 of def 10 (2) identical to 2 of def 10 (3) identical to 3 of def 10 (4) A propositional schema A of an opponent line may be defended against an attack in round n as often as is desired, but only once in an attack round n, and any number of times in defence rounds m." Lorenzen-Lorenz prove that the effective rule makes all theses of intuitionistic logic universally defensible (they can be defended against all possible strategies) while the classical rule makes all theses of classical propositional logic defensible. It is thus clear that definite logical results follow from argumentation-rules. Looking for the argumentative foundation of these rules is thus, so we find, a necessary continuation of the work begun there. We want to add however (as will become clear from the later paragraphs of our paper) that for us, logical rules should be derived from conditions necessary for "good" discussions and should rather appear in meta-languages and not as positions that can be defended in actual discourse. According to us logical rules are never argued about, neither defended nor attacked. This different attitude does not decrease however our appreciation for this valuable result.

(8) Jaakko Hintikka presents his language games as "a link between language and reality" (Saarinen, op cit, pp1). He selects a domain D of objects about which his games develop arguments. At each stage of the game, a sentence S' is being considered, and the game has as adversaries a thinker "I" and "Nature". We present two of the relevant rules because we want to comment upon them (Saarinen, op cit p 34-35) (G.E) "If S' is (Ex)F(x),I choose a member of D, give it a proper name, say b. The game is then continued with respect to F(b).(GU);If S' is (x)F(x) the same happens except that Nature chooses b. According to Hintikka, philosophically his games are very different from those of Lorenzen (see op.cit., note II, p76) because he uses them to connect reality with language while Lorenzen considers only relations between players that are speakers. In Saarinen however, Hintikka is aware of the fact that the use of Nature as a participant in a game is not plausible. He refers to his earlier publication Logic, Language-Games and

Information p101 where he reduces all universal quantifiers and all conjunctions to negated existential quantifiers and negated disjunctions. By these means Nature as such is eliminated. But, as he remarks, the properties of the negation become absolutely essential. In fact, he cannot reach this elimination of Nature without using classical, non intuitionistic logic. Doing this he precisely cannot even discuss the main result of Lorenzen and Lorenz. And moreover as a result of this reduction he eliminates the major original feature of his game theoretical approach (according to his own assertions). We are of the opinion that he would be ill advised to eliminate Nature (the price is too high: he loses the originality of his approach, and moreover ties himself irreversibly to one type of logic). But one cannot but share his misgivings as to the metaphorical use made of the concept of "Nature" (and, in consequence, as to the metaphorical use made of the concept of semantics). The problem needs further elucidation, especially because of the fact that Hintikka reaches also very valuable results in a) the study of partially ordered quantifiers b) the application of language games to modal statements c) the analysis of sentences from everyday language by means of games. Could these results not equally well be reached by an interpersonal game, rather than by a semantical game? At present the problem remains open. Our own point of view, in which the action concept (and primarily the interaction concept) is crucial will lead us to attempt a synthesis of interpersonal and semantical games. But - as explained in our text - our conception of argumentation makes us prefer other theories of argument than the game theoretical ones.

(9) C.Berge, Théorie générale des jeux à n personnes (Paris 1957).
R.D.Luce and H.Raiffa, Games and Decisions (Wiley, New York, 1957).

(10) A.Rapoport, Fights, Games and Debates (Ann Arbor, University of Michigan Press, 1960) and the same (editor), Game Theory as a Theory of Conflict Resolution (Reidel, 1973).

(11) For various essays on these concepts see Foundations and Applications of Decision Theory - Vol I: Theoretical Foundations (ed by C.A.Hooker, J.J.Leach, E.F.McClennan, Reidel, 1978).

(12) See note 10.

(13) See Jacob Marschak, Economic Information, Decision and Prediction, selected essays vol II, Reidel, 1974; chapter 21, "Elements for a Theory of Teams".

(14) See Hamblin, op.cit. note 2

(15) Again, see Hamblin, note 2.

(16) According to us, Hamblin's Fallacies, Naess' general introduction and Barth-Krabbe, even if they do not come immediately to grips with the

concrete properties of the differences between logical algebras, give to the theory of argumentation a wider scope than the better known and very valuable work of Hintikka and Lorenzen-Lorenz. Each of these authors has to reach a suitable pay-off between scope and depth. This is unavoidable. We want also to attract attention to chapters 6 and 7 of Naess's introduction. Without using any difficult technology he comes to grips with the basic problems the more formal contributions talk about.

(17) See Saarinen (op.cit.), Hintikka and Carlson "Conditionals, Generic Quantifiers, and Other Applications of Subgames" (pp. 179-214).

(18) "Persuasive Communication as Metaphorical Discourse under the Guidance of Conversational Maxims" (to appear in Logique et Analyse 1980, by L.Apostel).

(19) This paper is an extended version of a talk given in the Groningen Symposium on Theory of Argumentation, organised by E.M.Barth and J.L.Martens.

# THEORY OF ARGUMENTATION AND THE DIALECTICAL GARB OF FORMAL LOGIC

Erik C.W. Krabbe

The few remarks I shall venture to make on Theory of Argumentation and the Dialectical Garb of Formal Logic are intended as starting-points for our discussions and brain-storming sessions in this symposion. I'm not going to tell you things you don't know. Instead I'm going to tell you what I don't know. Of course, I hope that at the end of the week we'll all know better...

I'll start from the title of my talk and shall, accordingly, first discuss the very concept of a "Theory of Argumentation". I shall then explain what is meant by "the Dialectical Garb of Formal Logic", and finally comment on the relations between them.

What is Theory of Argumentation? I take it to be a field ("Argumentology" would be a name for it that duly ends in "ology") in which theories (plural) of argumentation are to be developed. We first need some sketchy, tentative definition of the field - a definition of the kind that appears in the introductions of textbooks. Such definitions may be incomplete, incorrect or unclear (they usually are), but they help to indicate what, according to some people, the field is about.

We find such a definition in [3] by van Eemeren, Grootendorst and Kruiger, all of whom are in our midst. I have made an attempt at translating some passages from their book. (This is not to take revenge on their activities as translators of a paper by E.M. Barth and myself - their work was excellent.) I'll first read out their definition of *argumentation*.

> Argumentation is a social, intellectual, verbal activity, concerned with opinions, aiming at their justification and consisting of a set of statements claiming to justify a given opinion in front of a rational audience. ([3], p. 13)

They then define *Theory of Argumentation*, as they describe its aims:

> Theory of Argumentation aims at drawing a distinction between proper[1] and improper starting-points for argumentation and between proper and improper schemata of argumentation. To achieve this, a description is called for (which is as precise and systematical as possible) of the following items:
> (1) items eligible as starting-points for argumentation;
> (2) items that may figure within a set of reasons;
> (3) norms applied, or applicable, in criticizing the propriety of starting-points or of schemata of argumentation. ([3], p. 24)

I don't want to discuss the details of this definition now, but there is one obvious problem: what difference is there between Theory of Argumentation, thus conceived, and logic? Check each item of the definition: Logic, too, is often defined as the science of arguments or reasoning, aiming at a distinction of valid and invalid arguments or argument forms. It, too, proceeds by description of (1) a set of admissible starting points (this is done in logical grammar or syntax) and (2) the structure of a correct derivation and (3) the underlying criteria. If we do not restrict the term "logic" to "deductive logic", but rather admit a somewhat wider conception of "logic", we may note that, since the substitution of "proper" for "valid" is a matter of mere words, the two fields - logic and Theory of Argumentation - coincide. Indeed, Van Benthem, who is also present here, in a recent paper expressed his doubt whether or not there is room for another discipline about arguments, beside logic ([2], p. 275). He deplores the neglect - within logic - of non-formal and non-mathematical aspects of the field, but deems it premature to start a new discipline; rather logic should mend its ways.

On the other hand, the two most influential works treated in [3] are the well-known treatises by Toulmin and by Perelman and Olbrechts-Tyteca ([5], [4]). Their authors are certainly not positively inclined towards formal logic. The insights of contemporary theoretical logic are largely dismissed as irrelevant to Theory of Argumentation. But if the fields coincided, these works would be themselves books on logic. Is "The New Rhetoric" a book on logic? Is Toulmin's book a book on formal logic?

I'm not certain whether we should regard the Theory of Argumentation as a subdiscipline of Logic (wider conception), or if, contrariwise, we should regard Logic (narrower conception) as a subdiscipline of the Theory of Argumentation. I don't think it's necessary to settle the matter before we proceed. We can have it either way. In either case Theory of Argumentation can be defined both extensively (pointing out pertinent publications) and by means of catchwords: "games", "definitions", "debates", "discussions", "fallacies", "practical argumentation", "burden of proof", "relevance of remarks", "convincing", "persuading", "plausibility", etc. Such catchwords may suffice to indicate the field and set it off against what is more commonly known by the name of "logic". Therefore, instead of trying to improve upon the *definition* cited above from [3] (I wouldn't know just how to go about it) and continuing to ponder upon the demarcation of fields, I propose the following *rule of strategy* for the theorist of argumentation so as to regulate his behavior with respect to formal logic:

*RULE 1* Do not discard the systems and results of "logic", but rather expand them, exploit them, amend them. Make them suit your own purposes.

Will this rule work? Will it lead to success in argumentational studies? As I told you at the beginning: I don't know. However, if we want to have *theories* of argumentation it seems to me that we must examine logic to find examples to which such theories might bear resemblance. Van Benthem remarks that the work of Toulmin and Perelman - who shunned logic - had no *theoretical* follow-up (*l.c.*).

I have a second rule of strategy to propose:

*RULE 2* Study primarily debates and discussions. Treat monological argumentation as a limiting subcase.

I'm quite willing to admit that theoretically it would be possible to treat monologue as the basic case and debates as cases where two or more parties together construct a "monologue". But wouldn't that be like constructing movement out of instantaneous rest - rest at each instant - instead of treating rest as a limiting subcase of movement (with zero deplacement)? Again, I don't *know* if this rule of strategy will lead to success. I think it plausible that it will, however, and therefore put it down as a proposal for your consideration.

The two rules of strategy taken together lead to an important and, I think, obvious consequence: Since the Theory of Argumentation should exploit Formal logic (rule 1) and since the dialectical point of view should have priority (rule 2) it at once follows that the Theory of Argumentation should be especially concerned with the "dialectical garb" of formal logic.

Let me explain what E.M. Barth and I mean by "the dialectical garb" of logic. There are - at present - at least three garbs (and many more subgarbs) that a contribution to formal logic may put on:

1. the *derivational* garb: here the "validity" of arguments is

defined as derivability in some system;

2. the *semantical* or *model-theoretical* garb: here "validity" is defined as immunity from counterexample;

3. the *dialectical* garb: here "validity" is defined as the existence of a winning strategy in a dialogue-game.

As you see, the "garbs" are distinguished according to the type of clarifying definition they apply to the concept of "validity". (They may easily be further divided into subgarbs, methods or techniques.) The classification into garbs is not equivalent to the familiar distinction of syntax, semantics and pragmatics. It is perpendicular to the distinction of constructive (intuitionistic) logic, classical logic, etc. Like all garbs, the garbs of logic come into and go out of fashion - though never completely. In this century, one may say, logic initially wore its derivational garb (axiomatic subgarb), though there was also an algebraic subgarb in vogue. Later logic put on a semantical garb and the derivational garb was often degraded to underwear. There is, since Lorenzen's work in the fifties, a dialectical garb at our disposal. I'm not saying that the semantical garb will now, in turn, be degraded, but I certainly want to stress that the dialectical garb is a garb in its own right and deserves more attention than it has previously had.

I hope that I've made myself clear: the dialectical garb of formal logic is not itself Theory of Argumentation. It is an approach to the concept of "validity".

The garbs may cover one another. For instance one may try to give the derivational and dialectical theories a semantic foundation, i.e., explain the rules of inference and of dialogue on semantic principles and present proofs of semantic completeness. On the other hand, there are well-known objections to a semantic foundation of logic, and one may, therefore, urge the priority of some other garb instead. I don't think that these questions of the priority of garbs - questions from the philosophy of logic - are of crucial importance to the Theory of Argumentation, though arguments put forward in this context sometimes are. This leads to my third rule of strategy:

*RULE 3* The Theory of Argumentation needn't be concerned with the priority of garbs (nor is it necessary that it takes a stand in the discussion about the priority of constructive over classical logic, etc.) but it should try to profit by the considerations concerning argumentation which are put forward in the battle of the garbs.

I venture to propose this rule. If I'm mistaken I shall surely be refuted during our sessions.

I stated before that the Theory of Argumentation should be especially concerned with the possibilities of exploiting the dialectical garb of formal logic. (Incidentally, this doesn't imply that Theory of Argumentation shouldn't consider semantics, I didn't say "exclusively concerned"). The dialectical garb has both *material games* and *formal games* to offer.

The *material games* are those in which the interpretation of the language - via the truth value of atomic sentences - has a bearing on the possibilities of winning and losing. They contain, one might say, some semantics. They model discussions which are partly indoors and partly outdoors. There are two debaters, but Nature too has a say in the game. It may be fruitful to consider material games from the point of view of the theory of 3-person games. I imagine they can be expanded into quite realistic models of argumentational situations.

The *formal games* are those in which the interpretation of the language plays no part. They figure in the foundations of logic, but one may well wonder, at first, how they could possibly serve as models for real or even for ideal debates. Isn't it *always* important in a discussion who is right? Doesn't it *always* matter if what is said is true or not? To this we may retort: in debates, what primarily matters is not whether or not sentences are true or false, but rather if the parties *agree* about their truth values, or agree about a method by which to come to such an agreement. And it certainly is not unrealistic to assume that in some cases the parties do not agree, and do not know how to come to an agreement about *any* (atomic) sentence. They may be so sceptical about all "material procedures" (observations, experiments, calculations, etc.) that they don't want to let them figure in their debates. Therefore, the formal games can, presumably, be given argumentational interpretations. In fact that is what Barth and I do in [1], and what I hope to do next Friday.

I'll end this talk today with a list of features, taken from the dialectical garb of formal logic, which I think any future theory of argumentation should incorporate:

1. There must be two or more *parties* in a debate.

2. There must be one or more *theses* in a debate.

3. There must be a possibility of pay-off, e.g. of *winning* or *losing* the debate (a mere exchange of information is inadequate).

4. The analysis of debates must proceed in terms of *rights* and *duties* of the parties.

5. What these rights and duties are depends solely on the previous *utterances* in the debate (perhaps also on the outcome of some tests), and not on the state of mind of the participants.

6. Moves must be *relevant* to the dialectical situation in which

they are made (the attacks and defenses given by Lorenzen are relevant).

7. The roles of the debaters are not necessarily equivalent. Debates *may be asymmetric:* their rules are not necessarily dualizable with respect to Proponent and Opponent.

8. The notion of a "permitted move" and its outcome must be *decidable* (and even: decidable by some practical method).

9. *Logical operators* are to be defined in terms of attacks and defenses.

10. The *lenght of debates* must be kept within limits - either by the subformula-property or by other means.

## NOTES

(1) I originally used the word "sound" here (to render "deugdelijk"), but the authors as well as Professor Provence Hintikka convinced me that this leads to confusion.

REFERENCES

[1] Barth, E.M. and E.C.W. Krabbe, *From Axiom to Dialogue. A Philosophical Study of Logics and Argumentation*, New York/Berlin: Walter de Gruyter, 1982, Ch. III and IV.

[2] Benthem, J.F.A.K. van, "Logika en argumentatietheorie", *Spektator* 7 - 5/6 (1978), pp. 263-276.

[3] Eemeren, F.H. van R. Grootendorst and T. Kruiger, *Argumentatietheorie*, Utrecht, etc. (1978). Aula-boeken 613.

[4] Perelman, Ch. and L. Olbrechts-Tyteca, *Traité de l'argumentation. La nouvelle rhétorique*, 3e éd., Brussels (1976). First edition Paris (1958).

[5] Toulmin, S.E., *The Uses of Argument*, Cambridge (1958).

# EIN KONSTRUKTIVER WEG ZUR SEMANTIK DER "MÖGLICHEN WELTEN"

Rüdiger Inhetveen

## 1. Dialogebenen. Spielregel

Wie Paul Lorenzen in seinem Referat über die dialogische Begründung von Logikkalkülen gezeigt hat, gelingt es mit Hilfe einer expliziten Definition des Delta-Operators und des aristotelischen Satzes über die Angemessenheit des Delta-Schrittes, eine konstruktive Begründung für effektive und klassische Modalkalküle anzugeben. Diese pragmatische Begründung reicht bis zu den Systemen M, M* und M*L = $S_4$. Für die in den Vollständigkeitsbeweisen auftretenden Interpretationshierarchien gibt es eine konstruktive Deutung über kumulierte Indizes, die zur Quantorenlogik zurückführt.

In einer kurz vor dem Abschluss stehenden Dissertation hat nun Marijan Marčinko in Erlangen gezeigt, dass sich diese Interpretationen zwangsläufig ergeben, wenn man den Zugang zur Modallogik geringfügig verallgemeinert. Ich möchte seine Ergebnisse, soweit und so, wie ich sie verstanden habe, kurz schildern.

Der Ausgangsgedanke besteht darin, die üblichen (effektiven und klassischen) Dialoge durch die Hinzunahme von sogenannten "Dialogebenen" zu differenzieren. Eine solche Dialogebene ist nichts anderes als ein Indexkomplex $L = l_1,\dots,l_n$ endlicher Länge $|L| = n$ (Die Bezeichnung L soll an "level of discourse" erinnern). Bei jedem Spielzug im Dialog ist die Ebene, in der er stattfindet, ausdrücklich anzugeben.

Während des Dialoges ist es (zuweilen) möglich, in Verbindung mit einem Angriff eine neue Dialogebene zu wählen. Die Art, wie solche Neuwahlen als zulässig eingerichtet werden, führt dann zu verschiedenen Spielsystemen. Diese Spielsysteme lassen sich *gemeinsam* wie folgt durch Dialogregeln beschreiben.

*Anfangsregel:* Der Proponent P beginnt mit der Behauptung einer These in einer Ebene L. Die Dialogpartner ziehen dann abwechselnd.

*Allgemeine Spielregel:*

(a) (effektives Spiel) P verteidigt sich gegen den - in einem Zweig - zuletzt erfolgten Angriff des Opponenten O oder greift eine der vom Opponenten gesetzten Formeln an. O verteidigt sich gegen den letzten Angriff des P oder greift die zuletzt von P gesetzte Formel an. Alles dies geschieht nach den Partikelregeln des jeweiligen Spielsystems. (b) (klassisches Spiel) P verteidigt sich gegen einen Angriff des O oder greift eine von O gesetzte Formel an. O spielt wie im effektiven Fall. Die Partikelregeln sind die gleichen wie im effektiven Fall.

*Gewinnregel:* P hat in einem Zweig gewonnen, wenn er eine in einer Ebene angegriffene Formel zu verteidigen hat, die O schon in derselben Ebene behauptet hat. P hat einen Dialog gewonnen, wenn er ihn in allen Zweigen gewonnen hat.

Die *Partikelregeln* müssen nun die Angabe von Ebenen berücksichtigen. Für den Fall, dass eine modalfreie quantorenlogische Formel vorliegt, wird die Ebene dieser Formel in Angriff und Verteidigung beibehalten. Liegt eine Delta-Formel in einer Ebene L vor, so erfolgt der Angriff durch die Angabe einer bezüglich L im jeweiligen System zulässigen (eventuell von L verschiedenen)

Ebene L' und die Verteidigung durch Behaupten des um Δ gekürzten Teils der Delta-Formel in der Ebene L'.

Abgesehen von dieser Ebenenbedingung sind das natürlich genau die alten Regeln für die Partikeln beziehungsweise für die Δ -Elimination. Für die verschiedenen Arten, Zulässigkeitsrelationen R zwischen den Ebenen zu definieren, liegen folgende Möglichkeiten nahe (mit $L = l_1,\ldots,l_n$ und $|L| = n$):

| | symm. | refl. | trans. |
|---|---|---|---|
| (o) $LR_0L' \leftrightharpoons L' = L$ | + | + | + |
| (1) $LR_1L' \leftrightharpoons L' = L,l_{n+1}$ | – | – | – |
| (2) $LR_2L' \leftrightharpoons LR_0L' \vee LR_1L'$ | – | + | – |
| (3) $LR_3L' \leftrightharpoons LR_0L' \vee L' = L,\ldots,l_{n+m}$ | – | + | + |
| (4) $LR_4L' \leftrightharpoons LR_0L' \vee LR_1L' \vee L'R_1L$ | + | + | – |
| (5) $LR_5L' \leftrightharpoons LR_3L' \vee L'R_3L$ | + | + | + |

Hier ist die triviale Relatiom $R_0$ aus notationstechnischen Gründen aufgenommen, damit die übrigen Relationen sich kurz definieren lassen.

Je nachdem, mit welcher Zulässigkeitsrelation die Partikelregeln konkretisiert werden, ergeben sich verschiedene Spielsysteme, die, um eine Beziehung zu den üblicherweise axiomatisch charakterisierten Modalsystemen herzustellen, jetzt daraufhin untersucht werden können, welche Formeln in ihnen gewinnbar sind.

## 2. *Beispiele*

Betrachten wir dazu einige Beispiele.

1\. Mit $R_1$ ist z.B. $\Delta.A\rightarrow B.\rightarrow\Delta A\rightarrow\Delta B$ gewinnbar. Ein Dialog sieht so aus:

| | |
|---|---|
| | L: $\Delta.A\rightarrow B.\rightarrow\Delta A\rightarrow\Delta B$ |
| 1 L: $\Delta.A\rightarrow B.$ | L: $\Delta A\rightarrow\Delta B$ |
| 2 L: $\Delta A$ | L: $\Delta B$ |
| 3 L'?2 | (7 L': B) |
| 4 L': $A\rightarrow B$ | L'?1 |

| | |
|---|---|
| 5 L': A | L'?2 |
| 6 L': B | L': A ?4 |

Dadurch, dass bei jedem Delta-Schritt ein echter Ebenenwechsel vorliegt, wird verhindert, dass im $R_1$ -Spiel inhomogene Formeln gewinnbar sind. Man macht sich das an einfachen Beispielen klar, wie etwa an der "Verifikationshypothese" $\Delta A \rightarrow A$

| | |
|---|---|
| | L: $\Delta A \rightarrow A$ |
| 1 L: $\Delta$ A | L: A |
| 2 L?1 | |
| 3 L': A | L'?1 |

Hier sind L und L' verschiedene Ebenen, so dass gemäss der Formulierung der Gewinnregel keine Gewinnstellung vorliegt.

2. Mit $R_2$ ist die gleiche Formel gewinnbar, weil der Proponent in Zeile 3 selbst L' = L wählen kann.

3. Mit $R_3$ lässt sich z.B. $\Delta\nabla A \rightarrow \nabla A$ gewinnen. Eine Strategie sieht so aus.

| | |
|---|---|
| | L: $\Delta\nabla A \rightarrow \nabla A$ |
| 1 L: $\Delta\nabla$ A | L: $\neg \Delta \neg$A |
| 2 L: $\Delta\neg$A | - |
| 3 L': $\neg\Delta\neg$A | L'?1 |
| 4 - | L': $\Delta \neg$A |
| 5 L"?4 | L": $\neg$A |
| 6 L": A | - |
| 7 L": $\neg$ A | L":?2 |
| 8 | L": A |

Man erkennt, dass der Angriff des Proponenten in Runde 7 auf Zeile 2 nur zulässig ist, weil $R_3$ transitiv ist. Eine andere wichtige Formel, die im $R_3$-Spiel gewinnbar ist, ist die Idempotenz

$\Delta A \rightarrow \Delta\Delta A$:

| | |
|---|---|
| | L: $\Delta A \rightarrow \Delta\Delta A$ |
| 1 L: $\Delta A$ | L: $\Delta\Delta A$ |
| 2 L'?1 | L': $\Delta A$ |
| 3 L"?2 | (5 L": A) |
| 4 L": A | L"?1 |

4. Ein typisches $R_4$-Spiel ist das um das sogenannte "Brouwersche Axiom".

| | |
|---|---|
| | L: $A \rightarrow \Delta\nabla A$ |
| 1 L: A | L: $\Delta\nabla A$ |
| 2 L'?1 | L': $\neg\Delta\neg A$ |
| 3 L': $\Delta\neg A$ | - |
| 4 L: $\neg A$ | L?3 |
| 5 - | L: A |

Hier wird in Zeile 4 vom Proponenten die Symmetrie von $R_4$ entscheidend benutzt. Im $R_3$-Spiel wäre dieser Angriff nicht erlaubt gewesen.

5. Schliesslich sei noch für $R_5$ die Gewinnbarkeit der Lewisschen Rechtsabsorption $\nabla\Delta A \rightarrow \Delta A$ gezeigt.

| | |
|---|---|
| | L: $\nabla\Delta A \rightarrow \Delta A$ |
| 1 L: $\neg\Delta\neg\Delta A$ | L: $\Delta A$ |
| 2 L'?1 | (7 L': A) |
| 3 - | L: $\Delta\neg\Delta A$ |
| 4 L"?3 | L": $\neg\Delta A$ |
| 5 L": $\Delta A$ | - |
| 6 L' : A | L'?5 |

Hier weiss man, dass $L'R_5L$ und $L''R_5L$ gilt. Damit der Angriff des Proponenten in Zeile 6 in der durchgeführten Weise möglich ist, muss $L'R_5L''$ gelten, was man in der Tat aus der Symmetrie und Transitivität von R unmittelbar erhält.

### 3. *Beziehung zu den modallogischen Standardsystemen*

Auf die Behandlung quantorenlogischer Beispiele wie der Barcanformel möchte ich hier nicht eingehen, weil die dafür nötigen technischen Details den Grundgedanken der Marčinkoschen Arbeit nicht weiter verdeutlichen. Doch die aussagenlogischen Beispiele, die eben behandelt wurden, sind natürlich so gewählt, dass sich die Beziehungen der $R_n$-Spiele (n=1,..,5) zu den Standardsystemen der Modallogik geradezu aufdrängt.

Um diese Vermutung in den Rang eines Theorems zu erheben, wird eine Normierung der $R_n$-Dialogspiele vorgenommen, die es, genau nach assertorisch-logischem Vorbild, erlaubt, zu entsprechenden *Entwicklungskalkülen* überzugehen.

Diese Kalküle lassen sich dann *erstens* mit den klassischen Modalsystemen vergleichen. Als Resultat ergibt sich der folgende

*Äquivalenzsatz:*

Der Kalkül zur Relation $R_1$ ist äquivalent zum System M
Der Kalkül zur Relation $R_2$ ist äquivalent zum System M*=T
Der Kalkül zur Relation $R_3$ ist äquivalent zum System M*L=S4
Der Kalkül zur Relation $R_4$ ist äquivalent zum System B*=Br
Der Kalkül zur Relation $R_5$ ist äquivalent zum System M*Lr=S5.

Auf die umfangreichen Beweise muss ich hier leider verzichten.

Ein *zweiter* wichtiger Teil der mit diesen Entwicklungskalkülen möglichen Untersuchungen betrifft deren Konsistenz, die über einen Beweis des Gentzenschen Schnittsatzes gewonnen wird:

Sind im $R_n$-Kalkül (n=2,..,5) die Stellungen $\Sigma \,\|\, L: A$ und $\Sigma_{L:A} \,\|$ abschliessbar, so auch die stellung $\Sigma \,\|$ .

Wäre nun für eine Formel A sowohl $\| A$ als auch $\| \neg A$ abschliessbar, so auch $\|A$ und $A\|$ . Anwendung des Schnittsatzes (mit leerem $\Sigma$) ergäbe die Abschliessbarkeit der Stellung $\|$ , was unmöglich ist.

Schliesslich lassen sich jetzt *drittens* die klassischen Untersuchungen zur Vollständigkeit aufnehmen. Lassen Sie mich darüber abschliessend noch ein wenig ausführlicher sprechen.

Es sei im folgenden $S_n$ der zur Relation $R_n$ (n=1,..,5) gehörende Entwicklungskalkül und S einer dieser Kalküle. Für Formeln von S muss zunächst die "Falschheit" definiert werden. Die dazu nötigen Termini sind die folgenden.

Eine Formelmenge $\lambda$ heisst *Basismenge,* wenn sie nur Primformeln oder Negate von Primformeln enthält. Eine Basismenge heisst *konsistent*, wenn sie mit keiner Primformel auch deren Negat enthält. Eine Basismenge heisst bezüglich einer S-Formal $\alpha$ *total,* wenn sie jede Primformel von $\alpha$ affirmiert oder negiert enthält. Ein System $\Lambda$ von Basismengen $\lambda$ heisst konsistent bzw. $\alpha$-total, wenn jedes $\lambda \varepsilon \Lambda$ kosistent bzw. $\alpha$-total ist. Kommen in $\alpha$ Quantoren vor, dann ist $\lambda$ $\alpha$-total bzgl. eines Variabilitätsbereichs $\omega$, wenn $\lambda$ alle Primformeln von $\alpha$ mit Elementen aus $\omega$ affirmiert oder negiert enthält. Es sei nun $\Lambda$ ein Basismengensystem, $\alpha$ eine S-Formel $\Delta\alpha_1$, und auf $\Lambda$ sei eine Relation R definiert. Dann heisst $\Lambda$ total bezüglich $\alpha$ über $\omega$, wenn gilt:

1) es gibt ein $\lambda^* \varepsilon \Lambda$ und ein $\lambda_i \varepsilon \Lambda$, so dass $\lambda^* R \lambda_i$ gilt;
2) jedes $\lambda_i$ mit $\lambda^* R \lambda_i$ ist eine $\alpha_1$-totale Basismenge (über $\omega$).

Mit diesen Hilfsmitteln definieren wir jetzt induktiv, was es für eine S-Formal $\alpha$ und ein $\lambda^*$ aus einem konsistenten, $\alpha$-totalen Basismengensystem $\Lambda$ heisst, dass $\alpha$ *S-falsch bezüglich* $\lambda^*$ *(über* $\omega$*)* ist. Das bedeute nämlich, dass

1) $\neg A$ in $\lambda^*$ ist, falls $\alpha$ eine Primformel A ist,
2) $\alpha_1$ S-wahr ist, falls $\alpha = \neg\alpha_1$ ist
3) $\alpha_1$ oder $\alpha_2$ S-falsch ist, falls $\alpha = \alpha_1 \wedge \alpha_2$ ist
4) $\alpha_1$ und $\alpha_2$ S-falsch ist, falls $\alpha = \alpha_1 \vee \alpha_2$ ist

5) $\alpha_1$ und $\alpha_2$ S-falsch ist, falls $\alpha = \alpha_1 \rightarrow \alpha_2$ ist

6) $\alpha_1 n$ für alle $n \varepsilon \omega$ S-falsch ist, falls $\alpha = \bigvee_x \alpha_1 x$ ist

7) $\alpha_1 n$ für ein $n \varepsilon \omega$ S-falsch ist, falls $\alpha = \bigwedge_x \alpha_1 x$ ist

8) $\alpha_1$ S-falsch bzgl. $\lambda_i$ über $\omega$ ist, falls $\alpha = \Delta\alpha_1$ und $\lambda^* R \lambda_i$.

$\alpha$ ist S-falsch bzgl. $\Lambda$ über $\omega$ genau dann, wenn $\alpha$ S-falsch bzgl. $\lambda^*$ über $\omega$ für ein $\lambda^* \varepsilon \Lambda$ ist.

Das klassische *Vollständigkeitslemma* lautet dann:

> Zu jeder in S nicht abschliessbaren Formel $\alpha$ gibt es ein bezüglich $\alpha$ totales konsistentes System $\Lambda$ von Basismengen und einen Variabilitätsbereich $\omega$, so dass $\alpha$ S-falsch bezüglich $\Lambda$ über $\omega$ ist.

Der Beweis geht von der (nichtkonstruktiven) Existenz eines endlichen oder unendlichen maximal entwickelten Zweiges aus, der nicht formal abgeschlossen ist. Mit Hilfe dieses Zweiges wird dann definiert:

1) $\omega$ : alle in diesem Zweig frei vorkommenden Variablen

2) $\lambda_L$: eine Basismenge aus den in der Ebene L links von $||$ stehenden Primformeln und den Negaten der rechts von $||$ stehenden Primformeln.

$\lambda_L$ ist wegen der Voraussetzung konsistent.

3) $\lambda_L$ wird erweitert zu einer konsistenten totalen Basismenge über $\omega$ bezüglich aller in der Ebene L vorkommender modalfreier Formeln.

4) Die Relation R zwischen den Basismengen wird über die Zulässigkeitsrelation in S definiert:

$$\lambda_L R \lambda_{L'} \leftrightharpoons LR_n L' \quad (n=1,..,5).$$

Mit diesen Definitionen gilt dann, dass $\alpha$ S-falsch bezüglich $\Lambda$ über $\omega$ ist.

Das Bemerkenswerte an diesem Beweis ist die Tatsache, dass die in der Kripke-Semantik auftretenden Relationen zwischen den Interpretationen einer Formel (den "möglichen Welten") hier direkt aus den jeweiligen Partikelregeln übernommen werden können. Man hat also nicht mehr die Situation, dass man von der Relation beispielsweise die Reflexivität verlangt, um für inhomogene Formeln überhaupt zu Interpretationen zu kommen.

# PART TWO:

# CHOOSING THE RULES

## INTRODUCTION TO PART TWO: CHOOSING THE RULES

Mr. Lorenz formulates the rules that distinguish the various dialogue games for logics in terms of *rights and obligations* of the players. Some informal remarks referring to obligations can be found in various papers by Lorenzen, but systematic expositions by other persons have usually been in terms of rights only - which is, I suppose, a natural point of view for mathematicians. Participants in a game "have", or "are given", certain rights, which may or may not differ from those of the other players. These rights can then be seen as constituting a simple generative base for the production of arguments - an image which resembles an axiom system and also the now well-known framework of so-called generative grammar.

Lorenz, however, chooses a more natural ("nature" here referring to daily life), and at the same time more "juridical", set of notions - there are rights, and there are *also*, and equally fundamentally, obligations. In Lorenz' paper both "right" and "duty" are primitive terms.

The second paper in this section refers to a longer paper by Barth and Krabbe (1978), in which one can find (p. 325f) remnants of discussions between the two authors concerning the desirability of emphasizing, in addition to rights, the notion of a player's obligations. One reason for doing this is that the notion of a player's obligations allows for a simpler formulation of some features of the various "games". In terms of the set of obligations of a player, one can say that in constructive dialectics the set of the proponent's obligations-to-defend is ordered, but that in classical dialectics it is unordered.

Ultimately we agreed to *define* someone's obligation at a certain stage as this player's *set* of rights at that stage. (Above, reference was made to sets of such sets.) In this sense, our set-up may be described as one in terms of rights only. Thereby the "juridical" aspect was somewhat weakened, but this is compensated for (we believe) by the aspects of our set-up that we have called Systematic and Orderly dialectics, together with our distinction of statemental dialogue attitudes. See also Barth and Krabbe (1982), Chs. III and IV.

Lorenz formulates and delves into certain "mathematical" problems concerning some conceivable choices of "structural" (i.e. , game-structuring), or "special" (i.e., game-type specifying), rules. These are the "$formal_3$" rules in the terminology employed by Barth and Krabbe. Our $formal_2$ rules correspond to what Lorenz calls "argument rules" or "general rules", being rules that concern the linguistic forms - the $forms_2$ - of the arguments (sentences) used in the game, and only these forms. Hence these $formal_2$ rules are common to all types of critical games, i.e., they are general rules, as against game-type specifying, or game-specific, rules.

# ON THE CRITERIA FOR THE CHOICE OF THE RULES OF DIALOGIC LOGIC

Kuno Lorenz

## *1. A game-theoretic pragmatic conception of truth*

The game theoretic approach to logic as worked out by P. Lorenzen[1] and K. Lorenz[2] resulted in a pragmatic conception of truth both in its material and in its formal sense: truth of a proposition A becomes defined as the existence of a winning-strategy for A in a dialogue-game about A, which in turn is defined as a certain finitary open two-person zero-sum game; the meta-truth of 'either $A \varepsilon \Upsilon$ or $A \varepsilon \lambda$' provable only classically by means of the saddle-point-theorem for such games is constructively reduced to the decidability of winning or losing for individual plays of a game about A. Hence, the fact that in general the concept of true proposition within a theory is neither decidable nor recursively enumerable even if we start with value-definite or bivalent (i.e. decidably true or false) elementary propositions[3] has forced us to drop the classical concept of proposition - propositions are entities which can be either true or false (principle of bivalence) - and to introduce a wider concept of proposition - propositions are entities which can, according to the rules of a dialogue-game, be either won or lost (principle of dialogue-definiteness) - together with a correspondingly wider concept of logical composition, since truth-tables, finite or infinite, are no longer generally applicable.

Furthermore, since we can infer from the principle of dialogue-definiteness that the dialogue-game must be finitary (i.e. each play of a game reaches a final position after a finite number of moves), the concept of *true* proposition, which is defined as the existence of winning-strategies in the game associated with each proposition, can now also be characterized as finitary. Only in special cases will the finitary concept of truth become recursively enumerable, or even decidable; e.g., under the restriction to only *formal* winning strategies, which are defined for the purpose of characterizing the formally true propositions within the class of all true propositions, it will be possible to prove that the concept of formally true proposition is recursively enumerable; the formal winning-strategies can be represented as derivable in a certain formal system, i.e. in one of the well known logical calculi.

## 2. *Specifying the game ("global" gamerules)*

The main idea of dialogic logic is that, for entities to be propositions, there must be a stipulation of rules which define possible argumentations to be finite sequences of arguments ending with win or loss for either player who argues both for and against that entity. This set of rules split into those independent of the kind of propositions in initial position - the *structural rule* - and the special *argument rules* dependent on the internal structure of a proposition. One of many not necessarily equivalent ways to stipulate a precise structural rule is:

(1) Dialogues about propositions consist of arguments which are put forward alternatively by an opponent O and a proponent P. The arguments follow certain rules of argumentation that belong to the game, so that each play ends up with win or loss for either player.

(2) With exception of the improper initial argument, each

argument either attacks prior ones of the partner or defends those of one's own upon such an attack, but does not act both ways simultaneously: the proper arguments split into attacks and defences.

(3) Attacks may be put forward at any time during a play of the game (rights!)

(4) Defenses must be put forward in the order of the corresponding attacks (to which the defence answers), yet may be postponed as long as attacks can still be put forward: that argument which has been attacked last without yet having been defended, must always be defended first (duties!)

(5) Whoever cannot - or will not - put forward an argument any more, has lost that play of the game, the other one has won it.

(1) and (5) may be accepted as natural, (2) accounts for the special dialogue character of the game by using just two types of arguments, attacks, i.e. a two-place predicate, and defences, i.e. a three-place predicate.[4] (3) and (4) define rank and order of attacks and defences in such a way that

(a) attacks are treated as rights independent of any special position reached during a single play of the game and hence not becoming void throughout a whole play,

(b) defences are treated as duties not to be cancelled throughout a whole play, yet subject to the permission to postpone their performance as long as rights of attack can be made use of,

(c) a special order of duties must be observed, namely that one which is induced by the sequence of the corresponding attacks: *last duty comes first.*

### 3. *Argument rules ("local" game rules)*

In order to give a justification for the imposition of this order of duties it is first better to specify the argument rules mentioned in (1). This can be done by laying down a *schema of attacks and defences* which shows all possible attacks against an argument as well as all possible defences of this argument upon each of these attacks. Among the possibilities for such schemata can be specified those which reduce a dialogue on a compound proposition completely to dialogues on its subpropositions. This leads to the concept of logical composition in such a way that a proposition A shall be called 'logically composed' out of propositions from a class K of given dialogue-definite propositions if the schema of attacks and defences associated with A - it represents the *particle-rules* - contains only propositions out of K. Purely finite combinatorial considerations show[5] that for a complete survey of finite and infinite compositions - infinite classes of propositions are restricted to those which are represented by propositional forms A(x), where x is an object-variable for specified classes of objects, e.g. those derivable in some calculus - it is sufficient to use only those *logical particles* which are defined by the following schema:

| | *A | attacks | defences |
|---|---|---|---|
| negation (not) | A | A | |
| | A*B | attacks | defences |
| conjunction (and) | A∧B | 1? | A |
| | | 2? | B |

| | | | |
|---|---|---|---|
| adjunction (or) | $A \vee B$ | ? | A |
| | | | B |
| subjunction ( if-then) | $A \to B$ | A | B |
| | $*_x A(x)$ | attacks | defences |
| universalisation (all) | $\bigwedge_x A(x)$ | ?n | A(n) |
| particularisation (some) | $\bigvee_x A(x)$ | ? | A(n) |

4. *Subjunction*

It is now easy to see that among the possible compounds the 'if-then'-particle plays a singular role, insofar as both attack *and* defence are subformulae of the compound called subjunction, and *only* here; hence, continuation of a dialogue about $A \to B$ will lead to subdialogues where the initial proposition is asserted by different players. This feature can be used to argue for the 'last duty comes first'-clause, if the following *dialogue-condition* (D) is accepted as an adequate criterion for the choice of the rules of a dialogue game.

(D) The obligation to perform the duty to defend $A \to B$ with B upon the attack A shall *not arise prior* to A's being defended upon a counterattack against A.

Condition (D) - an abbreviated and completely structural formulation is: neither player must defend upon an attack unless this attack has been defended upon a counter-attack - takes an intermediate position between the following two extremes, which are in general not even consistent with the rest of the structural rule:

(a) The obligation to perform the duty to defend $A \to B$ with B upon the attack A shall not arise prior to A's being true, i.e. a whole winning-strategy for A has to be presented before the player of $A \to B$ is obliged to assert B,

(b) The obligation to perform the duty to defend $A \to B$ with B upon the attack A arises if and only if A is not counter-attacked, i.e. unless a counter-attack against A does not cancel the duty to defend with B, B has to be asserted just after the mere assertion of A, in short: each player must choose whether he is going to defend upon an attack or to counterattack against that attack

Case (a) would turn $A \to B$ into the metaproposition $A\varepsilon\Upsilon \Rightarrow B\varepsilon\Upsilon$ and, hence, would make the concept of dialogue non-finitary as soon as winning-strategies for A cannot be found by finite procedures, whereas case (b) would make $A \to B$ dialogue-equivalent to $\neg A \vee B$ (i.e. both propositions can be substituted for each other at any place in a dialogue without affecting win and loss) and, hence, eliminate the singular role of 'if-then'. With respect to the concept of formal winning-strategy explained further down, case (a) makes that concept inapplicable and case (b) makes that concept empty[6]; in both cases there is no way to go from material truth to formal truth beside the usual classical procedure to define formal truth as general material truth which, in view of the universal quantifier in the meta-language, leads to just that restriction upon the domain of propositions treatable classically, namely to value-definite ones, which dialogic logic will overcome.

Now, it seems reasonable to understand the dialogue-condition (D) in such a way that the defence upon an attack need not be performed unless this attack has been defended upon *finitely many* counterattacks where the possible number of counterattacks has been chosen by the defender. This is the utmost postponement of the obligation to defend that can be stipulated without violating the rest of the structural rule. To secure the finitary character of the game with even this extended interpretation of the dialogue-condition the general regulation on the number of attacks permitted against a single argument during a given play which - as a final part of the structural rule - is still open should run as follows:

$(G_{\alpha,\beta})$ During a play of the game the sequence of attacks against one single argument must be correlated with a strict descending sequence of ordinals, $<\alpha$ by the opponent and $<\beta$ by the proponent ($\alpha$ and $\beta$ being constructive ordinals, the *bounds of attack* for either player[7]) representing the following duty: if $\zeta_n$ is the n-th attack against an argument such that .1. the ordinal $\gamma^*$ ($<\alpha$ resp. $<\beta$) of the (n-1)-th attack $\zeta_{n-1}$ against the same argument is the successor of an ordinal $\gamma$, the ordinal assigned to $\zeta_n$ shall be $\gamma$, .2. the ordinal $\lambda$ ($<\alpha$ resp. $<\beta$) of the (n-1)-th attack $\zeta_{n-1}$ is a limit-ordinal, the attacking player must choose an ordinal $\gamma<\lambda$ as the ordinal assigned to $\zeta_n$.

The necessity to use ordinals to represent the limitation of the number of attacks permitted against a single argument reflects the fact that the existence of winning strategies for or against a proposition will in general be dependent on how the choice of the upper limit of attacks gets split - following the corresponding choices of the other player - into a finite sequence of choices of upper limits. Since it can be proved that the (materially) true propositions in the union of $\alpha,\beta$-games, with no limitations on the ordinals $\alpha,\beta$ in the second number class, coincide with those in the union of $1,\alpha$-games which can be shown to be coextensive with the derivable formulae in a semi-formal system (i.e. a formal system with rules having infinite sets of premisses) using intuitionistic logic, the (material) truth concept of the dialogue-game with $\alpha,\beta$ being any choice of (denumerable) ordinals as bounds of attack, coincides with intuitionistic or effective truth[8].

## 5. *Formal winning-strategy and formal truth*

The next and final step concerns the introduction of a formal winning-strategy, hence, of formal truth within a dialogue-game. It starts with the observation that for certain logically compound propositions the existence of a winning-strategy can be ascertained, independent of any knowledge about the existence of winning strategies for or against prime constituents. To use this feature in a special rule for formal playing it is useful first to replace all prime propositions with propositional symbols, all predicates with predicate symbols and all constants with object symbols which serve as the universal domain for the object variables in formal playing[9]. We therefore stipulate

(7) (a) Prime propositional schemata (i.e. either propositional symbols or expressions of the form $\mathbf{p}\ (n_1 \ldots, n_l)$ with $\mathbf{p}$ being a predicate symbol and the $n_\lambda$ being object symbols) cannot be formally attacked; they may be asserted by O without restrictions, whereas P may assert a prime propositional schema $\mathbf{b}$ only if O has asserted $\mathbf{b}$ before.

Now it is easy to prove that a formal winning-strategy for a propositional schema $\mathbf{A}$ in a $1,\alpha$-game can be converted into a formal winning-strategy in a 1,n-game which means that for formal playing the infinite ordinals as bounds of attack can be replaced by finite ordinals, i.e. the natural numbers, as bounds of attack. If, furthermore, we define *logical implication* of a thesis $\mathbf{A}$ from hypotheses $\mathbf{A}_1, \ldots, \mathbf{A}_n$ (i.e. $\mathbf{A}_1, \ldots, \mathbf{A}_n \prec \mathbf{A}$) as usual through the formal truth of the subjunction $\mathbf{A}_1 \wedge \ldots \wedge \mathbf{A}_n \rightarrow \mathbf{A}$ it should be checked whether the following *two principles of logical reasoning* which govern the utility of formal truth for ascertaining material truth hold:

(P) (a) Invariance of formal truth against substitution, i.e. if $\mathbf{A}(a_1, \ldots, a_n)$ ε formally true then $\mathbf{A}(\mathbf{A}_1, \ldots, \mathbf{A}_n)$ ε formally true

(b) Hereditariness of material truth through logical implication, i.e. if $\mathbf{A}_1, \ldots, \mathbf{A}_n \prec \mathbf{A}$ and all $A_\nu$ε true then A ε true (where the $A_\nu$, A are interpretations of the schemata $\mathbf{A}_\nu, \mathbf{A}$, respectively)[10]

Part (a) of (P) can easily be seen to hold[11], if rule (7) is amended by

(7) (b) P may take over each prime propositional schema from O *at most* m-times, if m is the bound of attack for P.

In consequence we see that any proposition A derived by interpretation in the usual way from a formally true schema $\mathbf{A}$, will be materially true, though by construction independent of the truth or falsehood of its prime constituents. Since it is a consequence of a cut-elimination theorem for dialogic logic, part (b) of (P) can be made to hold by imposing the condition of O,P-symmetry on the rules of the game which had been fulfilled in advance[12]. It has the further consequence that dialogue-equivalence of schemata which is stronger than initial-equivalence (i.e. both schemata can be substituted for each other at initial position in a dialogue without affecting win and loss which, restricted to value-definite interpretations, is just the classical concept of logical equivalence: $\mathbf{A} \succ\!\prec \mathbf{B} \leftrightharpoons$ for all interpretations A,B of $\mathbf{A}, \mathbf{B}$: Aεtrue iff Bεtrue), is itself equivalent with logical equivalence. We have here the explanation that even within the restricted domain of value-definite propositions not every classically valid schema turns out to be an effectively valid schema. As a matter of fact, the classical theory does not even permit one to define this difference of general material truth and purely formal truth.

## 6. *A theorem of formal dialogic logic*

The main theorem of dialogic logic restricted to formal playing now states that the class of propositional schemata for which there are formal winning-strategies in the $\omega,\omega$-game is enumerable by a formal system of intuitionistic logic, essentially a Gentzen-type calculus for logical implications $\mathbf{A}_1, \ldots, \mathbf{A}_n < \mathbf{A}$.[13] And the classically valid schemata coincide with those theses which effectively follow from tertium-non-datur-hypotheses about certain subschemata of the thesis in question. i.e. schemata of the form $\mathbf{A} \vee \neg\mathbf{A}$ or $\bigwedge_x (\mathbf{A}(x) \vee \neg\mathbf{A}(x))$.

## NOTES

(1) P. Lorenzen, "Logik und Agon," in: Atti del XII Congresso Internazionale di Filosofia (Venezia, 12-18 Settembre 1958). Volume quarto, Firenze 1960 (repr. in: P. Lorenzen/K. Lorenz, Dialogische Logik, Darmstadt 1978)

(2) K. Lorenz, Arithmetik und Logik als Spiele (Diss.), Kiel 1961, selection in: P. Lorenzen/K. Lorenz, Dialogische Logik, Darmstadt 1978.

(3) It was L.E.J. Brouwer, who first observed that value-definite propositions do not generally transfer value-definitenes to their logical compounds; cf. L.E.J. Brouwer, "Ueber die Bedeutung des Satzes vom ausgeschlossenen Dritten in der Mathematik, insbesondere in der Funktionentheorie," J. für reine und angewandte Mathematik 154 (1925).

(4) The use of only one type of arguments, i.e. attacks, has been investigated in: R. Drieschner, Untersuchungen zur dialogischen Deutung der Logik (Diss. Hamburg 1963), with the result that one gets essentially a (classical) logic of propositions built up solely by means of $\downarrow$ (the junctor or connective 'neither - nor') and $\downarrow$ (the quantor or quantifier 'no') out of prime propositions which is nothing but L. Wittgenstein's procedure in his Tractatus logico-philosophicus 5.5 ff to generate truth functions by way of $N(\bar{\xi})$ for any number of propositional variables $\xi$. The use of three or more types of argument has not yet been investigated. Without the distinction of attack and defence, using the tripartite division of arguments into permanent, tabooed (relevant only for formal playing), and the other ones without any label, referring instead - together with the rules of argumentation - to relations between an argument and a whole sequence of arguments rather than to relations between single arguments, the investigations in: W. Kindt, Eine abstrakte Theorie von Dialogspielen (Diss. Freiburg 1972), are carried through. They aim at a unified account of a wide range of different dialogue-games in order to facilitate comparative studies among them.

(5) Cf. K. Lorenz, "Dialogspiele als semantische Grundlage von Logikkalkülen," Archiv f. math. Logik und Grundlagenforschung 11 (1968) (repr. in: P. Lorenzen/L. Lorenz, Dialogische Logik Darmstadt 1978)

(6) Cf. the results about 'reine Logik' in: K. Lorenz, Arithmetik und Logik als Spiele (Diss. Kiel 1961, selection in: P. Lorenzen/K. Lorenz, Dialogische Logik, Darmstadt 1978)

(7) A general theory of ordinals using the concept of dialogue-definiteness together with a solution of the apparent vicious-circle involved in proving a general $\alpha,\beta$-game to be finitary does not yet exist, hence, the restriction to constructive ordinals as, e.g. in: K. Schütte, Beweistheorie (Heidelberg etc. 1960).

(8) Cf. K. Lorenz, "Die dialogische Rechtfertigung der effektiven Logik," in: F. Kambartel/J. Mittelstraß (eds.), Zum normativen Fundament der Wissenschaft, Frankfurt 1973 (repr. in: P. Lorenzen/K. Lorenz, Dialogische Logik,

Darmstadt 1978).

(9) If formal playing is used with reference to some specified domain of objects, e.g. natural numbers (i.e. only the predicates are treated as mere symbols), it is possible to introduce a difference of formal truth logically and formal truth, e.g. arithmetically; non-restricted arithmetical induction is a case of a formally true proposition arithmetically though not logically within the effective dialogue-game.

(10) The 'if-then'-clauses in the meta-language used in ( P ) are dialogue-definite metapropositions and, hence, are subject to the same rules of dialogic logic as in the object-language.

(11) Cf. K. Lorenz, "Dialogspiele als semantische Grundlage von Logikkalkülen" (cf. note 5)

(12) W. Kindt (cf. note 4) has shown by counterexamples that cut-elimination does not hold in O,P-unsymmetric games as falsely claimed in:K. Lorenz, "Dialogspiele..." (cf. note 5)

(13) Cf. K. Lorenz, "Dialogspiele ..." (cf. note 5); another proof in: W. Stegmüller, "Remarks on the completeness of logical systems relative to the validity-concepts of P. Lorenzen and K. Lorenz," Notre Dame J. of Formal Logic 5 (1964). The idea derived from reading the semantic tableaux of E.W. Beth (e.g. in: The Foundations of Mathematics, Amsterdam [2]1964) as notations for winning-strategies of an underlying game.

## REFERENCES

[1] H.B. Curry, "Remarks on Inferential Deductions," in: A.-T. Tymieniecka (ed.), *Contributions to Logic and Methodology in honor of J.M. Bocheński* (Amsterdam 1965)

[2] E.C.W. Krabbe, "The Adequacy of Material Dialogue-Games." *Notre Dame J. of Formal Logic* 19 (1978)

[3] F. van Dun, "On the Modes of Opposition in the Formal Dialogues of P. Lorenzen." *Logique et Analyse* N.S. 15 (1972)

[4] K. Lorenz, "Rules versus Theorems." *J. of Philosophical Logic* 2 (1973)

[5] P. Lorenzen, "Dialogkalküle." *Arch. f. math. Logik und Grundlagenforschung* 15 (1972)
-----, "Zur konstruktiven Deutung der semantischen Vollständigkeit klassischer Quantoren- und Modalkalküle." *Arch. f. math. Logik u. Grundl.* 15 (1972)

[6] F. Kambartel, "Uberlegungen zum pragmatischen und argumentativen Fundament der Logik," in: K. Lorenz (ed.), *Konstruktionen versus Positionen. Beiträge zur Diskussion um die konstruktive Wissenschaftstheorie* (Berlin etc. 1968)

# A NORMATIVE-PRAGMATICAL FOUNDATION OF THE RULES OF SOME SYSTEMS OF FORMAL DIALECTICS[3]

E.M. Barth

## 1. *New foundations. Statemental dialogue attitudes*

The foundation which I shall talk about has been set up by mr. Krabbe and myself (1978; 1982). It pertains to the work of Lorenzen and Lorenz. Furthermore it has been inspired by practically everybody, except by Grice, whose work came into the picture at a rather later date. In the first place, and most strongly, by Arne Naess, furthermore by R. Crawshay-Williams and by C.L. Hamblin; and on a certain point also by Hintikka -- our notion of *statemental dialogue attitudes* is a development, in a "Naessian" direction, of the notion of *propositional attitudes* which we encountered in the work of Hintikka.

## 2. *Two purposes -- presentation of the dialectical systems, and the problem of fallacy*

We offer a new formulation of, and a new way of arguing in favour of the adoption of those systems of formal dialectics (as we shall call them, following Hamblin) that were constructed by Lorenzen and Lorenz. It seems to us that a theory of argumentation must contain their work on the dialogic of structural elements of language (logical constants) as a proper part.

Such an investigation into the normative-pragmatical basis of the dialectical rules as we have made serves two purposes. One is to find a way of *presenting* a dialectical system which will make this system acceptable to the majority of potential debaters, so that the system may become the cultural norm in a certain "company" (in the sense of Crawshay-Williams). The second purpose is to get a better grasp of the topic of *fallacies*, though this purpose is not dealt with directly in our paper (1978). The paper contains the results of our investigation into the possibilities for a normative pragmatical basis of the dialectical rules (as we call them). The result consists in a certain terminological apparatus together with a small number of pragmatical norms and ends and their stepwise implementations, issuing in a set of rules by which, at each stage of the discussion, some arguments are generated and other conceivable arguments are not. A debater will have to chose between the arguments that the system generates.

The non-generable arguments are the fallacious ones. One can better put it the other way round: a fallacious argument is, by definition, an argument that is not generated (at that stage of the discussion) by the system of dialectical rules. The study of fallacies can then move from the stage of catch-word classification that we know today to an investigation of the relation of a given argument (i) to the dialogical situation at the given stage of the discussion and (ii) to the dialectical rules (of a given system) that pertain to exactly that dialogical situation. A study of the pragmatic (e.g., of the socio-cultural) foundations of various systems of dialectical rules will then deepen our understanding of why, and on which pragmatic (e.g., on which socio-cultural) conditions, we are inclined to deem an argument fallacious.

### 3. *Basic norms and ends; implementations*

I shall start with the pragmatical norms and ends and shall come to the terminology later, although this may sound a bit strange under the prevailing tacit rules for the exposition of scientific theories.

The norms from which we set out are a number of *desirable characteristics of systems of rules for discussions* in cases of *overt conflicts of opinion*. We believe that these characteristics are so naturally seen as desirable in large parts of our culture that one may expect most potential debaters within our culture to be willing to subscribe to them, with the exception of one norm and with the exception of one part of our culture which may have difficulties with that one norm. I hope - and I trust - that it will come as a surprise to you what that norm is (FD D1 below).

In most cases, however, most people are probably willing to subscribe to these norms which are, if you like, prolegomena to any future $formal_3$ dialectics. I shall call these norms *primary rules* and their implementations *secondary rules*, and their implementations again *tertiary rules*, and so on.

Toward potential debaters we claim that the implementations have *problem-solving validity* (cp. my (1972))- a deeper (more fundamental) norm or rule sets a problem for the constructors of systems of dialectics, and the implementation is a solution (not necessarily the only one!) to that problem, and should be accepted for that reason by all who agree that it is. Let $X_n$ be a rule which has already been adopted and let $X_{n+1}$ be our implementation of it. The claim, then, is that if $X_{n+1}$ is adopted, then $X_n$ will be satisfied by our dialectical system, in the best way that the authors can think of consonant with the other primary rules and their implementations.

I cannot imagine that our set of primary rules (deepest

norms) or our argumentation in favour or their implementations is final, but we do claim that a set-up *of this type* is of considerable value, practical as well as philosophical.

## 4. *Dialectics should be systematic and thoroughgoing*

I shall run through the primary rules with you, and I shall mention their immediate implementations and perhaps the immediate implementations of these again. We suggest, first, that the following rule be adopted:

FD S1 A defender of an attacked statement shall always have the opportunity to attempt to defend it by means of *another remark* (unless restrictions to this rule or its application are introduced separately and are applicable in this case).

We shall call this the basic, or primary, rule of any system of *systematic* dialectics (abbreviated to 'S' in the name of the rule).

This rule is acceptable, I should think, to most potential debaters. It can be implemented as follows - *via* a number of terminological conventions which I shall not bother you with here:

FD S2 Every intermediary thesis $T_n$ is to be regarded as a *conditional defense* of the previous thesis $T_{n-1}$, in the sense that if at some stage $T_n$ has somehow been *unconditionally defended*, then $T_{n-1}$ is to be regarded as unconditionally defended, too.

Furthermore, we suggest that an acceptable system of dialectics should be *realistic*, in the following sense:

FD R1 This opportunity (of defending an attacked statement by means of a new utterance) shall be *realistic* in the sense that some attempts to defend an attacked statement unconditionally shall be successful.

This means that the constructor of the system must formulate and recommend *closure rules*, that is to say rules that state that under certain conditions the last intermediary thesis, and thereby the initial thesis, shall be regarded as unconditionally defended.

The next desirable basic characteristic to be mentioned here is that our system(s) should be a system (systems) for a *thoroughgoing* dialectical probing of the tenability of the initial thesis ($T_0$) against critical remarks. In terms of "proponent" and "opponent" of the initial thesis:

FD T1 At any stage of the discussion the opponent shall have the opportunity to test the tenability (against criticism) of the other party's statements, and the proponent shall have the opportunity to attempt to defend its statements in all possible manners that are consonant with the other rules of the system.

This leads the authors to the notion of a *chain of arguments* (cp. a sub-tableau in Beth's tableau methods) and to regard a discussion as consisting of any number of chains of arguments, whereas Lorenzen and Lorenz regard each chain of arguments as defining another discussion, albeit with identical initial parts. In our set-up there is the possibility of *retracing ones steps* back to a certain stage of the discussion and to start on a new chain of arguments from there, by supplanting ones speech act at that stage with another one which also was permissible at that stage (i.e. which also is generated by the system at that stage). A chain of arguments issuing from a remark made by the opponent may be called a *line of attack* and one issuing from a remark by by the proponent may be called a *line of defence*.

We believe that most people will agree that this characteristic of a dialectical system, viz. that it should allow for thoroughgoing discussions, is a desirable one.

## 5. *Dialectics should be orderly and dynamic*

However, even if it be accepted by a certain company (or, in a certain society) that the system under construction ought to be such that the dialectical process can be *systematic, realistic* and *thoroughgoing* in our sense, the constructor of the system still does not have much to go by. But there are more characteristics of possible dialectical systems which in all likelihood one can persuade a company to agree upon as desirable characteristics and hence as requirements for the system under construction to satisfy. One very important characteristic is that of *orderliness*. Formulated as a norm for a system of dialectics to satisfy it is this:

FD 01 The obligations (and hence: the rights) of each party should at any stage be decidable from a survey of the discussion (in that chain of arguments) up to that point; and the same should hold, for each party, for the relative priorities (urgency) of its obligations, if there be more than one.

Like all the other basic norms, this norm poses a *problem* for the constructor of dialectical systems. The present problem can be solved by the following rule together with other rules:

FD 02 Whenever a party, N, at some stage of some chain of arguments criticizes a statement, N shall lose the right to attack this statement again *in that same chain of arguments*, unless it be in (counteractive, indirect) defense of a certain attacked statement of its own that has not yet been defended. Similarly, whenever a debater has defended a certain attacked statement *in a direct manner*, i.e. not by means of a counter-attack, then this party is *no longer obliged* to defend it (against this attack), even if the defense was merely a conditional one.

Since we define N's *obligation* issuing from a move by the other party, $\bar{N}$, as the *set of rights* that N acquires as a concequence of $\bar{N}$'s move, it follows that one loses all ones *rights* (plural!) to defend a statement within the same chain of arguments as soon as one has defended it once in a direct manner, i.e. by a speech act which is not a counterattack.

The next desirable feature of a system of dialectics that we discuss in our paper is that the type of dialectical process it defines should be *dynamic*. Formulated as a condition to be satisfied by the system as a whole:

FD D1 The system of rules applied in a discussion shall be designed to promote the revision of the opinions of at least one of the parties, and thereby to speed up the flux of opinions generally, in any company in which these rules are adopted.

As said above, I expect it to come as a surprise to quite a few people to learn that this condition may be taken to be one of the basic norms for (sub-)systems of dialectics that are provably equivalent to systems of modern formal logic. For many (though not all) philosophers who have expressed qualms about modern logic as a whole have done so because, they say, modern logic is "static" and unfortunately conducive to "static modes of thought". Nothing could be more wrong - as correctly seen and expressed by two other critics, the Neothomist H.B. Veatch and the Calvinist K. Popma, both of whom are staunchly hostile to modern as against traditional forms of logic.

One way of implementing this rule is to decide that:

FD D2 The rules of the system shall be such that *unavoidable* decisions as to the outcome of discussions will be reached as soon as possible.

In order to satisfy this condition we suggest to arrange the system such that:

FD D4 The rules shall *aim at bringing about, as far as possible* that each chain of arguments *ends* within a finite number of steps.

How this can be implemented so as to yield rules that are directly applicable in practice, in an unequivocal manner, is discussed in our paper, as well as in our book (1982).

Another instrument for bringing about this "dynamic" property in the ensuing system or systems, and which can be used simultaneously with rule FD D2, is an agreement concerning the following implementation of FD D1:

FD D9 Only such structural operators/functors (logical constants) shall be employed in a discussion for which there are clear definitions of their meaning-in-use, informing the debaters how sentences containing them can be challenged and how one can try to defend them.

As it happens this blacklists a considerable number of uses of language as not suited for use in dynamic discussions. Many locutions which are characteristically used for - among other things - the purpose of expressing dogmatic beliefs, whether in theology or elsewhere, must be eliminated from the language to be used in discussions if this rule, which seems reasonable enough if one intends to enter into discussions at all, is adopted. I have written about this fact and its connections with the problem-history of logic and semantics in other publications (1971/1974; 1978).

Next question: How can one choose between the various ways of defining a meaning-in-use for the various logical constants? I take Lorenzen's defining "strips" to be known to everyone here. Many of you will have noticed that students and others fail to understand why they are as they are, and come with suggestions for alternative "strips". Why, they say, should one choose Lorenzen's definition of the word *not*, rather than one which permits a critic to attack a statement of a sentence *not p* by means of the statement *not* (*not p*)?

Here our answer is the following: Lorenzen's definition - which says that a statement of *not p* is to be challenged by a statement of *p* - leads to a systematic decomposition of the negative sentences that are uttered in the discussion, whereas to allow *not* (*not p*) as a critical move will have the effect of lengthening them. A rule that allows this clearly does not satisfy FD D4, which, through FD D2, serves the supernorm FD D1 in a special way, and such a rule will therefore not serve FD D1 in an optimal manner. In general:

FD D10 Definitions of the meanings-in-use of structural operators should, whenever possible, be such that they will bring about a *decomposition* of the sentences constituting the conflict or used in the discussion.

Lorenzen's defining "strips" for the sentence connectives - which we do not repeat here - all satisfy this norm whereas suggestions for alternative "strips", such as the one just mentioned or the suggestion to exploit De Morgan's laws, do not.

The "dialectical" rules we have formulated up to this point do not pertain to any one linguistic expression in particular, but "formalize" discussions only in the general Quinean sense of reglementing them, which is what we mean by the index "3" in "$formal_3$ dialectics". Lorenzen's strips are rules for exploiting sentence forms and are called "$formal_2$ rules", the index "2" indicating "formality" of type 2, the linguistic type. In this way we distinguish linguistic form from behavioural form. An index "1" is reserved for "platonic form".

## 6. *Epilogue: The three elementary phases of a critical discussion*

In our paper (1978; cf. 1981) we only deal with rules for $formal_2$ critical discussions. All this talk about the $formal_2$ aspects of discussions may give the impression -- to the outer world, and, worse still, to the theoreticians themselves -- that this is all there is, and all there is to say. In order to counteract this false impression, I would like to put into words that in a normal critical discussion issuing from a conflict of avowed opinions, several phases can be discerned.

In a normalized critical discussion one should probably distinguish *four* elementary phases (with possibilities for cyclical arrangements of any number of these). Let the initial situation be:

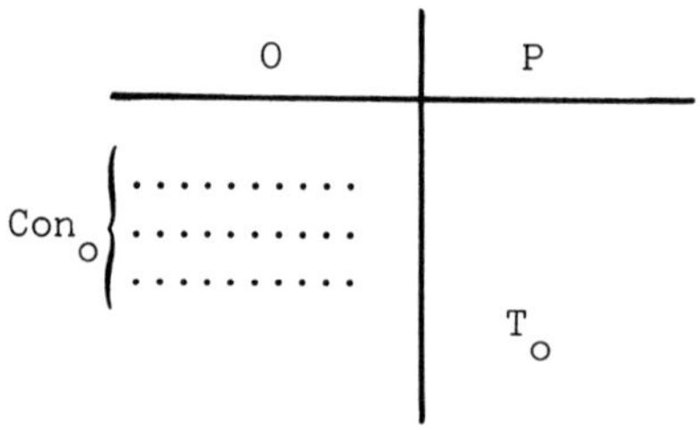


*Phase 1:* The most dynamic arrangement is to start with a Streitgespräch *ex concessis* (a $formal_{2,3}$ dialogue). If P can remove O's doubts as to (the truth of) $T_o$ on formal grounds ( = $formal_2$ grounds $\cup$ $formal_3$ grounds), then

STOP. Suppose, however, that when the participants have reached the n'th intermediate discussion, where $T_n$ is the (intermediate) thesis and $Con_n$ the (intermediate) set of concessions, the Opponent says -- whether in earnest or merely for the sake of the argument is not important -- that P cannot convince O on purely formal grounds. Then one should proceed to

*Phase 2:* -- a clarificational (hermeneutical, interpretational) discussion of $T_n$, on the basis of $Con_n$. Requests to explain formulations by more precise formulations (i.e., by formulations that eliminate some likely interpretations of the first formulations; cf. Naess 1966) belong to this phase. Let us call a formulation which is offered by one of the parties as more precise than another formulation, and which is accepted as such by the other party (or parties), a *meaning postulate of the discussion.* If O expresses withdrawal of doubt as to the meaning of the referential components in $T_n$, then proceed to

*Phase 3:* -- a Streitgespräch with meaning postulates, issuing from a new sequent $Con_n^+/T_n^+$. As far as I can see, it can be dealt with just as any other "formal" Streitgespräch *ex concessis* (cf. Phase 1), except that there are more concessions than before:

$$Con_n^+ = Con_n \cup \{\text{meaning postulates}\},$$

and $T_n^+$ may, but need not be, another formulation than -- a reformulation of -- $T_n$. If P still cannot remove O's doubt as to (the truth of) T (through removing O's doubt as to the intermediary thesis $T_n^+$) on "formal" grounds, then proceed to

*Phase 4:* -- a "material" discussion, i.e., a discussion including non-speech acts or truth-values for atoms, or both. (Notice that various non-equivalent definitions of "material dialogue" are found in the literature.)

The point of this epilogue is to draw attention to the fact that, in practical life, one should not try to distinguish between "formal", "hermeneutical" and "material" *discussions* -- these are ideal situations which come as aspects or phases of real discussions, and which have been isolated for theoretical purposes. (They should of course not be confounded with the phases of theory formation, described in the Preface.)

# PART THREE:

# DESCRIBING ARGUMENTATIVE DIALOGUES

## INTRODUCTION TO PART THREE: DESCRIBING ARGUMENTATIVE DIALOGUES

The authors of the contributions that now follow, Heidrich and Günther, are doing linguistic communications research, using the tools of the logicians not for the purpose of studying problems of corroboration and fallacy but for the wider purpose of studying the nature of dialogues generally.

They are studying the *interaction* between the participants in a dialogue (compare the definition of "dialectics" given in the Preface to this volume). Thus Günther defines a concept 'dialogue' on the basis of a concept he calls 'dialogue basis', and explains (p. 4) that this concept of a dialogue basis is introduced "in order to study two-person interactions constructively".

Heidrich writes: "In our opinion [ i.e., Günther's and his own] it would ... be inadmissible to represent only e.g. verbal acts as structural properties but, as is often done, leave out entirely representations of the internal states of persons" (p. 4). They are of the opinion that in order to come to grips with the development of dialogues theoretically it is necessary to study "the interrelation between the contents of the speech acts and the contents of the propositional attitudes which occur in the dialogue situations".

This was a topic of some discussion during the conference. Some of the participants defended the position that one ought to concentrate on linguistic behaviour and not get oneself entangled in entities as intractable as intentions and propositional attitudes, and proposed to replace the latter notion with that of statemental dialogue attitudes. Some general comments may be helpful in order to try to see what is happening (though what follows is certainly not meant as an argument for or against either approach).

In contemporary philosophy two seemingly opposed trends can be distinguished. There is, to start with, the very long, and very slow, cultural movement that might be called "externalization" -- of much that was earlier (sometimes, very long ago) taken to be features of a spiritual world, or anti-phenomenal human *logos* . That spiritual world, whether generic or individual, was seen as an "inner" world. Space, conflicts, judgements and proofs are examples of what was once taken to be features of that inner world. Today we study sentences, as the external counterparts of judgements, and the formalists' proof on a sheet of paper is the externalized counterpart of what Descartes and others in his time took to be the essential proof procedure -- a monologue carried on by, and *in* , (someones) mind (cf. Preface to this volume).

So much for the first trend, that of "externalization". Statemental dialogue attitudes (Barth and Krabbe, FATD) is a notion inspired by the trend toward externalization and criticism. The other trend is the recent analytic interest in intensions, intentions, and even internal states of human beings (see above). Propositional attitudes (cf. Hintikka's *Knowledge and Belief* , 1962; Günther, Heidrich, below) belong with this group. However, in analytic circles the latter trend is mostly -- and here, too -- super-imposed upon the former, in contradistinction to the treatment of intensions and internal states in earlier, e.g., phenomenological, philosophy. Furthermore, the papers presented here are sharply distinguished from phenomenological writings by their interactionist point of view.

Naess, Lorenzen, Lorenz, and others from whose work reference to internal states is totally absent, are ultimately interested in various problems of (intersubjective) *assessment of* arguments -- their succes in effectuating agreement or disagreement, winning or losing, once they have been adduced. Heidrich and Günther are developing *dialogue grammars,* and hold that they need internalistic concepts for the purpose of a detailed description of the *generation of* arguments.

# A SET OF CONCEPTS FOR THE STUDY OF DIALOGIC ARGUMENTATION*

Arnold Günther

## 1. *Introduction*

This paper presents the fundamentals for a range of constructive studies of dialogic argumentation by introducing a system of concepts which may be used for the representation of, among others, argumentative dialogues. This system of concepts was designed for a quite general study of two-person interactions, especially for the characterization of classes of dialogues but because of its generality also proved useful for the study of dialogic argumentation.[1]

Constructive studies of dialogic argumentation are conducted in logic as well as in linguistics; these studies in both disciplines, however, are severely limited. Logical studies of dialogic argumentation on the one hand tend to concentrate on (the principles of) correct argumentation and to consider only entities such as statements, or more precisely: speech act products, and their relations to one another. Linguistic studies of dialogic argumentation, on the other hand, tend to concentrate on linguistic forms of expressions used in argumentations, with the aim of finding rules or conditions characterizing well-formed sequences of verbal expressions which occur in argumentations, without much interest in the question whether argumentations are correct or not. My own approach to the study of dialogic argumentation is constructive but neither wholly logical nor wholly linguistic, although

I make use of logical and linguistic concepts and methods. I remove the limitations mentioned by placing the study of argumentation where it belongs: within the wider context of a study of communication and action. In this context not only questions of correctness can be discussed, but also relations of verbal expressions, speech acts and speech act products, among others. The plan of my paper is as follows: In section 2. I informally describe essential aspects of argumentation from the point of view of a theory of communication and action. In section 3. I present a system of concepts which can be used for the representation and construction of (models of) dialogues. In section 4. I sketch a treatment of argumentative dialogues and argumentations based on the system of concepts developed in section 3.

## 2. *Argumentation - informally described*

Instead of giving a full-scale informal description of argumentation, I'll just give a list of those five characteristics of argumentation I'm especially interested in.

(I) Argumentation occurs most naturally in multi-person interactions.

(For simplicity's sake let's confine our attention to two-person interactions. Consideration of multi-person interactions where 'multi' means 'more than two' would only complicate matters at the expense of understanding and naturalness.) Argumentation is something people do. The question whether argumentation *is* multi-person interaction need not be answered here; as for my purposes, it suffices to say that some properties of interactions are properties of argumentations. This difficulty results from the process/result ambiguity connected with the word "argumentation", according to which argumentation may be a process, i.e. an individual event, or the result (or structure) of such a process, i.e. some kind of abstract object. It will be advantageous to have both senses of the word at our disposal.

(II) Argumentation is intimately connected with language use.

Persons engaged in argumentation normally use words, phrases, sentences or texts of a language. Socrates' refutation of Parmenides' theory that there is no motion, by simply walking to and fro in front of Parmenides without saying anything, would not normally count as an argumentation. The degree of intimacy this connection between argumentation and language use has is a matter of dispute. One may hold, for example, that language is only necessary for the identification of propositions or statements relevant to an argumentation, or contrary to that one may hold that for an argumentation the form of verbal expressions used is of central importance. Both positions can be maintained consistently. The first position uses a concept of argumentation as an abstract object, the second position uses a concept of argumentation as a process.

(III) Argumentation involves at least the change of propositional attitudes of knowledge or belief in the people arguing.

It nearly goes without saying that each case of language use changes the (propositional) attitudes of the persons involved. Insofar this characteristic of argumentation is a consequence of (II). It is the character of the attitudes and the nature of their change effected by argumentation which allows a more precise characterization: Attitudes of belief or knowledge are to be changed by argumentation. These changes are generally of the following kind: A belief is justified or rejected by argumentation or knowledge is reached by argumentation.

(IV) Argumentation is action according to rules.

Although language use has been considered to be an action at least since AUSTIN this contention cannot be deduced from our contention in (II), as it is not yet clear which constellations of actions constitute another action. Thus, for example, not every temporal sequence of actions needs to be action, but of course there are complex actions which are sequences of (more elementary) actions. Argumentation is action governed by rules; without further analysis, however, it cannot be equated with sequences of speech acts. It is not clear whether rules are parts of actions and as I am not going to discuss this problem here, I have introduced them explicitly. It should be added that a process/result ambiguity is also connected with the word "action".

(V) Argumentation can at least be cooperative or competitive (eristic).

Among properties of interactions, which are also properties of argumentation, are cooperativity and competitiveness. Accordingly we distinguish between cooperative argumentation and competitive - or eristic - argumentation. It is not altogether clear how these properties should be defined, but something like the following seems to lie at the bottom of this distinction: In cooperative interactions partners help each other to reach a (common) goal, whereas in competitive interactions partners try to reach different or opposing goals with the intention to win.

## 3. *Dialogue bases*

In order to study two-person interactions constructively, i.e. by using logical and mathematical objects or concepts, I have introduced the concept of a dialogue basis. A dialogue basis is, roughly, a classified repertoire of objects which can be used for the construction of dialogues.[2] Given the concept of a dialogue basis one can define a concept of dialogue on a dialogue basis.[3] Dialogues on a dialogue basis are, strictly speaking, (possible) models or representations of dialogues, but for ease of formulation I shall simply call them dialogues or abstract dialogues. Here is a rough sketch of the kind of objects, i.e. (abstract) dialogues, which are to be constructed by means of a dialogue basis: A dialogue (on a dialogue basis) is a sequence of (dialogue-)steps, each step including a (characterization of a) speech act and (of) various relevant aspects of the dialogue partners.[4] In the 17 explicit definitions given below well-known set-theoretical concepts are used; among abbreviations note '$\wp$' for 'the power set of'. For ease of understanding I list various symbols used in the definitions together with an indication of their designata, before giving the exact definitions.

$\mathcal{P}$ is a set of persons (such a set has two elements).

X is a person, i.e., an element of some such set $\mathcal{P}$.

$\mathcal{E}$ is a set of indicators of - i.e., a set of marks indicating-propositional attitude type (such a set is non-empty and finite).

E is an indicator of propositional attitude type, i.e., an element of some such set $\mathcal{E}$.

$\mathcal{G}$ is a set of indicators of - i.e., a set of marks indicating - illocutionary force (such a set is non-empty and finite).

G is an indicator of illocutionary force, i.e., an element of some such set $\mathcal{G}$.

$\mathcal{J}$ is a system of objects of propositional attitude, i.e., a non-empty set of objects of propositional attitude together with a family of relations defined on that set.

u($\mathcal{J}$) is the set of objects of propositional attitude in, i.e., the "universe" of, the system $\mathcal{J}$.

p is an object of propositional attitude, i.e., an element of some such set u($\mathcal{J}$).

$\mathcal{L}$ is a language.

EXP($\mathcal{L}$) is the set of expressions of the language $\mathcal{L}$.

$\varphi$ is an expression, i.e., an element of some such set Exp($\mathcal{L}$).

(E,p) is a combination of a propositional attitude indicator and an object of propositional attitude; such a combination will be called a propositional attitude.

(X,E,p) is a combination of a person and a propositional attitude; such a combination will be called an occurrence of a propositional attitude.

($\varphi$,G) is a combination of an expression of a language and an illocutionary force indicator; such a combination will be called a speech act type.

(X,$\varphi$,G) is a combination of a person and a speech act type; such a combination will be called an individual speech act.

$\mathcal{R}$ is a set of dialogue rules.

R is a dialogue rule, i.e., a member of some such set $\mathcal{R}$.

Four types of dialogue rules are distinguished:

EE-rules, connecting propositional attitudes; they are sets of pairs of sets of propositional attitudes.

EG-rules, connecting propositional attitudes with speech act types; they are sets of pairs consisting of sets of propositional attitudes and speech act types.

GE-rules, connecting speech act types with propositional attitudes; they are sets of pairs consisting of speech act types and sets of propositional attitudes.

EGE-rules, connecting propositional attitudes and speech act types with propositional attitudes; they are sets of pairs the first elements of which are pairs consisting of sets of propositional attitudes and speech act types and the second elements of which are sets of propositional attitudes.[5]

Now exact definitions will be given.

Def 1

A *dialogue basis* $\mathfrak{D}$ is a 6-tuple ($\mathcal{P},\mathcal{E},\mathcal{J},\mathcal{G},\mathcal{L},\mathcal{R}$), where $\mathcal{P}$ is a two-element set, $\mathcal{E},\mathcal{G}$ are non-empty finite sets, $\mathcal{J}$ is a system, i.e., a non-empty set together with a family of relations, $\mathcal{L}$ is a language, $\mathcal{R}$ is a finite set of sets such that for each R $\in$ $\mathcal{R}$

$R \subseteq \mathcal{P}(\mathcal{E} \times u(\mathcal{J})) \times \mathcal{P}(\mathcal{E} \times u(\mathcal{J}))$
or $\mathcal{R} \subseteq \mathcal{P}(\mathcal{E} \times u(\mathcal{J})) \times (\mathrm{Exp}(\mathcal{L}) \times \mathcal{G})$
or $\mathcal{R} \subseteq (\mathrm{Exp}(\mathcal{L}) \times \mathcal{G}) \times \mathcal{P}(\mathcal{E} \times u(\mathcal{J}))$
or $\mathcal{R} \subseteq (\mathcal{P}(\mathcal{E} \times u(\mathcal{J})) \times (\mathrm{Exp}(\mathcal{L}) \times \mathcal{G})) \times \mathcal{P}(\mathcal{E} \times u(\mathcal{J}))$

$\mathcal{P}$ is the set of persons of $\mathfrak{D}$ ; $\mathcal{E}$ is the set of indicators of propositional attitude type of $\mathfrak{D}$ ; $u(\mathcal{J})$ is the set of objects of propositional attitude of $\mathfrak{D}$ ; $\mathcal{L}$ is the language of $\mathfrak{D}$ ; $\mathcal{G}$ is the set of illocutionary force indicators of $\mathfrak{D}$ ; $\mathcal{R}$ is the set of dialogue rules of $\mathfrak{D}$ .

Def 2

A *propositional attitude* on a dialogue basis $\mathfrak{D}$ is a pair (E,p), where E is an element of the set $\mathcal{E}$ of $\mathfrak{D}$ and p is an element of the set $u(\mathcal{J})$ of $\mathfrak{D}$.

Def 3

Let (E,p) be a propositional attitude on a dialogue basis $\mathfrak{D}$. An *occurrence* of (E,p) on $\mathfrak{D}$ is a triple (X,E,p), where X is an element of the set $\mathcal{P}$ of $\mathfrak{D}$.

If (X,E,p) is an occurrence of a propositional attitude, we say that X has a propositional attitude of type E concerning p.

Def 4

An *individual speech act* on a dialogue basis $\mathfrak{D}$ is a triple (X, $\varphi$,G), where X is an element of the set $\mathcal{P}$ of $\mathfrak{D}$, $\varphi$ is an expression of the language $\mathcal{L}$ of $\mathfrak{D}$ and G is an element of the set $\mathcal{G}$ of $\mathfrak{D}$.

A speech act s = (X,$\varphi$,G) is said to be a speech act with illocutionary force G performed by X by uttering the expression $\varphi$ , X is called the speaker.

Def 5

A *speech act type* on a dialogue basis $\mathfrak{D}$ is a pair ($\varphi$,G), where $\varphi$ is an expression of the language $\mathcal{L}$ of $\mathfrak{D}$ and G is an illocutionary force indicator from the set $\mathcal{G}$ of $\mathfrak{D}$.

If $(X,\varphi,G)$ is an individual speech act, we say that X performs a speech act of type $(\varphi,G)$, and that $(X,\varphi,G)$ is of type $(\varphi,G)$.

Def 6

R is an EE-*rule* of a dialogue basis $\mathfrak{D}$ iff $R \varepsilon \mathcal{R}$ and $R \subseteq \mathcal{P}(\mathcal{E} X\, u(\mathcal{J})) X\, \mathcal{P}(\mathcal{E} X\, u(\mathcal{J}))$.

I.e. an EE-rule is a set of pairs the elements of which are sets of propositional attitudes. If $r \varepsilon R$, then there are entities a, c such that $r = (a,c)$ and both a and $c \subseteq \mathcal{E} X\, u(\mathcal{J})$.

Def 7

R is an EG-*rule* of a dialogue basis $\mathfrak{D}$ iff $R \varepsilon \mathcal{R}$ and $R \subseteq \mathcal{P}(\mathcal{E} X u(\mathcal{J})) X\, (Exp(\mathcal{L}) X \mathcal{G})$.

I.e. an EG-rule is a set of pairs the first element of which is a set of propositional attitudes and the second element of which is a speech act type. If $r \varepsilon R$, then there are entities a, c such that $r = (a,c)$, $a \subseteq \mathcal{E} X u(\mathcal{J})$ and $c \varepsilon Exp(\mathcal{L}) X \mathcal{G}$.

Def 8

R is a GE-*rule* of a dialogue basis $\mathfrak{D}$ iff $R \varepsilon \mathcal{R}$ and $R \subseteq (Exp(\mathcal{L}) X \mathcal{G}) X\, \mathcal{P}(\mathcal{E} X\, u(\mathcal{J}))$.

I.e. a GE-rule is a set of pairs the first element of which is a speech act type and the second element of which is a set of propositional attitudes. If $r \varepsilon R$, then there are entities a, c such that $r = (a,c)$, $a \varepsilon Exp(\mathcal{L}) X \mathcal{G}$ and $c \subseteq \mathcal{E} X\, u(\mathcal{J})$.

Def 9

R is an EGE-*rule* of a dialogue basis $\mathfrak{D}$ iff $R \varepsilon \mathcal{R}$ and $R \subseteq (\mathcal{P}(\mathcal{E} X u(\mathcal{J})) X\, (Exp(\mathcal{L}) X \mathcal{G})) X\, \mathcal{P}(\mathcal{E} X u(\mathcal{J}))$.

I.e. an EGE-rule is a set of pairs, the first element of which is a pair consisting of a set of propositional attitudes and a speech act type, and the second element of which is a set of propositional attitudes. If r ε R, then there are entities a,b,c such that r = ((a,b),c), both a and c $\subseteq \mathcal{E}$ X u($\mathcal{J}$) and b ε Exp($\mathcal{L}$)X $\mathcal{G}$.

For ease of formulation I introduce the concept of situation. It can be given a more important status on my approach; here, however, it will be used as an abbreviation only.

Def 10

A *situation* in a dialogue basis $\mathfrak{D}$ is a set of occurrences of propositional attitudes on $\mathfrak{D}$.

Def 11

Situations S and S' are *connected* in a dialogue basis $\mathfrak{D}$ *by* EE-*rule* R iff there are r,a,c such that r ε R, r = (a,c) and for every propositional attitude in a there is an occurrence of that propositional attitude in S and for every propositional attitude in c there is an occurrence of that propositional attitude in S'.[6]

Def 12

An individual speech act s is *connected* with a situation S in a dialogue basis $\mathfrak{D}$ *by* EG-*rule* R iff there are r,a,c such that r ε R, r = (a,c), for every propositional attitude in a there is an occurrence of that propositional attitude in S, and s is an individual speech act of type c.

Def 13

A situation S is *connected* with an individual speech act s in a dialogue basis $\mathfrak{D}$ *by* GE-*rule* R iff there are r,a,c, such that r ε R, r = (a,c), s is an individual speech act of type a, and for every propositional attitude in c there is an occurrence of that propositional attitude in S.

Def 14

Situations S,S' and an individual speech act s are *connected* in a dialogue basis $\mathfrak{D}$ *by* EGE-*rule* R iff there are r,a,b,c, such that $r \varepsilon R$, $r = ((a,b),c)$, for every propositional attitude in a there is an occurrence of that propositional attitude in S, s is an individual speech act of type b, and for every propositional attitude in c there is an occurrence of that propositional attitude in S'.

Def 15

A *dialogue step* in a dialogue basis $\mathfrak{D}$ is a triple (A,s,E), where A,E are situations in $\mathfrak{D}$, s is an individual speech act on $\mathfrak{D}$, A and s are connected by an EG-rule and s and E are connected by a GE-rule, or A,s,E are connected by an EGE-rule.

Def 16

If (A,s,E) is a dialogue step in a dialogue basis $\mathfrak{D}$ and $s = (X, \varphi, G)$ is an individual speech act on $\mathfrak{D}$, then X is the *speaker* in (A,s,E).

Def 17

A *dialogue* on a dialogue basis $\mathfrak{D}$ is a finite sequence $D = (D_1, \ldots, D_n)$, where $D_i$, $1 \leq i \leq n$, are dialogue steps in $\mathfrak{D}$, and for every $i > 1$: if $D_i = (A_i, s_i, E_i)$ and $D_{i-1} = (A_{i-1}, s_{i-1}, E_{i-1})$, then $E_{i-1}$ and $A_i$ are connected by an EE-rule, and there are i, j $1 \leq i, j \leq n$, such that the speaker in $D_i$ is different from the speaker in $D_j$.

The concepts introduced in definitions 1 - 17, or concepts similar to them, make up the hard core of systems of concepts used in constructive studies of dialogues.

## 4. *Cooperative argumentative dialogues and argumentation*

With the concepts of dialogue basis and dialogue on a dialogue basis at our disposal, we will turn back to dialogic argumentation and try to answer the question: what use may be made of dialogue bases in the study of dialogic argumentation? That there is no lack of interesting problems to be solved is shown by a list of selected problems:

1) Define a concept of argumentative dialogue and characterize the class of argumentative dialogues on a dialogue basis.
2) Define an abstraction function which assigns an abstract structure called "argumentation" to every argumentative dialogue on a given dialogue basis.
3) Are there minimal requirements a dialogue basis must fulfil in order for there to be argumentative dialogues on that dialogue basis? And if there are, what are they?
4) Is there a dialogue basis such that all dialogues on it are argumentative dialogues?

In the following I'll be discussing some of the relations between certain dialogues on a dialogue basis and argumentations, concentrating on the problem of how to define an abstraction function which assigns to these dialogues a structure which may be called an argumentation. We cannot study the relations between abstract dialogues and argumentations precisely unless we use a method for representing argumentation. Representations of argumentation should be mathematical objects, just as representations of dialogues by means of dialogue bases are mathematical objects. When developing a method of representing argumentation one may use two policies: a strict one and a liberal one. The strict policy is to abstract as much as possible from the actual course of argumentation, e.g. to abstract the linguistic form of utterances away and simply to use arguments without recourse to their actual linguistic form. On this strict policy, language is used just for the identification of arguments, and is to this extent important, but only because of its identifying power. The liberal policy tries to be as explicit as possible and considers e.g. the linguistic form of arguments as of central importance also. The liberal policy should lead to a representation of argumentation considered as a process (or individual event), the strict policy should lead to a representation of argumentation considered as the "essential" structure of an argumentation; see remarks in section 2., (I) and (II). Looking now for representations of argumentation we see at once that the objects which logicians call arguments are representations of argumentation only on the strictest of policies. Arguments in the logicians' sense are pairs consisting of a set of premisses and a conclusion; the train of reasoning or argumentation leading from premisses to conclusion is completely left out of consideration. More suitable candidates for the title of representations of argumentation seem to be derivations in some logical system.[7] For definiteness let us consider the KALISH-MONTAGUE system of natural deduction, supposing that KM-derivations (short for "derivations in the KALISH-MONTAGUE system") are representations of argumentation.[8] Analysing this system from the point of view of a theory of communication and action, I have succeeded in defining a dialogue basis and a function which assigns to every completed KM-derivation a dialogue, KM-dialogue for short, on that dialogue basis. KM-dialogues are cooperative argumentative dialogues. I'll just sketch some points I consider to be of interest, without giving explicit definitions.[9] I start with a description of KM-dialogues, thus giving an informal description of the dialogue basis.

1) In KM-dialogues the partners may have propositional attitudes of the following six types: they may *want that* something is the case, they may *know that* something is the case, they may *know why* something is the case, they may *assume that* something is the

case, they may *presuppose that* something is the case, they may *consider* something *relevant* to something. This last type of propositional attitude is the type of a 2-place propositional attitude; it was introduced for its ability to relate steps in a KM-dialogue to the various tasks the dialogue partners try to fulfill.
2) Objects of propositional attitude in KM-dialogues are elementary propositions expressed by the language the dialogue partners use, or certain complex propositions constructed from elementary propositions, or states of affairs characterized by a dialogue partner having a propositional attitude. A dialogue partner, for example, may want his partner to make a certain assumption.
3) Dialogue partners in KM-dialogues use a language constructed on the basis of a sentential language by adding various functors. By uttering sentences of this language the dialogue partners may *ask questions, make statements, give orders* or *give information.*
4) The dialogue rules for KM-dialogues are of the four kinds introduced in section 3.: they characterize the various connections between propositional attitudes the dialogue partners have and speech acts they perform. The rules characterize how dialogue partners interpret speech acts, under which conditions they perform speech acts and how they reason. The rules are designed to handle the evolving, remaining and disappearing of attitudes.
5) Dialogue partners in KM-dialogues have different capacities: One of them is able to *recognize* argumentative *problems*, the main features of the *context* in which the problems arise and to *recognize* that something is a *solution* to a *problem*, while the other is able to *analyze* argumentative *problems* and to *draw elementary inferences.*
6) KM-dialogues can be generally characterized as social actions or processes in which dialogue partners cooperate in order to solve argumentative problems.
The concept of dialogue basis cannot be used to define the class

of KM-dialogues as the set of all dialogues on the dialogue basis I have just sketched implicitly.[10] The set of KM-dialogues is defined by means of a function, which assigns to any completed KM-derivation a certain dialogue on the dialogue basis. Consider a completed KM-derivation. Such a derivation is a sequence of lines containing formulas of a formal language: some of the lines and especially the first line, consisting of '~~Show~~' and a formula of the language; lines may be boxed, and there is a box containing all lines except the first line. A KM-derivation is constructed in a finite number of steps; corresponding to each KM-derivation there is an n-termed sequence of partial KM-derivations, where n is the number of steps needed for the construction of the derivation. The KM-dialogue assigned to a KM-derivation is an n-termed sequence of dialogue steps, where n is the number of steps needed for the construction of the derivation. If $i \leq n$, the i-th dialogue step corresponds to the i-th partial derivation so that the speech act in this dialogue step is determined by the last operation performed in constructing this partial derivation, and the situations in the dialogue step are determined by the preceding partial derivation. Taking KM-dialogues to be argumentative dialogues and KM-derivations to represent argumentations, we are justified in considering the inverse of the function just hinted at to be an abstraction function, that abstracts "the argumentation performed" from an argumentative dialogue.

## NOTES

(*) This paper benefitted from discussions I had with M. Böttner and C.H. Heidrich, from criticisms and help by E.M. Barth and from suggestions by L. Carlson and J. Hintikka. Readers with spare time or some interest in the study of imperfection are invited to speculate on the former state of the paper.

(1) An attempt to describe these ideas was made in A. Günther (1977); see the references there for earlier attempts and for the origin of some of the concepts.

(2) As dialogue bases are to include all those entities which the identity criteria of dialogues make use of, an analysis of the intuitive concept of dialogue is presupposed for their definition. For details see again A. Günther (1977).

(3) A dialogue basis does not contain principles for the construction of dia- logues and insofar the concept of dialogue on a dialogue basis is much too wide. The most important work to be done on dialogue bases will be to narrow down the class of dialogues on a dialogue basis.

(4) This characterization contrasts with other characterizations of dialogues, where e.g. a dialogue is understood to be a sequence of the verbal expressions used by the dialogue partners, or where a dialogue is understood to be a sequence of pairs, each pair consisting of the name of a person and the verbal expressions used by this person. For more details on the problem of how to represent dialogues see A. Günther (1977), § 5, and A. Günther (forthcoming).

(5) Compare W. Labov's classification of interaction rules in W. Labov (1970).

(6) As L. Carlson and J. Hintikka pointed out in discussion, EE-rules will have to incorporate principles of epistemic logic.

(7) For this idea I am indebted to J. Corcoran (1972) and D. Prawitz (1972).

(8) First presented in R. Montague & D. Kalish (1957) and later in textbook form in D. Kalish & R. Montague (1964).

(9) For details on this dialogue basis and explicit definitions see - as if you hadn't guessed - A. Günther (1977).

(10) This is due to the fact that a dialogue basis is not a "grammar of dialogues" but a repertoire of elements for the construction of dialogues.

## REFERENCES

[1] Corcoran, J. (1972) "The Conceptual Structure of Classical Logic", *Philosophy and Phenomenological Research* 33 (1972), 25-47

[2] Günther, A. (1977) *Dialogkonstruktionen auf der Basis logischer Ableitungen. IKP-Forschungsberichte* 68-I, Hamburg 1977

[3] Günther, A. (forthcoming) "Some Ways of Representing Dialogues", In: L. Vaina & J. Hintikka (eds) *Cognitive Constraints on Communication. Representations and Processes,* Dordrecht (forthcoming)

[4] Kalish, D. & R. Montague (1964) *Logic. Techniques of Formal Reasoning.* N.York 1964

[5] Labov, W. (1970) "The Study of Language in its Social Context", *Studium Generale* 23 (1970), 30-87

[6] Montague, R. & D. Kalish (1957) "Remarks on Descriptions and Natural Deduction", *Archiv für mathematische Logik und Grundlagenforschung* 3 (1957), 50-73

[7] Prawitz, D. (1972) "The Philosophical Position of Proof Theory", In: R.E. Olson & A.M. Paul (eds) *Contemporary Philosophy in Scandinavia,* Baltimore 1972, 123-34

# MONTAGUE-GRAMMERS FOR ARGUMENTATIVE DIALOGUES*

Carl H. Heidrich

## 1. *Introduction*

In this contribution I present by means of a dialogue example the method by which dialogues can be associated with a MONTAGUE-grammer.[1]

In section 2 I shall outline the methodological background for the construction of dialogues, their linguistic descriptions and their representations in MONTAGUE's semiotic. Section 3 contains the informel dialogue construction on the original dialogue as well as its representation. Section 4 contains the construction of a MONTAGUE-grammar on the dialogue example.

## 2. *Background and motivation*

The example I am going to discuss in section 3 and 4 is a dialogue of a type which we call *Begründungsdialog*, or in English, roughly, *explanatory dialogue*. That the class of these dialogues is important is obvious. In everyday life and in scientific work we are continually engaged in explanatory dialogues. I wish to point also to the debates in the theory of knowledge concerning the explication of the concept of *explanation*.

As far as I know no earlier research on the relations between dialogic theories of communicative actions and formal (logical) model theory has been based on MONTAGUE's Semiotic.[2]

Without mentioning the ontological problem of the existence of communicative actions, the range of problems to be studied should contain: i. The problems of correct descriptions of communicative actions. ii. The development of concepts and the explication of concepts for the study of communicative actions. iii. The development of a suitable methodology.

One possible way of attacking the problems just mentioned is to construct models of verbal communicative actions which may function as paradigms, i.e. of examples or of test instances.

## *2.1 A supplementation of MONTAGUE'S methodology*

If one tries to treat dialogues in MONTAGUE's semiotic, e.g. in the version of UG or PTQ, the following facts characterize the situation with which one is faced.[3]

i. MONTAGUE's theory is one for sentences and not one for texts or dialogues.

ii. The natural language objects described by a MONTAGUE-grammar are formal objects.

iii. The connection between informal grammars and standardized semiotic properties of formal grammars are not explicitly stated.

Parts of the standardizations, e.g. lexematic -or morphological- which MONTAGUE used for the investigations of fragments of natural language sentences followed from the methodology he adopted. He has expressed his point of view on various occasions in a general as well as in a more specific way:

> "It seemed to me desirable that pragmatics should at least initially follow the lead of semantics - or its modern version, model theory -...."[4]

Thus it is necessary to supplement MONTAGUE's methodology by working out standardizations for a useful treatment of dialogues so that their informal and formal investigations are related more explicitly. To this end the following maxims are adopted:

(1) A theory of verbal communicative actions should be developed informally and formally in pragmatics.

(2) The formal theory of pragmatics should follow the lines of MONTAGUE's proposals in the formal treatment of natural languages and their translations into intensional logic.

(3) Dialogues should be introduced as formal objects which are models of natural dialogues.

(4) A concept of dialogue structure and satisfaction should be introduced such that

i. natural dialogues may or may not satisfy a dialogue structure

ii. natural dialogues which satisfy a dialogue structure should be related to formal models of dialogues.

Concerning (2) MONTAGUE has used two related methods to correlate formal descriptions of natural languages with those of intensional logics. One can be found in EFL, the other in UG, PTQ. The intensional relations, which may or may not hold for different kinds of entities, are standardized according to types. Hence, an intensional language will be type theoretical. The established semantic-syntactic parallelism allows the construction of a model theoretic concept of interpretation.

The procedure by which MONTAGUE's methodology is supplemented and which satisfies maxims (2,3) is best sketched diagrammatically:

(5)

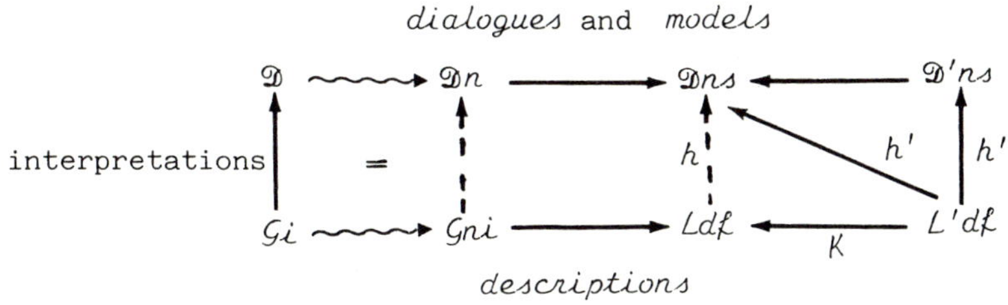

The diagram is separable into a left part and a right part. In the left part $\mathfrak{D}$ and $\mathfrak{D}n$ should be *natural dialogues* (taken as individual events) and *natural dialogues in standardized form* respectively; *Gi, Gni* are *informal language descriptions*, "grammars", of the corresponding natural dialogues such that the natural dialogues are interpretations of their linguistic descriptions. In the right part $\mathfrak{D}ns$ and $\mathfrak{D}'ns$ should be *set-theoretical dialogue models*, *Ldf* and *L'df* should be *formal languages* (formal grammars) of dialogue descriptions such that the dialogue models are interpretations of the formal languages relative to the interpretation assignments h, h' and a translation k. I.e. the right part should be a MONTAGUE-theory (in the sense of UG) - relative to two MONTAGUE-grammars *Ldf* and *L'df* for which the theorem of section 5,p. 233 UG holds.[5]

The relations (mappings) between the left and the right part assure that the explicit standardizations on the dialogue and on the level of description are preserved in the MONTAGUE-theory.

## 2.2 *Dialogue structure. Dialoguemodel, and the representation of dialogical properties*

One of the principal problems to be solved is to find such relations. Another principal problem is the following: If there are explicit relations on the dialogue level, there are also set-theoretical dialoge models. How can one introduce precise formal descriptions for natural dialogues and for dialogue models such that one has also relations between the respective formal descriptions?

To meet maxims (1,3,4) it is necessary to construct a suitable *dialogue structure*. I refer now to the paper of GÜNTHER in this volume, especially to definitions 1 - 17. The concepts are defined there as set-theoretical predicates. Definition 17 is the definition of the concept 'dialogue' as it is used in our research.

(6) i. An abstract (mathematical) object for which definition 17 holds true is a dialogue structure.

ii. A concrete, specified object for which definition 17 holds true is a dialogue model.

A natural dialogue *satisfies* the/a dialogue structure if it can be related to (mapped onto) an equivalent dialogue model.

It is perhaps useful to illustrate here the overall pattern of a dialogue step, for two persons X, Y, as it will be used in section 3, compare GÜNTHER's definition 15:

$$D=(A,s,E)\left(\begin{array}{l} \text{situation } A=\left\{\begin{Bmatrix}\text{prop.attitude}\\ \vdots\end{Bmatrix}_X , \begin{Bmatrix}\text{prop.attitude}\\ \vdots\end{Bmatrix}_Y\right\} \\ \quad \text{speech act} \quad s \quad \text{(explicit performative utterance)} \\ \text{situation } E=\left\{\begin{Bmatrix}\text{prop.attitude}\\ \vdots\end{Bmatrix}_X , \begin{Bmatrix}\text{prop.attitude}\\ \vdots\end{Bmatrix}_Y\right\} \end{array}\right)$$

It nearly goes without saying that it is necessary at the beginning of such an enterprise as ours, to concentrate on relatively simple, well known but non trivial communicative actions, which take into account the more or less accepted knowledge of philosophical and behavioural theories. In our opinion, it would thus be inadmissible to represent in an empirical model of dialogues only e.g. verbal acts as structural properties but, as is often done, leave out entirely representations of the internal states of persons.

On the other hand, with respect to the right part of (5), it is indispensable that the dialogue models contain adequate intensional relations to represent dialogic properties. What could be done to meet this requirement is to *reduce* the object dialogue to an intensional relation. [6] First of all it is necessary to show that the reductions can be treated formally and to elaborate some procedures for handling them. For special cases I have shown that reductions can be expressed as rules. [7] This fact was used to get information about reductions of entities such as 'dialogue', 'dialogue step', 'situation', 'attitude', 'speech act', etc. As soon as one looks at the problem that way it is obvious that the entity dialogue will not have a simple reduction. [8] One can imagine that according to GÜNTHER's definition 1 - 17 the representation of dialogues in MONTAGUE-grammars is not quite an automatic task. A dialogue structure in the sense of (6) contains, except for sets of points of references, the set-theoretical structure upon which the definitions of intensional relations will be based.

Another mass of problems to be solved is contained in the left side of the diagram. Because, at least for German, there is no informal grammar either for speech-acts or for attitude sentences, to say nothing of a semantic theory for both implicit and explicit forms of performative utterances and attitude sentences. What we have done to reach solutions by suitable standardizations appears partly in the example to be discussed.

On the language level the connection depends on the amount and detail of the standardized semiotic properties of the linguistic material contained in $\mathcal{D}n$ and $\mathcal{G}ni$. Hence, the relation between $\mathcal{G}ni$ and $\mathcal{L}d\ell$ is a translation from an informal into a formal grammar in the sense that a natural dialogue satisfying a dialogue structure exists as an interpretation. The connection between the two parts of the diagram depends, on the dialogue level, on the constructions of abstract set-theoretical structures in which natural dialogues can be embedded.[9]

In view of all the facts just mentioned it seemed to us necessary that the standardizations which follow from the demands in dialogue models should be made explicit. In fact the maxims (1-4) as well as (6) already contain standardizations not yet discussed in MONTAGUE grammars. As an example: BENNETT discusses in his dissertation some aspects of performative verbs.[10] But, actually, the property P of s, which is a dialogically relevant performative utterance of a person X addressed to Y, is not discussed. One needs also categorical representations of a feature such as 'the identity or non- of the utterer with the actor in an action expressed in a complement sentence' as in

I IMPLORE YOU TO HELP HIM, i.e.

I IMPLORE YOU THAT YOU HELP HIM but not

* I IMPLORE YOU THAT I HELP HIM.

In the next two sections I shall follow the path $\mathcal{D}$ - $\mathcal{D}n$ - *Gni* - *Ldf* of the diagram (5). In the present state of our research it is not possible to start by defining a dialogue basis for the dialogue example, as was already pointed out by GÜNTHER in his paper.[11] Section 3 contains the part $\mathcal{D}$-$\mathcal{D}n$-*Gni* of the diagram, i.e. the construction of the informal standardized description will be presented. Section 4 contains part *Gni* - *Ldf* of the diagram, i.e. it contains the MONTAGUE grammar of the dialogue description.

One could then define the dialogue basis, and a treatment of the dialogue in a MONTAGUE-theory would also be possible. But because of lack of space this part of the program must be postponed to a further paper.[12]

## 3. *An example of a dialogue*

### 3.1 *The original dialogue, and a completed version*

The example of the explanatory dialogue originates from

SCHNURRE's "Ich frag ja bloss", 1973.
"I'm only askin'"

*Original dialogue*

1A Wieso humpelst n?
Why ye limpin'?

2B Gelesen.
Was readin'.

3A Davon humpelste?
Izzat why ye limpin?

4B Ja.
Yea.

5A Wien das?
That (Izzat) why?

6B Nich aufgepasst.
Wasn't payin' attention.

7A Schweres Buch?
Heavy book?

8B Comic-Heft.
Comic book.

9A Was: Auf'n Fuss gefallen?
What! Fell on yer foot?

10B Quatsch; Fuss eingeschlafen.
Nonsense; My foot fell asleep

The added numbers distinguish the different utterances, A and B represent the two speakers.

This original dialogue $\mathfrak{D}$ is a natural dialogue but it does not satisfy the dialogue structure. The aim of the next steps is to construct a natural dialogue which does satisfy the dialogue structure. All of these steps should be expressed on the level $\mathfrak{Dn}$ of the natural dialogues (compare section 2). But because the aim of this paper is not the construction of a set-theoretical dialogue structure (of the original dialogue) in itself and also not the investigation of modeltheoretic properties of the dialogue structure, it suffices to work out only a few steps of the construction of the dialogue on the level $\mathfrak{Dn}$. The other steps can be worked out on the level $\mathcal{Gni}$ of the informal description of the dialogue which contains the linguistic material from which the MONTAGUE-grammar will be formulated. It is necessary to assure that essential properties of the original dialogue are represented in the description in a unique manner. The first step of standardization is to get a version of the original consisting of completed utterances. This version (and a translation of it into English) can be given as a result of the following reading of the original dialogue. This is one reading and it is a very rough description of the dialogue situation:

A sees that B is limping. Because of this experience he asks for a reason or cause by uttering 1A. B replies by uttering 2B that he read something. A does not know or is uncertain whether or not B's reading is a reason for B's limping and by uttering 3A he asks explicitly whether it is or is not. In reply 4B,B confirms that the reading actually was the reason. A does not understand that and informs B about it by uttering 5A. In 6B,B gives some more information in saying that he did not pay attention to something. A tries to reconstruct the case by making a hypothesis which he offers in 7A by asking whether B read a heavy (or difficult) book. B, by uttering 8B, confirms the hypothesis partly by saying he read a comic (= light (easy) book). (In German "schwer", "leicht" are ambiguous; the respective readings are possible for both adjectives.) A proceeds now by trial and error and asks in 9A whether the book fell on B's foot. In 1oB this is rejected by B who says that this foot had fallen asleep. This, apparently, satisfies A. In the completed version A expresses that by uttering 11A.

*Completed utterances (and translation)*

1A Warum humpelst Du?
Why are you limping?

2B Ich habe gelesen.
I was reading.

3A Weil Du gelesen hast, humpelst Du?
You're limping, because you were reading?

4B Weil ich gelesen habe, humple ich.
I'm limping, because I was reading.

5A Ich verstehe nicht, dass Du humpelst, weil Du gelesen hast.
I don't understand that you're limping, because you were reading.

6B Ich habe nicht aufgepasst.
I wasn't paying attention.

7A Hast Du ein schweres Buch gelesen?
Did you read a heavy (difficult) book?

8B Ich habe ein Comic (leichtes Buch) gelesen.
I was reading a comic book (light (easy) book).

9A Ist Dir etwas auf den Fuss gefallen?
Did something fall on your foot?

1oB Mein Fuss ist eingeschlafen.
My foot fell asleep.

11A Ich verstehe, dass Du humpelst, weil Du gelesen hast.
I understand that you're limping, because you were reading.

### *3.2 Descriptions of the (completed) dialogue*

The utterances in the original as well as in the stilistically completed version are primary performative utterances. The second step of standardization is to paraphrase (or translate) the completed version (synonymously) into an explicit performative version. The types of performatives used in the utterances are respectively: 1A: question, 2B: answer, 3A: question, 4B: confirmation, 5A: information, 6B: information, 7A: question, 8B: reply, 9A: question, 1oB: reply, 11A: information. The explicit performative versions of 1A, 2B are then:

1A Ich frage Dich, warum Du humpelst.
I ask you why you are limping.

2B Ich antworte Dir, dass ich gelesen habe.
I answer (you) that I was reading.

The explicit performative utterances of this version are to be taken as elements on the level $\mathfrak{D}n$. I shall go on with the construction of the dialogue on the level $\mathcal{G}ni$ of informal description. One common way of describing explicit performative utterances is to use proper names or third person pronouns, or variable names instead of first or second person pronouns. The following is then a possible description of the completed original dialogue in its explicit performative version:

*Description 1*

1A A fragt B, warum B humpelt.
A asks B why B is limping.

2B B antwortet, dass B gelesen hat.
B answers that B was reading.

3A A fragt B, ob B humpelt weil B gelesen hat.
A asks B whether (or not) B is (was) limping, because B was reading.

4B B bestätigt A, dass B humpelt, weil B gelesen hat.
B confirms A that B is limping, because B was reading.

5A A teilt B mit, dass A nicht versteht, dass B humpelt, weil B gelesen hat.
A informs B that A doesn't understand that B is limping, because B was reading.

6B B teilt A mit, dass B nicht aufgepasst hat.
B informs A that B wasn't paying attention.

7A A fragt B, ob B ein schweres Buch gelesen hat.
A asks B whether B had read (had been reading) a heavy book.

8B B erwidert A, dass B ein leichtes Buch gelesen hat.
B answers A that B has read an easy book.

9A A fragt B, ob B etwas auf den Fuss gefallen ist.
A asks B whether (or not) something fell on B's foot.

1oB B erwidert A, dass B's Fuss eingeschlafen ist.
B answers A that B's foot fell asleep.

11A A teilt B mit, dass A versteht, dass B humpelt, weil B gelesen hat.

A informs to B that A understands that B limps, because B was reading.

There are several reasons, some of which I shall discuss, not to use this type of description for the original dialogue. In this version pronominal references are definite. Referential ambiguities will occur with anaphoric pronouns in indirect complement phrases. In German special problems result from the choice of tense and mood. For both present tense and preterite indicative as well as subjunctive mood are possible in the descriptions of explicit performative sentences. Various morphological and sentence order changes in the complement sentences will occur and these changes may influence the pragmatic interpretations.

Instead of the sentences occurring in descrition 1, the following type of description using explicit performatives and quoted utterances will be used:

1A A fragt B: "Warum humpelst Du?"

A asks B: "Why are you limping?"

On level $\mathfrak{D}n$ the above mentioned form of 1A is necessary to fulfill the conditions of the dialogue structure. But in the case of explicit performatives on the description level $\mathcal{G}ni$ one can avoid indirect contexts: the explicit performative names the act which is performed in a unique way on both levels. The quoted utterances mention the wording of the utterance and "refer" to the content of the speech act (of asking someone), just as the indirect context "refers" to the content of the speech act; but perhaps both ways of referring may not be equivalent. As will be seen later, we shall not dispense with indirect contexts on level $\mathcal{G}ni$ but these occur only as indirect contexts of propositional attitudes.

The use of variable (or proper) names connected with explicit performatives is appropriate for another reason. It is necessary to describe the actual time of the dialogue too.[13] Although the description form of 1A above uses present tense as 1A itself, it is unclear whether this practice is the best possible. An ultimate way would be one in which a description of a speech act were given synchronously as the speech act is performed. One could perhaps discuss whether a description form like

Ich frage Dich: "Warum humpelst Du?"

I ask you: "Why are you limping?"

can be used. But I shall not go into this question here.

The final description will contain a few other standardizations. Instead of the description form of 1A above the following will be used

1A A fragt B:"Was ist der Grund dafür, dass du humpelst?"
A asks B: "What is the reason for the fact that you are limping?"

This standardization eliminates *warum* (why)-questions.The dialogue will contain only direct and *was* (what)-questions. The other description forms have to be changed accordingly. The advantage of this standardization will be apparent if one sees the interrelation between the contents of the speech acts and the contents of the propositional attitudes which occur in the dialogue situations. The final form of the description of the completed original dialogue is then:

*Description 2*

1A A fragt B: "Was ist der Grund dafür, dass Du humpelst?"
A asks B: "What is the reason for the fact that you are limping?"

2B B antwortet A: "Ich habe etwas gelesen."
B answers A: "I was reading"

3A A fragt B: Dass du etwas gelesen hast, ist Grund dafür, dass du humpelst?"

A asks B: "The fact that you were reading something is the reason for the fact that you are limping?"

4B B bestätigt A: "Dass ich etwas gelesen habe, ist Grund dafür, dass ich humple."
B confirms A: "That I was reading something is the reason for the fact that I am limping."

5A A teilt B mit: "Ich verstehe nicht, dass, dass du etwas gelesen hast, Grund dafür ist, dass du humpelst"
A informs B: "I don't understand that the fact that you were reading something is the reason for the fact that you are limping."

6B B teilt A mit: "Ich habe auf etwas nicht aufgepasst."
B informs A: "I wasn't paying attention to something."

7A A fragt B: "Hast du ein Buch gelesen?"
A asks B: "Did you read a book?"

8B B erwidert A: "Ich habe ein Comic-Heft gelesen."
B answers A: "I was reading a comic book."

9A A fragt B: "Ist dir das Comic-Heft auf den Fuss gefallen?"
A asks B:"Did the comic book fall on your foot?"

1oB B erwidert A: "Der Fuss ist mir eingeschlafen."
B answers A: "My foot fell asleep."

11A A teilt B mit: "Ich verstehe, dass, dass du etwas gelesen hast, Grund dafür ist, dass du humpelst."
A informs B: "I understand that the fact that you were reading something is the reason for the fact that you are limping."

### *3.3 The definitive description of the completed dialogue*

To complete the construction the dialogue situation has to be constructed. This means (compare section 2 and GÜNTHER, this volume, definition 15) that for each dialogue step the situations A,E have to be worked out.

With respect to the standardization of the description form of the occurrences of propositional attitudes a general remark should be made in advance. Since an occurrence of a propositional attitude means that a specific person X *has* this attitude, a natural representation for X's mental state on level $\mathfrak{D}n$ is a sentence containing a first person pronoun, e.g. with X=A:

> Ich weiss, dass B humpelt.
>
> I know that B is limping. [14]

On level $\mathcal{G}ni$ it is again convenient to use proper or variable names instead of pronouns because definite pronominal references are indispensable in description forms like:

> A vermutet, dass B weiss, was der Grund dafür ist, dass B humpelt.
>
> A presumes that B knows what the reason is for the fact that B is limping.

The construction below depends on some facts derived from the reading of the original given at the beginning of this section. The explanation going on in the dialogue is characterized by the fact that B knows a cause or reason for his limping. It could have happened that the dialogue did end with step 2B. If A had accepted the explanation at this point different things could have happened: He may have learned a new causal relation; he may have had enough causel relations available in his knowledge to develop a chain of causel relations which makes the explanation offered by B intelligible to him. Or he may have thought that B is simply crazy or is playing a joke on him. What happens after 2B is, probably, that A tries to find out what actually is the case.

The idea in constructing the dialogue and its situations was to shape a structure in the commmunicative situations sufficient to handle the knowledge, the intention, the will of A,B, the flow of information between A,B, and the logical apparatus by which A,B manipulate their attitudes and actions to keep the dialogue running and terminate it.

The following abbreviations are used in the completed description

Le : B hat *e*twas gelesen
Ls : B hat ein *s*chweres Buch gelesen
Ll : B hat ein *l*eichtes Buch gelesen

Ne : B hat auf *e*twas nicht aufgepasst
Nf : B hat auf den *F*uss nicht aufgepasst
Nb : B hat auf das *B*uch nicht aufgepasst

H : B *h*umpelt
F : B ist etwas auf den *F*uss gefallen
E : B ist der Fuss *e*ingeschlafen

In front of the first dialogue step two sets of sentences, OA1,..., OA7, OB1,..., OB1o, are listed which represent the latent knowledge of A,B. It contains knowledge of facts, causel relations, and some substitution rules such as 'if B reads something then he reads a heavy or a light book'. A has available a fundamental knowledge, OA1: if states of affairs exist, there are causes or reasons for them. The latent knowledge of A,B is part of their entire knowledge. In case of the example only those instances of knowledge are realized which are of immediate importance for the ongoing explanation. The decision has been made that A asks for a rational explanation and B tries to give one. B does not understand A's question as one for, say, a Freudian explanation. If different possibilities for different types of explanations were taken into consideration the latent knowledge would have to provide for that.[15]

In the complete description the horizontal lines separate the different dialogue steps. The numberings at the left and right are used for referring to sets or subsets of attitude sentences. Set braces have been omitted. A few abbreviations have been made: in some places '-' is used to indicate a propositional attitude which is mentioned in the preceding line. Instead of such longer description sentences as

A weiss, dass etwas Grund dafür ist, dass B humpelt.

A knows that something is the reason for the fact that B is limping.

or as

A interessiert, was die Begründung dafür ist, dab B humpelt.

A is interested in what the explanation is for the fact that B is limping,

the shorter sentences

A weiss, dass aus einem grunde H

A knows that for some reason H

or

A interessiert die Begründung für H

A is interested in the explanation of H

will be used in the description of the dialogue situations. The explicit sentences will be used in the construction of the MONTAGUE-grammar.

| | | | |
|---|---|---|---|
| oA1 | A weiss, dass, wenn Sachverhalte vorliegen, diese Gründe haben. | B weiss L1 | oB1 |
| 2 | – $((Ls \vee L1) \rightarrow Ne)$ } (causal relations) | – Nf } (Knowledge of facts) | 2 |
| 3 | – $(Nf \rightarrow (F \vee E))$ } | – E } | 3 |
| 4 | – $((F \vee E) \rightarrow H)$ } | – H } | 4 |
| 5 | – $(Ne \Rightarrow (Nf \vee Nb))$ } | – $(L1 \rightarrow Nf)$ } | 5 |
| 6 | – $(Le \Rightarrow (Ls \vee L1))$ } (subst. rules) | – $(Nf \rightarrow E)$ } (causal relations) | 6 |
| 7 | – $(L1 \Rightarrow Le)$ | – $(E \rightarrow H)$ } | 7 |
| | | – $((Nf \vee Nb) \Rightarrow Ne)$ } | 8 |
| | | – $((Ls \vee L1) \Rightarrow Le)$ } (subst. rules) | 9 |
| | | – $(Nf \rightarrow F \vee E)$ | 1o |

| | | | |
|---|---|---|---|
| 1A11 | A weiss H | | |
| 2 | A weiss, dass aus einem Grunde H | | |
| 3 | A weiss nicht den Grund für H | | |
| 1A21 | A interessiert die Begründung für H | | |
| 2 | A will wissen den Grund für H | | |
| 3 | A vermutet, dass B weiss den Grund für H | | |
| 1.S | A fragt B: "Was ist der Grund dafür, dass du humpelst?" | | |
| 1A1 - 1A2 | | B weiss H | 1B31 |
| 1A31 | A weiss, dass B weiss H | – , dass A weiss H | 2 |
| 2 | A weiss, dass B weiss, dass aus einem Grunde H | B weiss, dass A weiss, dass aus einem Grunde H | 3 |
| 3 | – , dass A weiss nicht den Grund für H | – , dass A weiss nicht den Grund für H | 4 |
| 1A41 | A weiss, dass B weiss, dass A will wissen den Grund für H | B weiss, dass A will wissen den Grund für H | 1B41 |
| 2 | A weiss, dass B weiss, dass A vermutet, dass B weiss den Grund für H | – , dass A vermutet, dass B weiss den Grund für H | 2 |

| | | | |
|---|---|---|---|
| 1AP(ost 1.h) | | 1BP(ost 1.h) | |
| | | B weiss Le | 2B11 |
| | | - (L1→H) | 2 |
| | | B will, dass A weiss Le | 2B21 |
| 2.s | B antwortet A:"Ich habe etwas gelesen." | | |
| 1A1 - 1A2 | | B weiss H | 1B31 |
| 1A31 | | B weiss, dass A weiss H | 1B32 |
| 2 | | B vermutet, dass A weiss den Grund für H | 2B42 |
| | A vermutet, dass B weiss, dass A weiss nicht den Grund für H | B vermutet, dass A weiss, dass B weiss den Grund für H | 2B43 |
| 1A42 | | | |
| 2A31 | A weiss Le | B weiss Le | 2B11 |
| | | B weiss (L1→H) | 2B12 |
| 2A41 | A weiss, dass B weiss, dass A weiss Le | B weiss, dass A weiss Le | 2B41 |

---

| | | | |
|---|---|---|---|
| 3A11 | A weiss H | 2BP | 3B |
| 2 | A weiss Le | | |
| 3 | - , dass aus einem Grunde H | | |
| 4 | A weiss nicht den Grund für H | | |
| 5 | A vermutet (Le→H) | | |
| 6 | A weiss nicht, ob (Le→H) | | |
| 3A21 | A interessiert die Begründing für H | | |
| 2 | A will wissen, ob (Le→H) | | |
| 3 | A vermutet, dass B weiss, ob (Le→H) | | |
| 4 | A weiss, dass B weiss, dass A weiss H | | |
| 5 | - - - Le | | |
| 6 | A vermutet, dass B weiss, dass A weiss nicht den Grund für H | | |
| 7 | A weiss, dass B weiss, dass A vermutet, dass B weiss den Grund für H | | |

| | | | |
|---|---|---|---|
| 3.s | A fragt B:"Dass du etwas gelesen hast, ist der Grund dafür, dass du humpelst?" | | |
| | | B weiss H | 1B31 |
| | 3A11 - 6 | B weiss Le | 2B11 |
| | 3A21 - 5 | B weiss (Le→H) | |
| | | B weiss (L1→H) | 2B12 |
| | A weiss, dass B weiss, dass A weiss nicht den Grund für H | B weiss, dass A weiss H | 1B32 |
| | 3A27 | | |
| | | - - Le | 2B41 |
| | | - , dass A vermutet (Le→H) | 3B31 |
| 3A31 | A weiss, dass B weiss, dass A vermutet (Le→H) | - , dass A weiss nicht, ob (Le→H) | 2 |
| 2 | - - , A weiss nicht, ob (Le→H) | | |
| | | B weiss, dass A will wissen, ob (Le→H) | 3B41 |
| 3A41 | A weiss, dass B weiss, dass A will wissen, ob (Le→H) | - , A vermutet, dass B weiss,ob (Le→H) | 2 |
| 2 | - - , dass A vemutet, dass B weiss, ob (Le→H) | | |
| 3AP | | 3BP | 4B21 |
| | | B will, dass A weiss (Le→H) | |
| 4.s | B bestätigt A:"Dass ich etwas gelesen habe, ist der Grund dafür, dass ich humple." | | |
| | A weiss H | B weiss H | |
| | A weiss Le | B weiss Le | |
| 4A31 | A weiss (Le→H) | B weiss (Le→H) | |
| | A versteht nicht (Le→H) | B weiss (L1→H) | |
| | A interessiert die Begründung für H | B weiss, dass A weiss H | |
| | A akzeptiert nicht (Le→H) | B weiss, dass A weiss Le | |
| 4A41 | A weiss, dass B weiss, dass A weiss (Le→H) | B weiss, dass A weiss (Le→H) | 4B41 |
| 4AP | | 4BP | |
| 5A11 | A weiss H | | |
| 2 | A weiss Le | | |
| 3 | A weiss (Le→H) | | |
| 5A21 | A interessiert die Begründing für H | | |
| 2 | A akzeptiert nicht (Le→H) | | |
| 3 | A versteht nicht (Le→H) | | |
| 4 | A weiss, dass B weiss, dass A weiss H | | |
| 5 | - - - Le | | |
| 6 | - - - (Le→H) | | |
| 7 | A vermutet, dass B nicht weiss, dass A versteht nicht (Le→H) | | |
| 8 | A will, dass B weiss, dass A versteht nicht (Le→H) | | |

| | | | |
|---|---|---|---|
| 5.s | A teilt B mit:"Ich verstehe nicht, dass, dass du etwas gelesen hast, Grund dafür ist, dass du humpelst?" | | |
| | 5A11 - 3 | 4BP | |
| | 5A21 - 6 | B weiss, dass A versteht nicht (Le→H) | |
| 5A41 | A weiss, dass B weiss, dass A versteht nicht (Le→H) | B vermutet, dass A nicht akzeptiert (Le→H) | |
| 5AP | | 5BP | 6B11 |
| | | B weiss Ne | |
| | | B vermutet, dass A nicht weiss Ne | 6B21 |
| | | B vermutet, dass A wissen will Ne | 2 |
| 6.s | B teilt A mit:"Ich habe auf etwas nicht aufgepasst." | | |
| 5AP | | 5BP | |
| 6A31 | A weiss Ne | B weiss Ne | |
| 6A41 | A weiss, dass B weiss, dass A weiss Ne | B weiss, dass A weiss Ne | 6B41 |
| 5A11 - 3 | | 6BP | |
| 5A21 - 6 | | | |
| 5A41 | | | |
| 6A31 | | | |
| 6A41 | | | |
| 7A11 | A vermutet (Le→Ne) | | |
| | A vermutet Ls | | |
| | A vermutet (Ls→Ne) | | |
| 7A21 | A will wissen, ob Ls | | |
| | A vermutet, dass B weiss ob Ls | | |
| 7.s | A fragt B:"Hast du ein Buch gelesen?" | | |
| 7A(nte 7.h) | | 6BP | |
| 7A31 | A weiss, dass B weiss, dass A vermutet Ls | B weiss, dass A vermutet Ls | 7B31 |
| 7A41 | A weiss, dass B weiss, dass A will wissen, ob Ls | B weiss, dass A will wissen, ob Ls | 7B41 |
| 2 | - - , dass A vermutet, dass B weiss, ob Ls | B weiss, dass A vermutet, dass B weiss, ob Ls | 7B42 |
| 7AP | | 7BP | |
| | | B weiss L1 | 8B11 |
| | | B will, dass A weiss L1 | 8B21 |
| | | B vermutet, dass A will wissen, dass L1 | 2 |

| | | | |
|---|---|---|---|
| 8.s | B erwidert A:"Ich habe ein Comicheft gelesen." | | |
| | A weiss H | 7BP | |
| 8A31 | A weiss L1 | B weiss L1 | 8B41 |
| | A weiss (Le$\rightarrow$H) | B weiss, dass A weiss L1 | |
| | A weiss Ne | | |
| | A interessiert die Begründung für H | | |
| | A akzeptiert nicht (Le$\rightarrow$H) | | |
| | A versteht nicht (Le$\rightarrow$H) | | |
| | A weiss, dass B weiss, dass A weiss H | | |
| 8A41 | – L1 | | |
| | – (Le$\rightarrow$H) | | |
| | – , dass A versteht nicht (Le$\rightarrow$H) | | |
| | – , dass A weiss Ne | | |
| 8AP | | 8BP | |
| 9A11 | A vermutet (L1$\rightarrow$Ne) | | |
| 2 | A vermutet (Ne$\Rightarrow$Nf) | | |
| 3 | A vermutet (Nf$\rightarrow$F) | | |
| 4 | A vermutet Nf | | |
| 5 | A vermutet F | | |
| 9A21 | A will wissen, ob F | | |
| | A vermutet, dass B weiss, ob F | | |
| 9.s | A fragt B:"Ist dir das Comicheft auf den Fuss gefallen?" | | |
| | | 8BP | |
| 9A31 | A weiss, dass B weiss, dass A vermutet F | B weiss, dass A vermutet F | 9B31 |
| 9A41 | A weiss, dass B weiss, dass A will wissen, ob F | B weiss, dass A will wissen, ob F | 9B41 |
| 4A42 | – , dass A vermutet, dass B weiss,ob F | B weiss, dass A vermutet, dass B weiss, ob F | 2 |
| | | B vermutet, dass A nicht akzeptiert (Le$\rightarrow$H) | 9B32 |
| | | B vermutet, dass A vermutet, dass (Ne$\Rightarrow$Nf) | 3 |
| | | (Nf$\Rightarrow$F) | 4 |
| | A weiss H | B weiss H | |
| | A weiss L1 | B weiss E | 1oB11 |
| | A weiss (Le$\rightarrow$H) | B weiss L1 | |
| | A weiss Ne | B weiss (L1$\rightarrow$Nf) | |
| | | B weiss (Nf$\rightarrow$E) | |
| | A interessiert die Begründing für H | B weiss (E$\rightarrow$H) | |

| | | | |
|---|---|---|---|
| | A akzeptiert nicht (Le→H) | B weiss (Nf→F∨E) | 1oB12 |
| | A versteht nicht (Le→H) | B weiss, dass A weiss H | |
| | | – L1 | |
| | A weiss, dass B weiss, dass A weiss H | – (Le→H) | |
| | – – L1 | – , dass A versteht nicht (Le→H) | |
| | – – (Le→H) | B vermutet, dass A akzeptiert nicht (Le→H) | |
| | – – Ne | B vermutet, dass A vermutet, dass (Ne⇒Nf) | |
| | – , – , dass A versteht nicht (Le→H) | (NF→F) | |
| | A vermutet(L1→Ne) | | |
| | A vermutet(Ne⇒Nf) | B weiss, dass A vermutet F | |
| | A vermutet Nf→f) | B weiss, dass A will wissen, ob F | |
| | A vermutet Nf | – , dass A vermutet, dass B weiss, ob F | |
| | A vermutet F | | |
| | | B will, dass A akzeptiert (Le→H) | 1oB21 |
| | A will wissen, ob F | B will, dass A weiss E | 2 |
| | A vermutet, dass B weiss, ob F | | |
| | A weiss, dass B weiss, dass A vermutet F | | |
| | – , – , dass A will wissen, ob F | | |
| | – , – , dass A vermutet, dass B weiss, ob F | | |
| 1o.s | B erwidert A:"Der Fuss ist mir eingeschlafen." | | |
| 1oAA | | 1oBA | |
| ausser: | 9A15, 9A21 – 2, 9A31, 9A41 – 2 | ausser: 1oB22, 9B31, 9B41 – 2 | |
| 1oA31 | A weiss F | | |
| 1oA41 | A weiss, dass B weiss, dass A weiss F | B weiss, dass A weiss F | 1oB41 |

---

1. [ A weiss H      1oBP
   A weiss L1
   A weiss (Le→H)
   A weiss Ne
   A weiss E ]

2. [ A interessiert die Begründung für H
   A weiss, dass B weiss, dass A weiss H
   – L1
   – (Le→H)
   – Ne
   – E
   – , dass A versteht nicht (Le→H) ]

3. [ A vermutet (L1→Ne)

A vermutet (L1→Nf)
- (Nf→E)
- (E→H)
- (L1→H)
- (L1⇒Le)

- (Le→H)

A versteht (Le→H)
A akzeptiert (Le→H)
A weiss die Begründung für H
A will, dass B weiss, dass A versteht (Le→H)
11.s A teilt B mit:"Ich verstehe, dass, dass du etwas gelesen hast, Grund dafür ist, dass du humpelst."
1oBP

| | |
|---|---|
| 11A41 A weiss, dass B weiss, dass A versteht (Le→H) | B weiss, dass A versteht (Le→H) 11B41 |
| | B vermutet, dass A akzeptiert (Le→H) 2 |

### *3.4 Reconstruction of the communication in the dialogue, on the basis of the definitive description*

To illustrate the machinery let us look at the first dialogue step. The subset 1A1 expresses the actualized knowledge of A as he sees B limping, he knows that there is a reason but he doesn't know what it is. So in the subset 1A2 an intention evolves from 1A1 to ask for a reason, which, so A conjectures, B knows. He utters 1s. After the uttering of 1s the attitudes change. So e.g. 'A knows, that B knows, that A does not know the reason for H' and B' knows, that A wants to know the reason for H'. Which of the attitudes remain and which disappear is indicated by repeating the numbers. 1AP, i.e. 1APost1s, indicates in the initial situation of the second dialogue step that the whole set of attitudes of the final situation of the first step remains for A. Only for easier reference are some attitude sentences repeated unnumbered in later steps. The initial situation of B is empty in the first dialogue step. Instead one could identify this initial situation of B with the whole or part of OB. But this is inconvenient above all for psychological reasons. A,B draw upon their latent knowledge only if it is needed in actual manipulations of their dialogical situations to understand what is said or to make a contribution in the ongoing dialogue.

It is not possible here to discuss all dialogue steps in detail. The most important parts of the situations of A,B and changes of situations are: A's,B's knowledge originating from information and from actualizations of the latent knowledge, knowledge about the other person, presumptions of facts, causes, causel relations, doubts about success of the explanation, intentions for further steps to achieve a successful explanation. This appears very clearly e.g. in step 1oB. In the last step 11A, A has enlarged knowledge of facts, reasons or causes, first group. He still looks for an explanation and he knows what B knows about him and his knowledge, second group. In the third group, by referring to his presumptions, A establishes a causal chain on the basis of some substitutions and logical consequences. He accepts the explanation and informs B about this fact.

## 4. *A MONTAGUE-grammar*

### 4.1 *The informal grammar*

I shall consider only "the" grammar for the dialogue example. Thus, in the present context I shall use the term *the fragment* to refer to the linguistic material appearing in the dialogue (cp. Montague's EFL).

The choice of the performative and attitude verbs, and the performative sentences as well as the indirect constructions of attitude sentences can be justified. The standardizations for performatives and attitudes have been discussed in papers by LUTZ-HENSEL and RODEWALD-RÖVER. For both linguistic types a *Grundform* and some variations of it are developed. The sentences in the example correspond to these forms. It turned out that the semantic factors of the base forms strictly separate classes of performative verbs from attitude verbs.[16]

The intensional object expressed by object complements in one class of attitude verbs, to which all verbs of the example belong, refers to states of affairs. In another class the intensional object is obligatorily a person. These are not used here. The absence of these attitudes simplifies the iteration of attitude constructions. In the example it is arranged that in iterated attitudes the intensional objects are always expressed as proposition denoting phrases. Other subclassifications concern e.g. temporal properties combined with the interpretation of the subject in the complement. Here it turns out that e.g. "Wissen" has nearly no limitations in use. On the contrary the temporal aspect in the intensional object of "Wollen" always points to the future, hence its importance for intentions.

It is obvious that informative and information asking explicit performatives contribute to the cognitive component. As can be seen, the performatives in the example are all of this kind. One class of performative verbs contains only verbs in which the addressee is not obligatory. Another class, to which all verbs of the example belong, contain only verbs with an explicit occurring addressee. Both classes are subdivided into two subclasses whether or not performatives for speech acts depend on other speech acts. Only "mitteilen" does not depend on other speech acts.

The inventory for the dialogue can be classified according to the sentence structures contained in it, because each sentence structure is organized in accord with the syntactic-semantic properties defined in the base forms. The inventory can be summed up in the following way.

*Nominals* are person names and personal pronouns: A,B, ICH, DU, *concrete object nouns*: FUSS, BUCH, COMICHEFT; *Definite and indefinite articles:* DER, DIE, DAS, EIN, EINEN; and the *indefinite pronoun* ETWAS. The *verbs* are classified as follows: 1. HUMPELN, 2. LESEN, AUFPASSEN AUF, 3. FALLEN AUF, 4. EINSCHLAFEN, 5. GRUND SEIN FÜR, BEGRÜNDUNG SEIN FÜR, 6. WISSEN, WISSEN WOLLEN, VERMUTEN, VERSTEHEN, AKZEPTIEREN, 7. INTERESSIERT SEIN AN, 8. FRAGEN, ERWIDERN, ANTWORTEN, MITTEILEN, BESTÄTIGEN. The only occurring *adverb* is NICHT, and the occurring *adjectives* are LEICHT, SCHWER.

The overall shape of the sentence structures is

(n) Subject - $\text{verb}_n$ - 1. object - 2. object.

The following *subject phrases* will occur: person names and personal pronouns, concrete object nouns, DASS-, WAS-sentences and ETWAS. *Object phrases* are: person names and personal pronouns, concrete object nouns, DASS-, OB-, WAS-sentences and ETWAS. Concrete subject nouns occur only with verbs 3 and 4. ETWAS subjects occur only with verbs 3 and 5. DASS-, WAS-sentence subjects occur only with verb 5. The subject phrases of all other verbs are persons or personal pronouns.

As to the verb objects the following holds: ETWAS and concrete object nouns occur as first objects only with verbs 2, 3. DASS-, OB-, WAS-sentences occur as first objects with verb 5 and all attitude verbs 6 and 7. Quoted sentences are first objects of all performative verbs 8. Quoted sentences do not occur within quotes and not in other positions. Second objects if they occur in verb 3-, 4-, 8- constructions are persons and personal pronouns. Apart from possible variations in subject and object positions there are only 8 sentence structures.

UND, ODER, WENN-DANN are used as sentence conjunctions. The latter is used in the formulation of the substitutions as well as in the causal connections.

### *4.2 The formal grammar*

I shall now describe the MONTAGUE-grammar into which the informal grammar of the dialogue sentences, represented by the 8 sentence structures and the sentence conjunctions just discussed, is translated. The following sets of basic expressions $B_A$ for the category A are defined:

$B_t = \emptyset$ truth value expressions

$B_q = \emptyset$ yes-no questions

$B_{q'} = \emptyset$ substitution questions

$B_T = \{A, B, ICH, DU, ETWAS_0\}$ terms

$B_{T'} = \{ETWAS_1\}$ proposition and indirect proposition terms

$B_{T''} = \emptyset$ quoted phrase terms

$B_{IV} = \{HUMPELN\}$ intransitive verbs

$B_{IV'} = \emptyset$ - " -

$B_{TV} = \{LESEN, AUFPASSEN\ AUF\}$ transitive verbs with TV as IV/T

$B_{TV/T''} = \{FRAGEN\}$ transitive verbs

$B_{TV'}$ = {EINSCHLAFEN} transitive verbs with TV' as IV//T

$B_{TV'/T}$ = {FALLEN AUF } transitive verbs

$B_{TV'/T''}$ = {ERWIDERN, ANTWORTEN, MITTEILEN, BESTÄTIGEN} trans.vbs

$B_{TV''}$ = {WISSEN, WISSEN WOLLEN, AKZEPTIEREN, VERSTEHEN, VERMUTEN, INTERESSIERT SEIN DARAN} transitive attitude verbs with TV" as IV//T'

$B_{TV'''}$ = {GRUND SEIN DAFÜR, BEGRÜNDUNG SEIN DAFÜR} transitive verbs with TV''' as IV//T'

$B_{CN}$ = {FUSS, BUCH, COMICHEFT} common nouns

$B_{AD}$ = {LEICHT, SCHWER} adjectives

The sets $P_A$ of *phrases* of category A can be introduced in a way similar to EFL or PTQ. To this end the following nineteen syntactic rules depending on nineteen syntactic functions are necessary. There are seven *base rules*, ten rules of *functional application*, one rule for conjunction, one rule for *relations of agreement* of terms, tenses, and negation.

To simplify matters I shall not use variables for the term phrases. As a consequence rules for quantification, which are somewhat intricate, will not occur. Therefore ETWAS-terms could not be handled as would be possible within quantification rules. I shall also dispense with explicit formulations of the lengthy conditions for word order and morphological changes resulting e.g. from conjugation and declension. But in a few important cases I shall make reference to an aspect of change in a note like [WM - dat ] to indicate that dative case and (possibly) word order must be respected.

*Syntactic rules*

The *base rules* produce term phrases, propositional term phrases for DASS-, WAS-, OB- contexts, quotations, two types of questions. The *functional rules* arrange the production of two placed transitive out of three placed transitive verb phrases, which contain the construction of the two placed transitive verb phrases for performative phrases containing quotations, the intransitive verb phrases out of the two placed transitive verb phrases, complete sentence structures out of intransitive verb phrases, and common noun phrases.

*Base rules*

$S_1$. $B_A \subseteq P_A$ for all $A \in CAT$

$S_2$. If $\alpha \in P_{CN}$, then $F_0(\alpha), F_1(\alpha) \in P_T$, where
$F_0(\alpha) = \text{EIN}\ \alpha$, $F_1(\alpha) = \text{DER/DAS}\ \alpha$ .

$S_3$. If $\varphi \in P_t$, then $F_2(\varphi), F_3(\varphi) \in P_{T'}$, where
$F_2(\varphi) = \text{DASS}\ \varphi'$ [WM]
$F_3(\varphi) = \text{OB}\ \varphi'$ [WM]

$S_4$. If $\varphi \in P_{q'}$, then $F_4(\varphi) \in P_{T'}$, where
$F_4(\varphi) = \varphi'$. [WM]

$S_5$. If $\varphi \in P_t \cup P_q \cup P_{q'}$, then $F_5(\varphi) \in P_{T''}$, where
$F_5(\varphi) = "\varphi"$.

$S_6$. If $\varphi \in P_t$, then $F_6(\varphi) \in P_q$, where
$F_6(\varphi) = \varphi'?$ [WM]

$S_7$. If $\delta \in P_{IV'}$, then $F_7(\delta) \in P_{q'}$, where
$F_7(\delta) = \text{WAS}\ \delta'$ [WM]

*Rules of functional application*

$S_8$. If $\delta \in P_{IV}$ and $\alpha \in P_T$, then $F_8(\delta,\alpha) \in P_t$, where
$F_8(\delta,\alpha) = \alpha\delta'$ [WM - conj]
$\alpha = \text{ETWAS}_0$ allowed for $\delta' = \delta''\alpha'$ and $\delta'' \in B_{TV'/T}$.

$S_9$. If $\delta \in P_{IV'}$ and $\alpha \in P_{T'}$, then $F_8(\delta,\alpha) \in P_t$, where
$\alpha = \text{ETWAS}_1$ is allowed .

$S_{10}$. If $\delta \in P_{TV}$ and $\alpha \in P_T$, then $F_9(\delta,\alpha) \in P_{IV}$, where
$F_9(\delta,\alpha) = \delta\alpha'$ [WM - acc.]
$\alpha = \text{ETWAS}_0$ allowed for $\delta \neq \delta':\alpha''$.

$S_{11}$. If $\delta \in P_{TV'}$ and $\alpha \in P_T$, then $F_{10}(\delta,\alpha) \in P_{IV}$, where

$F_{10}(\delta,\alpha) = \delta\alpha'$ [WM - dat.]

$\alpha \neq ETWAS_0$ .

$S_{12}$. If $\delta \in P_{TV''}$ and $\alpha \in P_{T'}$, then $F_{11}(\delta,\alpha) \in P_{IV}$, where

$F_{11}(\delta,\alpha) = \delta\alpha$ .

$S_{13}$. If $\delta \in P_{TV'''}$ and $\alpha \in P_{T'}$, then $F_{11}(\delta,\alpha) \in P_{IV'}$ .

$S_{14}$. If $\delta \in P_{TV'/T}$ and $\alpha \in P_T$, then $F_9(\delta,\alpha) \in P_{TV'}$ .

$S_{15}$. If $\delta \in P_{TV/T''}$ and $\alpha \in P_{T''}$, then $F_{12}(\delta,\alpha) \in P_{TV}$, where

$F_{12}(\delta,\alpha) = \delta{:}\alpha$ .

$S_{16}$. If $\delta \in P_{TV'/T''}$ and $\alpha \in P_{T''}$, then $F_{12}(\delta,\alpha) \in P_{TV'}$ .

$S_{17}$. If $\zeta \in P_{AD}$ and $\alpha \in P_{CN}$ - {FUSS, COMICHEFT}, then

$F_{13}(\zeta,\alpha) \in P_{CN}$, where $F_{13}(\zeta,\alpha) = \zeta\alpha$ .

*Rules of conjunction*

$S_{18}$. If $\varphi,\psi \in P_t$, then $F_{14}(\varphi,\psi)$, $F_{15}(\varphi,\psi)$, $F_{16}(\varphi,\psi) \in P_t$, where

$F_{14}(\varphi,\psi) = \varphi$ UND $\psi$,

$F_{15}(\varphi,\psi) = \varphi$ ODER $\psi$,

$F_{16}(\varphi,\psi) =$ WENN $\varphi$, DANN $\psi$ .

*Rules of tense and sign*

$S_{19}$. If $\delta \in P_{IV}$ and $\alpha \in P_T$, then $F_{17}(\delta,\alpha)$, $F_{18}(\delta,\alpha)$, $F_{19}(\delta,\alpha) \in P_t$, where

$F_{17}(\delta,\alpha) = \alpha\delta'$ [WM - neg.]

$F_{18}(\delta,\alpha) = \alpha\delta'$ [WM - perf.t.]

$F_{19}(\delta,\alpha) = \alpha\delta'$ [WM - neg.perf.t.] .

With the aid of rules S1 - S19 the sentences occurring in the dialogue description, except for OA1, can be constructed as meaningful expressions. The rules allow to construct more meaningful expressions than existing in the dialogue. For the aim of this paper it seemed appropriate to formulate no further restrictions for the rules.

The following derivation trees illustrate the application of the syntactic rules for the derivation of two sentences. The sentences 1s and 3A23 of the dialogue description are used as examples:

1s A fragt B: "Was ist der Grund dafür, dass Du humpelst?"

3A23 A vermutet, dass B weiss, ob (Le→H), i.e.
A vermutet, dass B weiss, ob wenn B etwas gelesen hat, dann B humpelt.

As usual, in the derivation tree 'φ,n' indicates that φ is the resul of an application of the syntactic function n, 'φ , – ' indicates that φ is a basic expression.

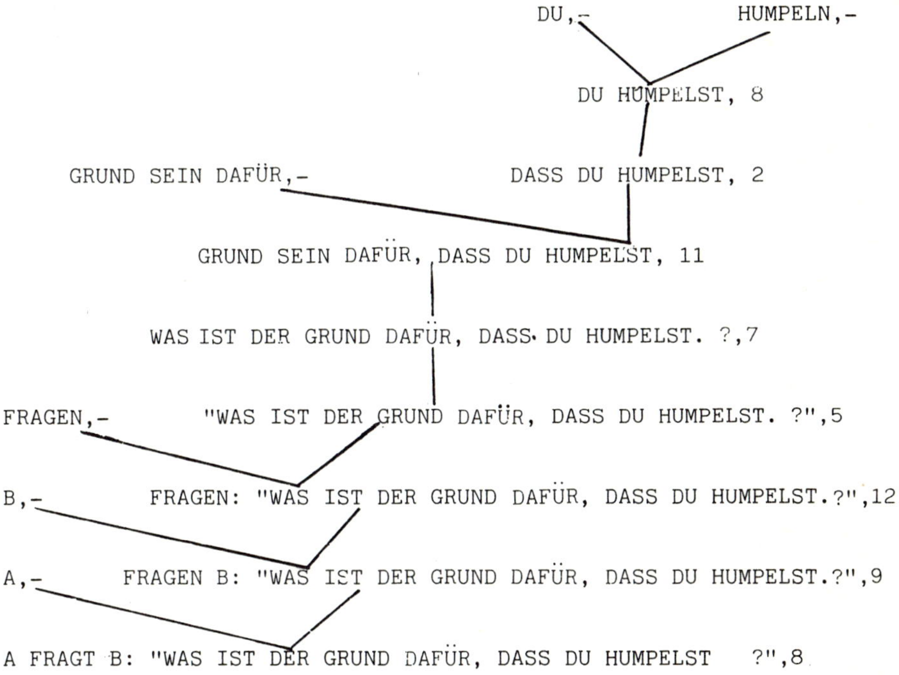

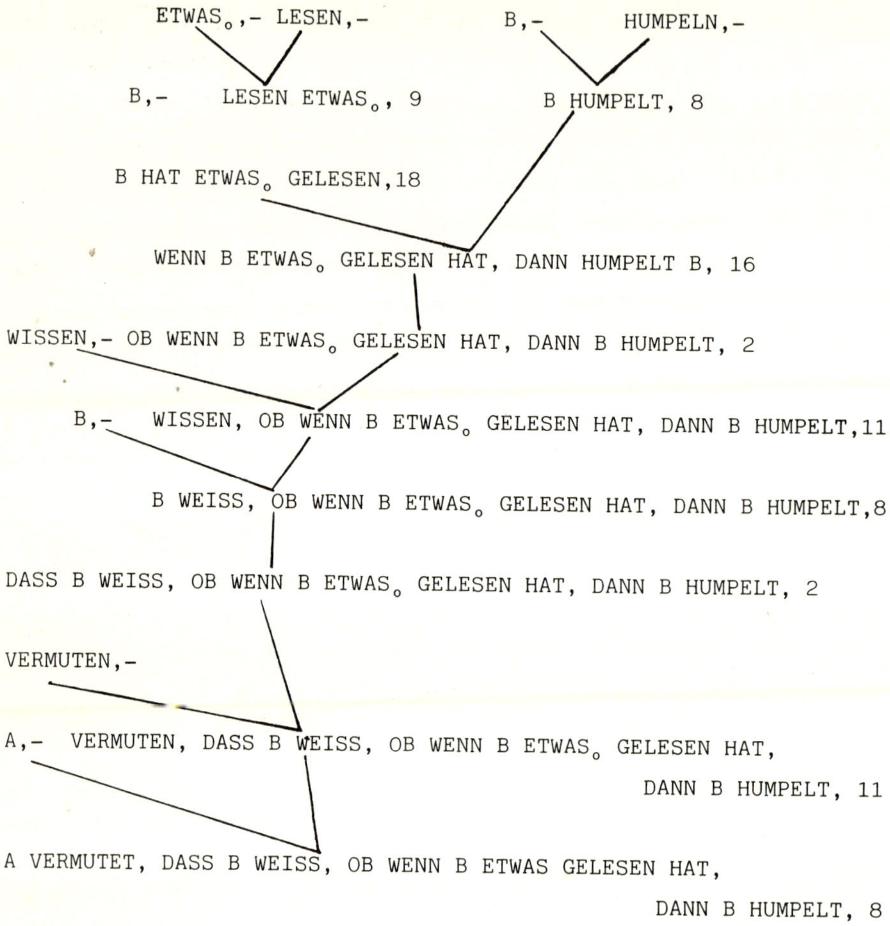
ETWAS$_0$,- LESEN,-
B,- HUMPELN,-
B,- LESEN ETWAS$_0$, 9
B HUMPELT, 8
B HAT ETWAS$_0$ GELESEN,18
WENN B ETWAS$_0$ GELESEN HAT, DANN HUMPELT B, 16
WISSEN,- OB WENN B ETWAS$_0$ GELESEN HAT, DANN B HUMPELT, 2
B,- WISSEN, OB WENN B ETWAS$_0$ GELESEN HAT, DANN B HUMPELT,11
B WEISS, OB WENN B ETWAS$_0$ GELESEN HAT, DANN B HUMPELT,8
DASS B WEISS, OB WENN B ETWAS$_0$ GELESEN HAT, DANN B HUMPELT, 2
VERMUTEN,-
A,- VERMUTEN, DASS B WEISS, OB WENN B ETWAS$_0$ GELESEN HAT, DANN B HUMPELT, 11
A VERMUTET, DASS B WEISS, OB WENN B ETWAS GELESEN HAT, DANN B HUMPELT, 8

NOTES

(*) I wish to thank D. Chisholm, Univ. of Arizona, for correcting the English of the final version of this paper.

(1) The material of this paper depends on work of M. Lutz-Hensel, A. Günther, C. Rodewald-Röver and myself. I report here on work in progress.The research was partly financed by DFG-grant He 9o5/1+1z. For details of the contributions of my colleagues see notes 9 and 16.

(2) Of course, this statement is not true for our own research.

(3) References to Montague's papers are made with respect to Montague (1974). I use the well known abbreviations for the titles of the papers.

(4) Montague (1974), p. 12o, compare also p. 96. More special formulations are in EFL on p. 189. See also Heidrich (198o), sect. 2.

(5) The theorem is mentioned in UG on p. 233 as "remark". 'Montague-grammar' and 'Montague-theory' are defined in Heidrich (1980), sect. 2.

(6) An informal example of a reduction is given in Heidrich (1980), sect. 3.

(7) Compare Heidrich (1977a), ch. 4 and 5.

(8) One reduction we made contains fourteen different intensional relations. See Heidrich (1976), p. 186ff. Compare Günther (forthcoming).

(9) References to the results of our research can be given with respect to diagram (5). Concerning the left part, most of the work on performatives and attitudes was done by Lutz-Hensel and Rodewald-Röver. The extensive material is published in Heidrich (1977b). Lutz-Hensel and Günther elaborated the first version of a dialogue model, published in Heidrich (1976), p. 141-18o. Günther developed the concept of a dialogue basis as well as a prototype of a set-theoretical dialogue model, see Heidrich (1977b).Günther(1977) is a study on the realtion of natural dialogues and dialogue models. Concerning the right part, Heidrich (1977a) contains a solution for speech acts.

(10) Bennett(1975), p. 72 and 69.

(11) Günther, in this volume, note 2.

(12) As a consequence the dialogue rules, see Günther, in this volume def. 6 - 9, are only implicitly stated in the dialogue. In the construction of the Montague-theory, especially in the construction of the models for

NOTES

Montague-grammars of dialogues, a system of languages will be introduced such that the modals can be formulated on this system of languages.

(13) Logical or functional time is of course reflected in the sequent dialogue steps. Compare Günther (1977), p. 59, and Günther (forthcoming).

(14) The problematic conclusions from having an attitude to the ontological state of the attitude's propositional content cannot be discussed here.

(15) A very important part of knowledge relevant for dialogues and not expressed in the example concerns knowledge of pragmatic conditions of communication, e.g. conventions of speech situations, which are presuppositions for any succeeding communication. For recent work in this direction compare Meggle (1979). It should also be pointed out that apart from "interest", "volition" (intention) and perhaps "acceptance", no part of the affective components of persons is used.

(16) The papers of Lutz-Hensel and Rodewald-Röver are published in Heidrich (1977b). The papers contain the linguistic characterizations of classes of about 200 verbs. Other classes are under work. Further extensive material on syntactic semantic analyses of performative verbs done by Lutz-Hensel is not yet published.

REFERENCES

[1] Bennet, M.R. (1975) *Some extensions of a Montague fragment of English.* Bloomington, 1975.

[2] Günther, A. (1977) *Dialogkonstruktionen auf der Basis logischer Ableitungen,* Hamburg, 1977.

[3] Günther, A. (forthcoming) "Some Ways of Representing Dialogues."

[4] Heidrich, C.H. (1979) (ed) *Formale Betrachtungen in Sprach- und Kommunikationstheorie* I, Hamburg, 1976.

[5] Heidrich, C.H. (1977a) *Intensionale Analysen von Sprechhandlungen,* Hamburg, 1977.

[6] Heidrich, C.H. (1977b) (ed) *Konstituenten dialogischer Kommunikation,* Hamburg, 1977.

[7] Heidrich, C.H. (1980) "Formal Capacity of Montague - grammars." In: L.J. Cohen, J. Los, H. Pfeiffer and K.P. Podewski (eds.) *Logic, Methodology and Philosophy of Science* VI. Proceedings of the 6th International Congress of Logic. Amsterdam, 1981.

[8] Meggle, G. (1979) "Eine kommunikative Handlung verstehen." In: Grewendorf, G. *Sprechakttheorie und Semantik,* Frankfurt, 1979.

[9] Montague, R. (1974) *Formal Philosophy,* New Haven, 1974 (Ed. by R.H. Thomason)

# PART FOUR:

# ANALYSING PHILOSOPHY

## INTRODUCTION TO PART FOUR: ANALYSING PHILOSOPHY

The first paper below (by Krabbe) is an analysis of so-called "immanent" criticism, or, better, of immanent criticism-and-defence, of philosophical systems. The other two papers (Naess, Barth) concern modes of argumentation that are actually found in philosophical texts from earlier centuries.

What Krabbe has to say can be applied to every system of opinion such that all relevant facts are determined -- in some way or other -- from the system itself. It would seem that these are precisely the systems of philosophy and science which one calls the rationalistic ones.

It is interesting to contemplate points of affinity between Krabbe's paper and that of Naess. We have therefore put the former first and the latter second.

Naess offers a theory about the types of argument contained in Spinoza's *Ethics*. The *Ethics* was set up *more geometrico*, and it was not -- and is not -- usual to connect geometrical proofs with discussions and geometrical proof theory with a theory of argumentation. However, though the *Ethics* does not have the form of a dialogue, Naess holds that Spinoza, while composing this text, did see himself as involved in a discussion with his contemporaries, and that he chose and formulated his arguments accordingly.

Neither did the rationalistic strain in Leibniz succeed in erasing this philosopher's respect for critical arguments and their importance for semantics and for proof theory (cf. paper by Barth).

That all this is no trivial matter appears from the study of other influential thinkers. As to René Descartes, whose revival in "analytic" circles by Noam Chomsky is known to all, there is an interesting paper by W.Marcizsewski (1975). On the assumption that Descartes -- consciously or unconsciously -- assumed the validity of *reductio ad absurdum,* Marciszewski shows that, for Descartes, there simply cannot be any controversial issues. Thereby Marciszewski gives an "immanent" explanation, based on Descartes' own logical and semiotical principles, of Descartes' professed negative attitude toward discussions. The Cartesian attitude -- which has other and deeper sources besides Descartes, influential though he was -- has penetrated more recent continental philosophy to a terrifying extent, particularly its more "idealist" branches and their materialist offspring. I may refer to Th. Adorno's impressive characterization -- and approval -- of the "dialectical" attitude of the excessively influential philosopher G.W.F. Hegel:

> "Hegel deeply distrusts argumentation, and he is right in doing so. A dialectician intuitively knows what was later to be rediscovered by Simmel, that whatever remains in the sphere of argumentation thereby always exposes itself to refutation...The ideal is non-argumentative thinking...in the medium of relaxed thought" (Adorno 1963, p. 158f, translated by me -- E.M.B.).

In *The Foundations of Mathematics*, pp. 9-14, E.W. Beth discusses some of the uncountably many applications that have been made by philosophers and "Cartesian" (my term) rationalistic scientists of what Beth calls "Aristotle's Principle of the Absolute". This principle of "the Absolute" is an important element in all anti-argumentative "idealist", or "dialectical", rationalism, not in the last place in its neo-platonic form as found, e.g., in the 15th century philosopher of "the Infinite", the speculative mathematician and theologian Nicholas of Kues/Cusa (of whom Beth seems not to be aware). Hegel's thought is strongly related to that of Cusanus, whether he was influenced by him or not.[1]

Outside philosophy proper things are not always all that much better. Monological "cartesian" rationalist cognition in general, idealist or not, with its monological understanding of semantics and logic, still has such a firm grip on mathematicians' minds (to say nothing of contemporary philosophers' minds) that what is dialogically clear and simple is, even today, made monological and well-nigh ununderstandable. Weierstrass' "method" in the differential calculus is a case in point, Leibniz (and Robinson) notwithstanding (paper by Barth).

The three papers that follow may be read as attempts to retrieve what was left of the spirit of criticism and debate in philosophy after the onslaught of Cartesianism and idealism.

## NOTES

(1) References are to: Th. Adorno, Drei Studien zu Hegel. Frankfurt a.M., 1963; Evert W. Beth, The Foundations of Mathematics - A Study in the Philosophy of Science. Amsterdam, North-Holland Publ. Cy, 1959; W. Marciszewski, "The Cartesian Concept of Conviction", Poznań Studies in the Philosophy of the Sciences and the Humanities, vol.1, no. 4, 1975.

# FORMAL DIALECTICS AS IMMANENT CRITICISM OF PHILOSOPHICAL SYSTEMS

Erik C.W. Krabbe

## 1. *Introduction*

In the following* I shall present a new argumentational interpretation of the formal dialogue-games which we owe to Professors Lorenzen and Lorenz. This interpretation differs from that given in [1] in that it is restricted to conflicts arising from a context of immanent criticism, whereas [1] dealt with pure conflicts in general. It will become apparent that the attacks and defenses in Professor Lorenzen's "strips" can be given *two different interpretations*, according to what happens to be the dialectical role of the utterer of the attacked statement. There are also a number of quite natural consequences pertaining to the structural rules.

My starting-point shall be a remark by Frank Van Dun ([3], p. 106)

> (..) *formal* dialogues - these being dialogues where one participant has all the facts and the other all the logic, so to speak.

Let us call the party with "all the facts":Black (Black, too, has logic of course), and the one with nothing but logic: White. You will presently understand why it is I don't call them Opponent and Proponent.

## 2. *The provocative thesis*

Imagine the following dialectical situation: Black is the "proponent" of a philosophical system, i.e., he/she/it knows or pretends to know what the world is like and what there is; this philosophy is laid down in a set of statements. White wants to attack this philosophy by immanent criticism, i.e., he/she/it wants to beat Black on its own ground. This is a situation where Black has all the facts, for the facts are determined by the system. White, on the other hand, has nothing but logic. Actually, White doesn't even have logic, at least not until the parties agree upon a system of formal dialectics...

I shall argue that Lorenzen's and Lorenz's formal dialogue-games constitute particularly suitable instruments for the resolution of conflicts in this kind of situation.

In the formal dialogue-games the party which has nothing but logic has some thesis to defend, and is called: Proponent. In the situation I depicted it is the party with al the facts (Black) which has a thesis (the philosophical system). Therefore, if I were to use the words "Proponent" and "Opponent", I would assign the name of "Proponent" to Black, and the name of "Opponent" to White. This, however, would be very confusing, as the dialectical role of Black will turn out to be equal to that of Lorenzen's Opponent and the role of White to that of the Proponent. I, therefore, stick to the names "Black" and "White".

One way in which White can start its immanent criticism is to put forward a statement which is known to be unacceptable to Black and to claim that it is part and parcel of Black's system. (Indeed, presumably all immanent criticism can be presented in this form.) For instance, in an attack on a theistic system, White can put forward the STONE-proposition: "God is able to make a stone He cannot Himself lift". Or, if White thinks that Black's system is inconsistent or otherwise absurd it may put forward a *falsum-statement* i.e., employ a sentence $(\wedge)$ which, in the system of formal dialectics agreed upon, expresses an absurdity. I shall call the statement put forward by White at the start of the discussion: *provocative thesis*. It is unimportant whether or not this thesis is believed to be true by White. Not only that this is *dialectically* unimportant, for that is always the case if the dialectics is externalized (see The Principle of Externalization of Dialectics in Section III.4 of [1]), but it is also unimportant for our judgment of White's veracity. Whereas in most situations you are supposed to adhere to your thesis (at least until your defeat in debate), this is not the case here. By its *provocative thesis*, *T*, White is merely announcing that Black cannot reasonably doubt T[1], unless Black is willing to abandon or modify its system.

The provocative thesis can have any grammatical form. If a first order language is employed, the following forms seem particularly well suited to express a provocation: the disjunctive form (dilemma: "God is either not loving or not omnipotent"), the existential form (strange entities: "Some circles are square"), denial (of pieces of common sense knowledge: "There is no knowledge") and the atomic form ("You're nuts"). The STONE-proposition can be expressed in existential form: "there is some way in which God....", or "there is some possible world such that....".

What if Black accepts the provocative thesis without more ado? In that case, we can either say that there was no discussion at all or that an abortive discussion has taken place. If someone has to be called the winner of such an abortive discussion it must be White. However, even if White is called the winner, this party has failed in its attempt at immanent criticism through picking an unsuitable provocative thesis. The provocative thesis should be unpalatable to Black.

### 3. *Critical interpretation of the logical constants*

If Black rejects the provocative thesis the result will be a *simple conflict of avowed opinions* (Def. 1. of Ch. III, [1]):

$$\langle \mathit{SYST}, T, \text{Black}, \text{White} \rangle,$$

where "*SYST*" stands for the uttered or published part of Black's system ( *SYST* is a set of statements), and "*T*" for the provocative thesis. The debaters may now pick a system of formal dialectics to resolve their conflict. In [1] an argument is developed in favor of several systems of formal dialectics (coinciding with the dialogue games of Lorenzen and Lorenz) as suitable instruments for conflict resolution, provided that the parties in the conflict want to implement various fundamental norms. Nothing is said about the origin of the conflict. I now want to show that, if the origin of the conflict is such as sketched above, the systems of formal dialectics in [1] become particularly appealing.

What forms can Black's rejection of the thesis take? The attacks described in Lorenzen's "strips" are, I think, quite acceptable. (They were recently accepted by the present company!) I would only like to add (as is done in [1])the possibility of a rejection of an atomic thesis by means of a simple expression of doubt (indicated by "?"). Hence there are now three cases in which Black can reject the thesis by a simple "how come?", viz., when the thesis is atomic, when it is disjunctive, and when it is existential. Let us consider the other forms which provocation and rejection can take:

If $T = T_1 \& T_2$ , I think we can understand White's provocation to imply that Black must admit both $T_1$ and $T_2$ (unless Black abandons or modifies its system). So it is presumably in order to have Black choose one of them for rejection. It makes little sense to have an initial provocative thesis of this form, since you may as well put forward either conjunct. However, conjunctive provocations may very well occur later on in the discussion.Similar considerations apply to $(\forall x)Ax$.

If $T = T_1 \rightarrow T_2$, we may take White's provocation to imply that, if Black enlarges its system by a statement $T_1$, it will become unreasonable for it to maintain doubt about a provocative thesis $T_2$. In order to reject this, Black should, *for the sake of argument*, become the advocate of an enlarged system $SYST \cup \{T_1\}$ (Black needn't *believe* $T_1$) and then reject $T_2$.

The case $T = \sim T_1$ may be treated similarly, equating $\sim T_1$ with $T_1 \rightarrow \wedge$. Here, White's provocation consists of a claim that $SYST \cup \{T_1\}$ is absurd.

In all these cases, where the rejection involves more than a simple "how come?", it is obvious that White should answer immediately by a protective defence move according to Lorenzen's strips. We may even merge attack and defence move, and go from a situation

$SYST/_{BLACK} A \ \& \ B$ (Black is to be the speaker)

immediately to:

$SYST/_{BLACK} A$ (Again, Black is to be the speaker).

On the other hand, it is convenient to stick to the principle that the parties take turns; we may then stipulate:

*Special Rule* 1 A rejection (by Black) of a conjunction, a conditional, a negation or an universal statement should be answered immediately by White by means of a protective defence, constituting a fresh provocation.

We cannot have this rule in the case of atomic statements, for in that case I wouldn't know of any protective defence, at least not within the context of an indoor game.[2] We cannot have it for disjunctive or existential statements either. White's provocation $\bar{T}_1 \vee \bar{T}_2$ doesn't imply either a provocation $\bar{T}_1$ or a provocation $\bar{T}_2$; hence, in this case it seems appropriate to grant White a right to postpone its choice of a protective defence. Similarly for $(\exists x) Ax$.

## 4. *Information-seeking interpretation of the logical constants*

Once Black has rejected a provocative thesis of a form to which the special rule doesn't apply, i.e., a thesis which is either disjunctive or existential or atomic, White may start to cross-examine Black, on account of its system, with the following ends in view:

(i) to make Black the advocate of a system which contains a statement of the very sentence used in the provocative thesis, or otherwise:

(ii) to make Black the advocate of a system stated in sufficient detail for White to choose a protective defence.

For the forms of these questions (by White) and answers (by Black) we should again consult Lorenzen's "strips". However, this time we interpret these strips in a *strikingly different way* : not as rejections and provocations, or even as attacks and defences of some sort or other, but us (information-seeking) questions and answers. White doesn't doubt the system or reject any statement of it *within* the game of immanent criticism. *White asks questions to get more information* about the system.

Black has, so we assumed, all the facts (as they are determined by the system). It therefore seems reasonable to require of Black that it answer all questions without delay:

*Special Rule* 2 All questions put to Black by White should be answered by Black in its next move.

Note that this implies that Black must, on demand, specify one of the alternatives contained in a statement $S_1 \vee S_2$. When $(\exists x) Ax$ is the object of a question, Black must point out an example $Aa$. In strip-form:

| Black | White | Black |
|---|---|---|
| $S_1 \vee S_2$ | which? | $S_1$ / $S_2$ |
| $(\exists x)Ax$ | example? | $Aa$ |

(all choices to be made by Black)

When $S_1 \rightarrow S_2$ is a statement in Black's system, and Black is questioned on account of this statement, we may imagine White remarking:

> You say that in your system $S_2$ would be the case if $S_1$ were the case. Well, I would say that, from your point of view, you cannot reasonably doubt that $S_1$ is the case - So I'm willing to put forward a provocative thesis $S_1$, instead of the one we are presently discussing. On the other hand, if you don't reject $S_1$, you must incorporate a statement $S_2$ in your system (for that's the content of your remark $S_1 \rightarrow S_2$). I'm also willing to continue our discussion about the present thesis, if you explicitly make a statement $S_2$, i.e., if you submit such a statement to questioning or other dialectical use.

Again Black ought to answer without delay. Schematically we have:

| Black | White | Black | White |
|---|---|---|---|
| $S_1 \to S_2$ | Shall I put $S_1$ or will you put $S_2$ ? | Please put $S_1$ | $S_1$ (fresh provocation) |
| | | $S_2$ (added to the system) (Black chooses) | (next question, or protective defence) |

Compare:

| White | Black | White |
|---|---|---|
| $T_1 \to T_2$ | $T_1$ (for the sake of argument) | $T_2$ (fresh provocation) |

For $\sim S_1$ we may, similarly, imagine White remarking:

> You system, would, you say, be absurd if $S_1$ were the case. Shall I put forward a provocative thesis $S_1$ or do you admit the absurdity of your system (by stating $\wedge$)?

The last option may or may not constitute a loss for Black (Cp. Sections IV.1 and IV.2 of [1]). Information-seeking questions on account of atomic statements are not admissible, as there is no more detailed information to be had.

How long may this questioning go on? White should be allowed to ask all relevant questions, i.e., all questions which are relevant to the uttered statements of the system. So White may ask both L? and R? on account of each conjunctive statement made by Black. In the course of the questioning more and more statements are added to the system and White should be allowed to put forward questions on account of these new statements as well. If no universal statement appears on Black's side the number of questions will always be finite. There are several techniques available in order to secure that only a finite number of questions can be asked, even when universal statements appear. One may require of White that it announces, and keeps within, a fixed limit before the discussion begins, or one may use techniques which employ ordinal numbers as in [2]. Anyhow, the discussion is naturally segmented into *local discussions*, as in Section III.6 of [1], each with its own local provocative thesis. Such a new thesis can either be the result of a protective defence move or the "fresh provocation" which results from a question aimed at a conditional or a negation; it marks the end of the previous local discussion and the beginning of the next one. Throughout the discussion Black employs the critical interpretation of the logical constants as to White's statements and White employs the information-seeking interpretation as to Black's statements.

White *wins* a local discussion if and only if

(1) the local provocative thesis is stated by Black, or

(2) (optional) $\wedge$ is stated by Black, or

(3) White wins the local discussion L' which orginates in L, (i.e. which starts with the rejection of the new provocation which ended L).

Blacks wins if White does not win, i.e., in the last local discussion: if White exhausts its rights of putting questions (without reaching situation (1) or (2)) and if, moreover, there is no possibility of protective defence. White/Black wins the discussion (or the chain of arguments, [1]) if and only if it wins the first local discussion. The effects of winning and losing can be determined as in [1], Section III.8. In some cases it seems reasonable that Black, having lost, should either announce a change in the system or abandon it or admit the provocative thesis into the system, but we cannot oblige Black to do so, unless it has been defeated in every possible way.

NOTES

(*) I would like to thank Prof. E.M. Barth and J. Vrieze for their advice whil preparing my two contributions to this volume.

(1) I use roman capitals as sentence-variables and corresponding italic capital as variables for statements (utterances) of sentences.

(2) What is wanted is a structural protective defence. For, a general protectiv defence is not a statement and hence would not constitute a fresh provoca tion. Moreover, it would obviously be unfair to White to require an imme diate reaction of the latter type. Cp. [1], Section III.7.

## REFERENCES

[1] Barth, E.M. and E.C.W. Krabbe, *From Axiom to Dialogue. A Philosophical Study of Logics and Argumentation*, New York/Berlin: Walter de Gruyter, 1982, Ch. III and IV.

[2] Lorenz, K., "Die dialogische Rechtfertigung der effektiven Logik". In F. Kambartel and J. Mittelstrass (eds.), *Zum normativen Fundament der Wissenschaft*, Frankfurt am Main (1973), pp. 250 - 280. Reprinted in P. Lorenzen and K. Lorenz, *Dialogische Logik*, Darmstadt (1978), pp. 179 - 209.

[3] Van Dun, F., "On the Modes of Opposition in the Formal Dialogues of P. Lorenzen," *Logique et Analyse, N.S.*, 15e Année (1972), pp. 103 - 136.

# AN APPLICATION OF EMPIRICAL ARGUMENTATION ANALYSIS TO SPINOZA'S "ETHICS"

Arne Naess

[This paper should be read as a sequel to the short paper by Naess in Part One of this volume.]

## 1. *The propositions of the "Ethics" conceived of as arguments in a debate*

Nobody today maintains that Spinoza is not an original philosopher. Harry Austryn Wolfson -- that extremely learned historian of ideas -- however, set himself the task of finding out which sources Spinoza used, or may have used, in formulating each detail of his main work, the *Ethics*. With extraordinary success, Wolfson traced *influences* upon Spinoza's formulations. One task of argumentation analysis is to transfer the historians' results, which are formulated in terms of influences, into a rich set of patterns of argumentation. This is a task of hypothetical reconstruction. It clarifies the cognitive content of an historical text by pointing out contrasts and by explication of agreements and disagreements. It rejects the existence of sovereign pronouncements having been made in a kind of communicational vacuum.

While the term "influence" is primarily a causal term, it also has wider connotations, including the transfer of opinion through verbal deliberation and argumentation. Wolfson's conclusion is that Spinoza, perhaps more than any other great philosopher, picked up opinions from others, but that he never did so slavishly. He subtly changed *everything* in his own direction. Thus, when studied deeply, every single proposition in the *Ethics* is seen to have a distinctive Spinozist color or flavor. It is, in my opinion, as if to Descartes, to Hobbes, and to a host of other thinkers, Spinoza has said: "Yes, but ...".

Furthermore, I take Spinoza to have had an intensive intuition concerning existence in general, a genuine *Weltanschauung* (stressing *Schauen* ), which simplifies many things and which unifies his own views.

With these two assumptions in mind -- the "Wolfsonian" assumption of "Yes, but ..." and my own assumption of a unifying and simplifying intuition -- I shall now comment on the vast set of theses of equivalence in the *Ethics*.

## 2. *Spinoza's theses of equivalence*

Spinoza connects about 90 basic terms in his *Ethics* by means of a great number of theses containing what I shall call *expressions of equivalence*:

A is one and the same thing as B
A, which is the same as B
A is nothing other than B
A cannot be anything other than B
A signifies the same as B
A and B signify the same
By A and B I understand the same
A is called B
A, that is, B
We say A when B

Some expressions I classify as expressions of equivalence even though they do not always suggest a close relation between

A and B:

| | | |
|---|---|---|
| A or B | as in | *Deus sive Natura* |
| A or B | as in | *Causa seu ratio* |

If all sentences containing equivalence expressions in a straightforward way are marked by "A eq B", it is clear that they make up a large class of important formulations in the *Ethics*. A list of about 250 equivalences is still not a complete list.[1] Each of the following eight central terms occurs either as A or as B in more than 15 sentences of equivalence: *causa, Deus, essentia, idea, natura* (or *Natura*), *potentia, ratio, virtus*.

If it is tentatively accepted that such relations of equivalence are transitive, then a vast network of equivalences is created.

Sentences expressing equivalence occur in great numbers in Spinoza's proofs and thus are clearly indispensible in his argumentations. Of 67 equivalences extracted from Propositions 1 to 73 in Part Four of the *Ethics* , 57 are made use of in proofs.

In a list of equivalences in this set of 90 basic terms:

| | | | |
|---|---|---|---|
| *aeternitas* | occurs in | 5 | equivalences |
| *affectus* | " | 19 | " |
| *amor* | " | 10 | " |
| *anima* | " | 8 | " |
| *beatitudo* | " | 8 | " |
| *bonum* | " | 7 | " |
| *causa* | " | 22 | " |
| *cognitio* | " | 19 | " |
| *conatus* | " | 16 | " |

It should be noticed, however, that some of Spinoza's equivalences do not really help us much to understand what he means. The frequently found expression *causa seu ratio* , traditionally translated as "cause or reason", is an example. It functions today mainly to remind us of the differences in meaning of *causa* and *ratio* at the time of Spinoza from the usages of "cause" and "reason" today.

The strings of equivalences

A eq B, B eq C, C eq D ...

are of particular interest from the point of view of simplification and univocality. I shall give an example involving the words *virtus*, *potentia* , *conatus* , *essentia*. The numbers in the diagram below refer to the list mentioned on p.247.

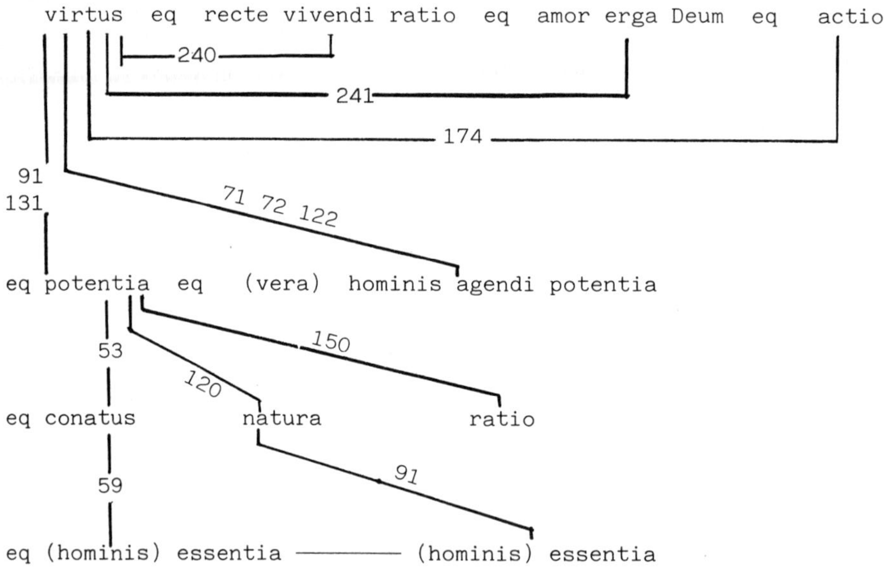

| Equivalence no. | is found in |
|---|---|
| 53 | Part 3, Prop 7, Demonstratio |
| 59 | 3, P9, Scholium |
| 71 | 3, P55, Sch |
| 72 | 3, P55, Cor 2, Dem |
| 91 | 4, Def 8 |
| 120 | 4, P33, Dem |
| 122 | 4, P52, Dem |
| 150 | 4, App 3 |
| 174 | 5, P4, Sch |
| 240 | 5, P41, Dem |
| 241 | 5, P42, Dem |

From the diagram it is seen that *virtus* occurs in five different equivalences. These five equivalent expressions are connected with yet others. If the equivalences (except a small number of them) are taken seriously as statements of extensional equivalences obeying the law of transitivity, there is *a possibility of vast simplification of the articulation of Spinoza's system.* If "A eq B eq C" is taken to imply substitutability, new versions of the *Ethics* may be constructed: one in which A has been inserted where we now find B or C, another in which B is written where now A and C occur, etc. Depending on the way in which the terminological reduction is carried out, one obtains different versions, or reconstructions, of the system.

An example: the terms "power" and "virtue" are connected with several strong expressions of equivalence. There is also an equivalence between "virtue" and "love of God". In the proof of theorem 42 in Part Five, it is said that love of God (*amor erga Deum*) is virtue itself (*ipsa virtus est*). Now, if in the *Ethics* we put the term "virtue" wherever we find "power", we get a text that sounds very Christian and very tender-minded (in the sense of William James). If, on the other hand, we substitute "power" for "virtue" everywhere, we get a text sounding like Machiavelli or Thomas Hobbes, and very tough-minded (in the sense of William James).

The so-called 'rationalism' of Spinoza can be constructed by taking *ratio* as a kind of primitive term and using some of the above equivalences to define other terms in terms of *ratio*. But one may also start with *amor erga Deum* and use the above equivalences to construct a kind of religious mysticism.

For several reasons, neither of these new texts brings us nearer to the system as intended by Spinoza. One reason is that *few equivalences are intended to be as strong as is required for substitutability*. Another reason is of a still more fundamental character: It may have been Spinoza's intention to suggest that behind, or beyond, a pair of terms said by him to be equivalent there is a single reality that can, and must, be approached through the differing connotations of each of the two terms.

Through the two attributes of extension and thought, human cognition grasps the one substance. Both avenues are essential for human cognition of what 'is in itself'. Each of them contributes to this. A limitation on one of them would make human cognition a poorer instrument even though each attribute is supposed to be a complete expression of substance or God.

In an analogous manner, one may explain the intended functions of many of the theses of equivalence in the *Ethics*. Thus the power-terminology refers to a reality that is also referred to by the virtue-terminology and the self-causation-terminology; yet to restrict the exposition of the system by eliminating the latter two terminologies would restrict unnecessarily our apprehension of that reality -- so he may have thought.

Whatever the merits of a partial explanation in this vein of Spinoza's use of equivalences, it does not lessen the relevance and importance of an approach by argumentation analysis.

### 3. *Equivalences as arguments*

The text of the *Ethics* can be seen as a set of answers to questions raised by Spinoza's contemporaries, forcing him to adopt the terminology of his time. The function of Spinoza's equivalences in argumentation may be illustrated by short dialogues between opponents (Op) and Spinoza (Sp):

> *Op:* Mr. Spinoza! According to my religion, a human being may attain a state of glory ( *gloria* ). But neither do you have anything to say about glory, nor does your philosophy permit you to attain glory. What do you have to say to that?
> *Sp*: The glory you talk about *is the same as* genuine self-satisfaction or peace of mind (*acquiescentia in se ipso, animi acquiescentia*) (5, P36, Sch).

-- The questioner is thereby referred back to one of the themes about which, in the *Ethics*, Spinoza says a great deal.--

> *Op:* I understand what you say about men's love for God, but what about God's love for human beings? In my religion we draw comfort from meditating on a God who loves us. Your philosophy does not permit you to indulge in a loving God, and that illustrates the difference between a warm religion and a cold philosophy.
> *Sp:* "God's love for men and the understanding love of the mind for God are one and the same." (5, P36, Cor).

-- In this last quotation, I have translated *intellectualis* by "understanding" because the term "intellectual" is heavily charged with modern, narrow conceptions of the intellect.

Spinoza's answer is, of course, not very enlightening for a religious person. But it certainly brings a complex of theological problems -- viz., those concerning God's love of humans -- within the circle of Spinoza's explicit and carefully worked-out philosophy of the third kind of knowing, the intuitive. --

> *Op:* Descartes distinguishes clear and distinct ideas from the confused. You seem to presuppose certain criteria of clarity and distinctiveness, for you use these expressions profusely in your *Ethics* without explaining them. Thus your *Ethics* is fragmentary.
>
> *Sp:* Genuinely clear and distinct ideas are those and only those "which refer to the third kind of knowledge." (5, P28, Dem).

-- Again, Spinoza brings an important range of problems within the circle of those problems that he treats in some detail.--

> *Op:* You speak favorably about seeking what is useful to us, and you explain in detail what it implies. But what is needed is a similarly deeply-founded teaching on how to live virtuously. You lack that: you cannot satisfy those who are striving to attain virtue.
>
> *Sp:* "The foremost and only principle of virtue or of the right way of living is the search for that which is useful for us." (5, P41, Dem).

-- In this example, it is presupposed that Spinoza has already formulated many propositions on seeking what is useful, but that he has not yet formulated any propositions on virtue. Through his answer, he now furnishes his opponents with a theory of virtue. The fight for virtue is a fight for what is 'really' useful. As we can see from Parts 4 and 5 of the *Ethics*, what is 'really' useful in his terminology is such behavior as we today would on the whole classify as virtuous (in the sense of being at an ethically high level).

Now consider the possibility that Spinoza has already formulated, more or less completely, his theorems on virtue, but not those on seeking what is useful. The opponent may then object:

> *Op:* You have lofty theorems on virtue, but as a sympathizer with Thomas Hobbes and a believer in the fundamental principle of self-preservation, I miss a more realistic ethics as part of your philosophy.
>
> *Sp:* The principle of seeking what is useful for us *is* the principle of virtue and the right way of living. There is no other principle.

-- Again Spinoza delivers the goods. He is able to do so because his basic intuitions allow for a vast simplification of metaphysics. But he cannot express it through a small number of terms; he *must include all the basic terms of all his opponents and rivals*. Or, not talking in the terms of argumentation analysis, he must include all the important terms of the different traditions and paradigms he is reacting to -- in part favorably, saying "Yes" and in part less favorably, saying "Yes, but...". (Rarely, or never, "No").

He implicitly says "Come to me! Whatever good and true there is in your own world view, you will find also in my philosophy. Whatever is bad or misleading in your own view, you will get rid of with my help."

The *Ethics* is a small book about big issues. It ranges over ontology, epistemology, basic physics (between 2, P13 and 2, P14), basic parts of psychology, some general sociology and pedagogics and, of course, a lot of ethics. Furthermore, it contains theology in the sense of doctrines about God, as well as some sociology of religion and morals.

How was it possible for Spinoza to furnish deep answers to the formidable variety of questions that were *asked* in his own time about all those themes? The question is pertinent because his aim was to convince the people of his own time and his own environment to *change* to some extent their opinions on practically all fundamental problems.

Tentative answer:

By means of his theses of equivalence.

One aim of this paper has been to exemplify a combined interest in speculative philosophy and an empirical, 'positivistic' analysis of argumentation. The understanding of a great philosophy such as that of Spinoza poses a variety of semantical and argumentational problems. In the above, it has been possible to illustrate only a very special application. It should, however, need little reflection to imagine the possibilities of fruitful applications of, among other things, the various tools mentioned in my first contribution to this volume.

## NOTES

(1) A. Naess, *Equivalent Terms and Notions in Spinoza's Ethics,* published by *Inquiry*, Philosophical Institute, University of Oslo, 1975.

# FINITE DEBATES ABOUT "THE INFINITE"

E.M. Barth

## 1. *Two philosophical paradigms*

In our time it is *de rigueur* to discuss the importance of scientific "paradigms", and to reflect on the attitudes of established science upon arrival of new or exotic paradigms. Unfortunately the discussion is usually carried out at a comfortable distance from the struggle that is taking place in our own age between two paradigms that I shall call the ontology-ratio paradigm and the dialogical two-role paradigm. Each of them has deep historical roots with wide and often unsuspected ramifications. The involvement of recent and contemporary science with each paradigmatic set of assumptions cannot very well be understood if the historical background of each of the competing theories is not brought into the picture. Below I shall give a simple, clear, and important example involving mathematics, classical physics and logic.

## 2. *"Tongue-twisting for the sake of consistency": a recent description of the Weierstrass method*

In 1972 *The Scientific American* published an expository article by two mathematicians, Martin Davis and Reuben Hersh. It was an exposition of Abraham Robinson's introduction, in 1962, of a notion of infinitesimals into the theory of the analysis of mathematical functions. Robinson's infinitesimals are quite different from the old philosophical notion. In a manner that satisfies contemporary mathematicians' standards of rigour, Robinson's model is able to supplant the standard (Cauchy-Weierstrass) foundation of the "infinitesimal calculus", or calculus of differentials and integrals, as it is better called, since nothing deserving the name of infinitesimals occurs in that theory.

In this otherwise excellent paper by Davis and Hersh an extremely telling passage can be found, reflecting an attitude to the Weierstrass formulation which I believe is quite common even today. Their outlook is a consequence of the "rational" epistemological attitudes and habits of exposition that still prevail in most parts of the exact sciences (to say nothing of other cultural and intellectual pursuits). I want to show that the Cauchy-Weierstrass theory is most easily understood in another light, the logico-epistemological outlook - "paradigm" - of critical discussion.

The cognitive shift from the adoration of *ratio* (*Vernunft*) to a critical-dialogical outlook has not yet taken place in culture at large, not even in analytical circles. It is a conceptual shift of the same order as that which Dijksterhuis called "the mechanization of the world picture", in fact it is an extension and complementation of the former shift in, or rather into, the social sphere. One might therefore speak of the *externalization* of the "rational" world picture, a process that has mechanization and socialization as complementary aspects. The dialogical outlook was a common ingredient in culture as late as in the twelfth century, but was expelled from European philosophy by the notion of *ratio* which came up in the thirteenth century and which has now dominated so-called "modern" (post-medieval) philosophy for centuries. One important consequence of this is that the exposition and the analysis of otherwise excellent scientific results still usually presupposes the meta-physics of *ratio*.

Traces of the critical outlook can be found, however, even in Leibniz, heir to many traditions. Weierstrass' foundation of the calculus that Leibniz invented shows the power of the critical approach at its full, though the habitual formulation of this foundation never shows this in an explicit manner - that would be inconceivable in the *ratio* -ridden epoch in which the epsilon-delta "method" was arrived at.

Davis and Hersh do not see this, for they have apparently not made this shift themselves. Most scholars have not. Consequently they treat the standard definition of velocity as "unnatural". They write:

> "To find an instantaneous velocity according to the Weierstrass method we abandon any attempt to compute the speed as a ratio. Instead we define the speed as a limit..... The intuitively clear and physically measurable quantity, the instantaneous velocity, becomes subject to the surprisingly subtle notion of "limit". If we spell out in detail what that means (according to Weierstrass - E.M.B.), we have the following *tongue twister* (they say - italics mine, E.M.B.):
>
> > The velocity is $v$ if, for any positive number $\varepsilon$, $\Delta s/\Delta t - v$ is less in absolute value for all values of $\Delta t$ less in absolute value than some other positive number $\delta$ (which will depend on $\varepsilon$ and $t$)."

Now we can probably all agree with Davis and Hersh not only that this is indeed the modern definition in the formulation in which it is taught in the schools and universities today, and we can also agree that to very many students it is a tongue-twister indeed; but listen to what they write next:

> "By this very definition we have defined the instantaneous velocity $v$ by means of a *subtle relation* between two new quantities, $\varepsilon$ and $\delta$ , which *in some sense* are irrelevant to $v$ itself. At least ignorance of $\varepsilon$ and

> δ never prevented Bernoulli or Euler from *finding* a velocity. The truth is that in a real sense we already knew what instantaneous velocity was before we learned this definition; *for the sake of logical consistency we accept a definition that is much harder to understand* than the concept being defined. Of course, *to a trained mathematician* the epsilon-delta definition is intuitive" (all italics mine, E.M.B.),

- and then they add, schoolmaster-wise,

> "this shows what can be accomplished by proper training."

So training, and nothing else than training, is what makes the definition finally become "intuitive" or natural, for those happy few who have time enough to undergo this training. Davis and Hersh themselves do not attempt to spell out the "subtle relation", as they call it, between ε and δ , or the sense in which ε and δ are irrelevant to the velocity in question (see quotation). They are willing to accept the "tongue-twisting" Weierstrass definition for the sake of logical consistency, although they consider the definition "harder to understand" than the undefined concept of an instantaneous velocity. Logical consistency is the only argument they offer in favour of that definition.

### *3. Two-role logic and the notion of 'limit'*

I am pretty sure that whoever writes and thinks in this way about the Weierstrass definition cannot have read what Leibniz wrote in the year 1702, in a reply to John Bernoulli, De Volder and Bayle. He wrote:

> "... the mathematicians' demand for *rigor* in their demonstrations will be satisfied if we assume, instead of infinitely small sizes, sizes as small as are needed to show that the *error* is less than that which *ANY OPPONENT* can assign, and *consequently* that *no error* can be assigned at all" (Loemker (ed.), p. 584, italics and capitals mine - E.M.B.).

Here Leibniz characterizes, in perfectly clear, dialogical terms, what would count as a *rigorous* proof, for instance as a rigorous proof that a velocity has the instantaneous value $v$, in terms of conceptual and of verbal interaction between an opponent and a proponent of a thesis, much as in classical (Archimedean) mathematical thought. In his own characterization of rigorous proof the notions of infinity and of "infinitesimals" have dropped out of the picture. That of an opponent, i.e. a user of language taking a critical or skeptical attitude in a discussion (contra-position, as I call it) to a proposed mathematical result (statement), has entered - in fact, has re-entered - the philosophical scene, compensating for the absence in this definition of the notion of an infinitesimal, and - in Leibniz' opinion - even surpassing it in its capacity of yielding a rigorous proof procedure.

How can one define "the surprisingly subtle notion of 'limit'"? Notice, first, that no one today would attempt a definition of the word "limit" in isolation. We rather ask: what does it mean *that* an entity, say S, is the limit of a series - which may be infinitely long - of entities $S_n$ characterized by increasing values of the index n - assuming that this series has a limit at all? The answer can be given as a definition of the meaning-in-use of the sentence form

(1) $$\lim_{n \to \infty} s_n = S$$

(where the condition: $n \to \infty$ ought to be written: $n \to$, without "$\infty$", which has no more than a historical justification in this connection). Before Weierstrass no one was able to give a clear account of what this meant. The definition not only may, but *should* be formulated in terms of interaction between the person who uttered a sentence of this form and a critical instance (which may be another person but which may be his or her *alter ego* as well). The critical instance who feels that he/she does not entirely understand the locution, and who somehow expresses that he does not, may be taken to ask for a *more precise* locution, i.e. one that excludes a number of misunderstandings about the speaker's claims by narrowing down the set of possible (connotative) interpretations of (1). The Weierstrass formulation has this characteristic, it is what Naess' English translator (Naess 1966) would call *a precization* of (1) - a technical neologism deriving from the Norwegian *en presisering*, German *eine Präzisierung*. In the tableau below I have formulated it in the current symbols for first-order predicate logic. The locution (1) is the initial thesis, $T_0$, the Weierstrass formulation is the next thesis of the verbal interchange, $T_1$, and so on.

| Opponent | Proponent | |
|---|---|---|
| (The opponent concedes the arithmetic of real numbers) | | |
| | $\lim_{n \to \infty} s_n = S$ | $[T_0]$ |
| Prec.? (I.e., can you express more precisely just what your claims are?) | | |
| | $(\varepsilon)(\exists N)(n)[n>N \rightarrow \lvert S - s_n \rvert < \varepsilon]$ | $[T_1]$ |
| (Assuming that the opponent understands the claim "for all":) $\varepsilon_0$ ? (I.e., *do you* defend this for $\varepsilon_0$?) | | |
| | $(\exists N)(n)[n>N \rightarrow \lvert S - s_n \rvert < \varepsilon_0]$ | $[T_2]$ |
| ? (I.e., *how do you* defend that?) | | |
| | $(n)[n>N_0 \rightarrow \lvert S - s_n \rvert < \varepsilon_0]$ | $[T_3]$ |
| $n_0$? (where $n_0 > N_0$) (I.e., *do you* defend this for $n_0$?) | | |
| | $\lvert S - s_{n_0} \rvert < \varepsilon_0$ | $[T_4]$ |
| ? (I.e., *how do you* defend that?) | | |

(The proponent now has to show, given the arithmetic of real numbers, that $|S - s_{n_0}|$ is indeed smaller than $\varepsilon_0$; if this can be done for every conceivable opposition, however small $\varepsilon$ is chosen and however large n is chosen, then the proponent's initial thesis $T_0$ is mathematically true.)

Observe that no mention is made in $T_1$ of an "infinitieth" term $s_\infty$, or of "infinitely small sizes" (such as $|S - s_\infty|$ might be, if "$s_\infty$" were to have a meaning at all). Even the sign "$\infty$" has disappeared.

Instead we have the proponent's claim that any opponent of $T_1$, and hence of $T_0$, may freely choose a tolerated (tolerable, to the opponent) error $\varepsilon$ - as minute as he/she might wish. No more, and no less, is expressed by the prenex "universal quantifier " - horrible expression - in $T_1$.

## 4. *Instantaneous velocities*

The limits of series of increment-quotients $\frac{\Delta s}{\Delta t}$ with decreasing values of the Cauchy-variable $\Delta t$ form a special case: if

(2) $s=f(t)$,

then the meaning of a statement of the following form:

(3) $\lim\limits_{\Delta t \to o} \frac{\Delta s}{\Delta t} = v(t)$

is defined as follows: for every value of "t",

(4) $\lim\limits_{\Delta t \to o} \frac{\Delta s}{\Delta t} = v(t) \quad =_{Df} \quad (\varepsilon)(\exists\delta)(\Delta t)\,[\Delta t < \delta \rightarrow |v(t) - \frac{\Delta s}{\Delta t}| < \varepsilon]$

($\varepsilon$): opponent's choice
($\exists\delta$): proponent's choice
($\Delta t$): opponent's choice

(Observe that one defines the meaning-in-critical-use of a whole statement form, and not of the *limes*-term in isolation.) The logic of a proof of the correctness of (3) can be shown in a dialogue tableau:

| Opponent | Proponent |
|---|---|
| (As above) | |
| | $\lim\limits_{\Delta t \to o} \frac{\Delta s}{\Delta t} = v(t)$ $[T_0]$ |
| Prec.? | |
| | $(\varepsilon)(\exists\delta)(\Delta t)[\ t<\delta \to \lvert v(t) - \frac{\Delta s}{\Delta t}\rvert < \varepsilon]$ $[T_1]$ |
| $\varepsilon_o$? | |
| | $(\exists\delta)(\Delta t)[\Delta t<\delta \to \lvert v(t) - \frac{\Delta s}{\Delta t}\rvert < \varepsilon_o]$ $[T_2]$ |
| ? | |
| | $(\Delta t)[\Delta t<\delta_o \to \lvert v(t) - \frac{\Delta s}{\Delta t}\rvert < \varepsilon_o]$ $[T_3]$ |
| $(\Delta t)_o$ ? (where $(\Delta t)_o < \delta_o$) (I.e., I have chosen a $\Delta t$ which is indeed smaller than your $\delta_o$; do you defend it in this case?) | |
| | $\lvert v(t) - \frac{\Delta s}{\Delta t_o}\rvert < \varepsilon_o]$ $[T_4]$ |
| ? (I.e., why should I believe this?) | (The proponent now has to show, given the arithmetic of real numbers, that $\lvert v(t) - \frac{\Delta s}{\Delta t}\rvert$ is indeed smaller than the proposed tolerance (acceptable error) $\varepsilon_o$; if this... however small $\varepsilon$ and $\Delta t$ are chosen, then (etc.).) |

## 5. *Paradigmatically misleading expressions*

The part from $T_1$ to $T_4$ corresponds to the "tongue-twister" of the textbooks, in the following sense: the tongue-twister is an attempt, dictated by the fashion of monological *ratio*, to *condense* what are in fact six steps of a discussion into one formula (sentence, formulation), and a formula at that which mentions neither proponent nor opponent. The way of reading the formula

$T_1$ which is common today - see the first quotation from the article by Davis and Hersh - contains ontological expressions, and suggests that the formula or sentence is used to express ontological claims, i.e. that it is primarily used *in order to refer*, and to describe what can be referred to: "for every...... *there is* ......". Notice that though some people have at last become wary of the expression "quantifier", recognizing that quantities are not defined unless the identity relation is involved, and for this reasons prefer the expression "operator", everyone still speaks of these operators as "existential" or "universal"; they thereby demonstrate that they accept them as references to or as claims concerning a (one) cognitive sub-stratum called "ontology", common to both parties and philosophically more fundamental than the parties and their verbal moves.

If, as I expect to hold of many of you who are present here, one treats these operators as expressions with which to make dialogical claims and give instructions for possible verbal action by other users of language, then one will have to admit that the existential quantifier is no more existential than it is quantifying.

This ought to be made clear in the symbolism. Hence the " $\exists$ ", or the "V" and the " $\Lambda$ ", will have to go. The symbol $\ulcorner(x)\urcorner$ is to be replaced by $\ulcorner x^{c}\urcorner$ , indicating that the critic is free to choose any value $\ulcorner x\urcorner$ that he might wish to mention, however small or large, and $\ulcorner(\exists x)\urcorner$ is to be replaced by $\ulcorner x^{s}\urcorner$ , indicating that the speaker has a free choice.

Applying this to the Weierstrass "method", it - i.e. our reformulation of $T_1$ - runs (assuming t to be given):

$$\varepsilon^{c}\ \delta^{s}(\Delta t)^{c}\ [\Delta t<\delta \rightarrow |v(t)-\frac{\Delta s}{\Delta t}|<\varepsilon].$$

The first part of the formula, the sequence

$$\varepsilon^{c}\ \delta^{s}\ (\Delta t)^{c}$$

has no other function than to indicate the order in which, in this case, the speaker or his or her critic (*alter ego* or someone else) is to choose a value for a variable between the brackets, and which variable.

## 6. *Conclusion*

Recent attempts to describe the logic of quantum physics in dialogical terms have brought about a non-intended association of the two, to the practical exclusion of other possible links with the history of theoretical and practical ideas. The attention of the scientific world should now be directed towards the possibility that enlightenment is to be had by a dialogical or two-role X-raying and re-interpretation of classical physics. One example has been given above. Interpreting the Weierstrass "method" in this two-role paradigm also shows more convincingly, I think, than anything else that points of time are not involved and need not be assumed. The domain of the variable "$\Delta t$" (oftened rendered as "h") need not contain infinitesimals in order that we can explain and discuss statements about limits, such as statements about instantaneous velocities. The expression "instant" in "instantaneous velocity" may itself well be a remnant of the earlier paradigm and in any case will contribute to the suggestion that "the velocity at an infinitesimal interval (a point) of time" is meant. In the two-role paradigm, however, the variable "t" is more appropriately described as a variable for readings of clocks. A reading of a clock I take to be a certain action together with its outcome ("o9.55.53 AM"). To read the variable "t" as referring to one "instant" of time in a linear order of such "instants" is to assume an ontological substratum of instants and to regard this ontological sub-stratum as *logically*, if not physically, prior to the readings. This seems to me to run counter to the inspiration behind the Weierstrass method, which cannot have been entirely different from the spirit of the quotation from Leibniz.

Owing to the preponderance in earlier philosophies of the assumption of non-extended and weightless "extremes", "limits", or "infinitesimals"[1] there must be a great many more cases to be found in which struggle with the notion of infinitesimals, and with the whole rational-ontological paradigm[2] in which it belonged, can be shown to have influenced the development of scientific theories,[3] and to still influence the way in which we are prone to interpret those theories today. It seems to me that there is a lot of work to be done.[4]

NOTES

(1) The philosophy, or mathematics, of "the infinitely large/small" of Nicholas of Cusa is brought into the picture in my (1979).

(2) The contrast: unextended infinitesimals or human individuals as supreme values is a consequence of this philosophical paradigm (in the first case) and of the rejection of that paradigm (in the second case). This is the central topic of my (1979).

(3) Cf. my (1977), in which the connection is discussed between (i) this paradigm with its central assumption of non-extended, "potent" infinitesimals (which should not, of course, be confounded with Abraham Robinson's infinitesimals) and (ii) the development -- which took place in Germany -- around 1800 of homoeopathic medicine and (iii) the development -- which likewise took place in Germany -- around 1850 of the Principle ("Law") of Conservation of Energy.

(4) A more extensive bibliography is found in my (1977) and (1979).

## REFERENCES

[1] Davis, Martin and Reuben Hersh, "Non-Standard Analysis," *Scientific American* Vol. *226* no. 6 (June 1972), pp. 78-86.

[2] Leibniz, G.W., *Gottfried Wilhelm Leibniz: Philosophical Papers and Letters*. A selection translated and edited, with an introduction by Leroy E. Loemker. Dordrecht, Holland, $^{2}$1969 (1956).

[3] Naess, Arne, *Communication and Argument. Elements of Applied Semantics*, Oslo and London 1966. Translation by A.Hannay of: *En del elementaere logiske emner*.

[4] Barth, E.M., "The Logical Paradigm in Dialectical Philosophy and Science," *Erkenntnis 11* (1977), pp. 291-322.

[5] Barth, E.M., "Perspectives on Analytic Philosophy." *Mededelingen der Koninklijke Nederlandse Akademie van Wetenschappen, afd. Letterkunde, Nieuwe Reeks, deel 42 - No. 2*. Amsterdam, Oxford, New York 1979.

# PART FIVE:

# ANALYSING INTERACTION

## INTRODUCTION TO PART FIVE: ANALYSING INTERACTION

The relevance of game theory and decision theory to practical disciplines, such as economics and ethics, is well known. Leopold-Wildburger discusses the relation of dialogue analysis to statistics and decision theory. She regards Bayesian thought as appropriate for the conduct and analysis of non-repeated discussion, and suggests that Harsanyi's extended and generalized n-person game theory -- where n may be greater than 2 -- should be used in developing an analytic theory of super-games and polylogues issuing from a system of somehow "opposed" interests, a "conflict", between n persons (or purposes). The full paper is presented elsewhere.

See in this connection also the paper by R. Giles (1976) and W. Hofstee (1980), both of which are listed in the Bibliography at the end of this volume; they discuss models of wager.

The paper by van Dun closes the book. It begins with a discussion of what it means to be reasonable, and goes on to formulate a basic principle for morality, in terms of respect for others, or self, as (a) *rational* creature(s). The last section of van Dun's paper contains a novel theoretical move in ethics. He formulates Lorenzen-strips (dialogical attack-defense rules) for statements concerning x's respect, or lack of respect, for y as a rational being.

It is interesting to contemplate the fact that on the definition of "being moral" that seems to follow from van Dun's fundamental principle of morality, Thomas Aquinas, Fichte, Hegel, and some others were immoral in the first degree towards female humans.

It remains to be seen what possibilities there are for developing van Dun's approach to ethical theory into a body of insights that may be applied as guidelines to practical situations. It would seem possible to exploit his ideas for the purpose of coming to grips with certain types of fallacy or "irrational" modes of argumentation. In fact, this may well turn out to be the first contribution to the systematic treatment of what I have elsewhere called higher-order rules -- all those rules in a theory of argumentation that regulate human intercourse, verbal or other, prior to and conducive to the coming into being of "rational" discussion (the first-order rules being those that regulate the moves *in* a "rational" discussion).

A deepened insight into what constitutes such proto-argumentative behaviour should satisfy anybody's desire for socio-cultural relevance, in fact such insight is, in all probability, the abstract commodity that mankind is most urgently in need of.

# A DECISION-THEORETICAL INTERPRETATION OF DIALOGUES

Ulrike Leopold-Wildburger

The main point of this paper is to demonstrate an analogy between the structure of dialogues and the structure of decision problems under conditions of uncertain information.

Let us first look at the situation where *one* agent tries to maximize his expected profit or utility. This agent can be a single person, a group, or an institution with in each case just *one* common opinion and pursuing *one* single purpose. This agent argues against nature and in consequence makes the decision on his (or her) own. This type of interplay (discussion) with nature is referred to as a *monologue*.

The consequences of argumentation within such a monologue and the eventual consequences of the decision of this agent depend upon the actions chosen by the decision-maker, but they are also functions of the state of the world. This state cannot be predicted with certainty, although complete ignorance does not prevail. We have some information about the different possible states of the world and are therefore able to formulate estimates about them. This way of estimating uses subjective probabilities, and Bayesian statistics should be used to tackle these problems. SAVAGE (1950) - adopting B. de Finetti's principles - proposed an axiomatisation of the rules of action which aim at maximizing subjectively expected utility of the consequences by applying subjective estimates for the probabilities of the different states of the world. If we follow their advice it is rational to be guided by the Bayesian principle: "Choose your decision so as to maximize your subjectively expected utility."

A monologue which is interpreted as a one-person-decision-problem with a finite number of decision-alternatives $a_i$ and with a finite number of possible states of the world $z_j$ can be described by a decision-matrix $\mathcal{D}$ in which a certain pay-off or utility is associated with each pair $(a_i, z_j)$.

In a concrete example [1)] that alternative remains as the optimal one which leads to the maximal expected utility.

We must, however, take into account the fact that both the estimates of the utilities of our possible actions and the estimates of the probabilities $p_i$ of the possible states of the world are subjective ones.

However, the fact that these estimates are subjective does not exclude the possibility that they are derived in a logical way from the structure of the situation. In this connection, we may think of Carnap's theory of logical probabilities (Carnap, 1962).

Bayesianism is thoroughly normative in the sense that it does not aim the description of actual decision behavior, but at a definition of the ideal of absolute rationality. Therefore, it seems to be adequate to adopt the Carnapian view of subjective probabilities rather than an interpretation which looks at subjective probabilities as purely psychological.

The literature on dialogue games aims at the clarification of fundamental philosophical questions. It is not concerned with the way in which dialogues take place in real life, but rather with an idealized picture of rational exchange of arguments. Therefore, it is natural to look at such dialogues in the light of

Bayesian decision theory.

Dialogues are situations in which the uncertainty of each dialogue-partner is partially caused by the arguments and by the actions due to the other decision-makers. We can inquire into *dialogues* and *n-person dialogues*, respectively, ($n \geq 2$) which give rise to n-person-decision-problems (with $n \geq 2$) in which each agent knows the existence of the other actors and knows their arguments. As a consequence, the actions $a_i$ of each agent likewise influence the state of the other agents, both their arguments and their decisions. This should reveal, on the one hand, the role of the subject matter of the discussion and the role of the decisions and, on the other hand, the role of the interaction between the agents. These situations can be described by strategic n-person games studies in the mathematical theory of games [2]. Before we can proceed with the discussion of these problems one should clarify the strategies and the pay-off-functions of the players (discussants). Rules for dialogical games of the kind employed, e.g. by HINTIKKA (1977) will be needed in defining the rules for n-person dialogical-games. The general setting of the game, for instance rules concerning the initial and non-initial moves of deductive and interrogative nature as well as the rules for winning and losing the dialogue, have to be established before starting the discussion of its purely decision- and game-theoretical aspects. After we have called attention to all these questions [3] (not to be discussed here any further), we can represent a n-person-game G in the following normal form:

$G = (A_1, \ldots, A_n; H)$

$A_i$ set of strategies of the player i; ($i = 1,2, \ldots, n$)

H assigns to each combination of strategies $a = (a_1, \ldots, a_n)$ $(a_i \in A_i)$ a pay-off-vector $H(a) = (H_1(a), \ldots, H_n(a))$; where H is called the pay-off-function of G.

The most important solution concept that can be used in the study of non-cooperative games is the concept of 'Nash Equilibrium'[4]. Such an equilibrium is a combination of strategies where a change of a player's strategy cannot yield a higher pay-off to this player if the other players use the prescribed strategies. Finally, it should be noted here that Bayesian theory, and by the same token the theory of games, is conceived of as being applied to non-repeated situations as they are very often found both in discussions and in decisions. If a monologue or dialogue is played several times a so-called super-game emerges which can again be handled by the same techniques. Super-games, however, can have properties which differ from those of unrepeated games. In the available literature on dialogue games the following question has not yet been posed ; Should dialogue games be analysed as one-shot games or as supergames? Probably at the present state of investigation it is advisable to restrict one's attention to dialogue games which are played just once. The task of analysing such games will be difficult enough.

*Appendix 1*

Bayesianism is concerned with axioms for rational behaviour in non-repeated discussion and decision situations where the aim of the game is the maximation of one's expected utility.

| | | state of the world | | | | expected utility |
|---|---|---|---|---|---|---|
| | | $z_1$ | $z_2$ | $z_3$ | $z_4$ | |
| probabilities | | $p_1=0.2$ | $p_2=0.1$ | $p_3=0.1$ | $p_4=0.4$ | |
| actions | $a_1$ | 1 | 2 | 4 | 9 | 4.8 |
| | $a_2$ | 2 | 4 | 4 | 8 | 5.2 |

Example *D*

*Appendix 2*

For a long time game-theoretical research was concentrated on two main areas: the study of solutions for two-person zero sum games and the development of concepts for cooperative games. Both areas are too restricted to cover satisfactorily those dialogue-situations where the dialogue-partners do not have exactly opposite interests. Recently, one can observe an increased tendency to do research in non-cooperative n-person game theory. The new equilibrium selection theory by HARSANYI and SELTEN is of special interest in this respect (Harsanyi-Selten, 1980). It aims at the rational selection of one equilibrium point out of many.

The new approach also permits the analysis of partially cooperative games as they sometimes arise in a dialogue-situation.

*Appendix 3*

See HINTIKKA (1977)

*Appendix 4*

$q^* = (q_1^*, \ldots, q_n^*)$ is an equilibrium if

$$H_i(q^*) = \max_{q_i \varepsilon Q_i} H_i(q^* | q_i) \quad \text{for } i = 1, \ldots, n$$

where $q^* | q_i = (q_1^*, \ldots, q_{i-1}^*, q_i, q_{i+1}^*, \ldots, q_n^*)$

and $Q_i$ is the set of all strategies of player i.

## NOTES

(1) Appendix 1

(2) Appendix 2

(3) Appendix 3

(4) Appendix 4

## REFERENCES

[1] Carnap, R., *Logical Foundations of Probability*, Chicago, 2 1962.

[2] Harsanyi, J. and R. Selten, *A General Theory of Equilibrium Selection in Games*, 1980, Chapter 1 and 2, Working Papers of the Institute of Mathematical Economics, University of Bielefeld, W-Germany; Chapter 3 and 4, Working Papers of the Center for Research in Management, University of California, Berkeley.

[3] Hintikka, J., "Language Games," *Dialectica, 31*, Nr. 3-4, p.225 - 245, 1977.

[4] Luce, R.D. and H. Raiffa, *Games and Decisions*, John Wiley and Sons, New York, 1957.

[5] Savage, L.J., *The Foundation of Statistics*, John Wiley and Sons, New York, 1950.

# ON THE PHILOSOPHY OF ARGUMENT AND THE LOGIC OF COMMON MORALITY.

F.van Dun

"The only desirable object which is
"quite satisfactory without any ul-
"terior reason for desiring it, is
"the reasonable itself."
C.S. PEIRCE

## 1. *Dialectical argument and first principles*

To say that man is a rational animal is to say that he is both an animal and a rational creature. But saying man is a rational creature is not at all like saying he is an animal creature. At least, the two are different for man himself, even if they might be instances of the same logical class for a non-human being. For us, human beings, the statement "Man is an animal creature" is an empirical statement, and if true, an empirical truth. But "Man is a rational creature" is not an empirical statement. Rather, for us, human beings, it is a dialectical truth.

The difference between the two statements is not one of logical form. Both are synthetic, logically contingent and hence carriers of information about the world. The difference follows from the fact that when arguing about the truth of these statements, we find ourselves in wholly different positions, depending on whether it is the truth of the one, or the truth of the other, which is being disputed.

We cannot reasonably deny that man is a rational creature.

True, given what we know as a result of the progressive accumulation of anatomical, physiological and bio-chemical data, we cannot reasonably deny that man is an animal creature either. But that does not make the latter proposition a dialectical truth. We can easily imagine circumstances in which it would indeed be very reasonable to refuse to believe that man is an animal creature. After all, there have been times and there are cultures still in which "enlightened opinion" was or is in favour of such a refusal. Moreover, why should all these "scientific data" matter?

On the other hand, however, one cannot, as a human being, imagine circumstances in which it would be reasonable for a human being to believe man is not a rational creature - not a creature endowed with rational abilities ("reason"), such as the ability to conceptualize, to construct logical complexes, propositions and norms, to interpret signs and to identify with some measure of success the meanings they carry; the ability to judge and to think, to apply the knowledge of the distinction between true and false, logically valid and logically invalid, desirable and undesirable, f a c i e n d u m and e v i t a n d u m ; the ability to "size up" (W.L. Matson's term), devise plans and carry them out or drop or revise them, and so on.

It would be unreasonable to refuse to believe man is a rational creature, not because of evidence, which might or might not strike us as relevant, nor of conjectures and hypotheses, which might or might not appear to be self-evident, but because of the existential situation created by the question itself: whether to believe man is a rational creature or not to believe it. There are perhaps, as Nietzsche warned us, no eternal facts. Still, that "I" and "you" are rational creatures is the one and only inescapable, necessary, fact in all arguments, and is untouched even by the objection that the argument itself may be illusory: *as an objection* that remark is but one move in the argument, although it may of course not be intended to be an objection, but then it is no longer part of the argument - as when it is intended to be the equivalent of "Get lost". Brought to light by our argument, i.e., by the a c t i v i t y itself of arguing, it is in no way dependent upon what our arguments qua propositions are: it is a dialectical truth that "You" and "I" are rational.

But that it is, in this sense, a necessary fact that we are rational, does not in itself constitute a reason why we should recognize it as such, why we ought not to deny it. We cannot r e a s o n a b l y deny it, but we c a n deny it. Why should this inability to reasonably deny it signify that we ought not to deny it? Again the answer is strictly dialectical in nature: the question is self-answering. We ought to be reasonable, to respect our rational nature, i.e. we ought to use our rational abilities and use them correctly, according to their immanent laws: that we ought to believe only what is true, and ought to desire only what is desirable, that we ought to make our judgments carefully, taking into account all the relevant considerations, that we ought to respect the distinction between validity and invalidity in making inferences, by seeking the former and avoiding the latter, and that we ought to apply the conclusions of correct inferences from true premisses in devising our plans of action.

It is apparently within our power to be unreasonable, but we cannot reasonably deny we ought to be reasonable. Whatever reasons I may give you for denying with me that we ought to be reasonable, they'd better be good ones, i.e. reasons which will make you (and me) understand why we ought not to be reasonable - propositions which you ought to judge to be true and appropriate and conclusive. But if I could find such reasons, if I could convince you that we ought not to be reasonable, I would in the same breath have convinced you that my "reasons" are not to be taken to be propositions whose acceptance should be followed by the acceptance of my conclusion, or at least, propositions whose acceptance should incline you, given our common background knowledge, to accept my conclusion. I cannot reasonably *argue* that we ought not to be reasonable - and neither can you. It is easy to deceive ourselves into believing we are arguing reasonably, by accepting the conclusion on the grounds that we ought to be reasonable, when the conclusion is that we ought not to be. As soon as this incongruence, this dialectical contradiction, is pointed out, we should admit that we cannot reasonably refuse to believe we ought to be reasonable.

Can't I object that this does *not* prove we ought to be reasonable? Of course I can - only I should not go on to argue that there can be a reason why we should conclude we ought not to be reasonable. I can choose not to argue, but once the choice is made I can only stick to it or repudiate it - and I do not stick to it by getting into an argument, trying to prove or make it plausible that my choice was *the right choice to make*. There is and can be no justification for my refusal or denial. I should not even go on to ask why there should be a justification, or, maybe, why I should look after my reputation as a bona fide person. A flat refusal to justify my refusal is all I can permit myself.

As soon as I attempt to justify my refusal, as soon as I say "Well, we ought not to be reasonable, and here is why...", I identify the validity of that norm as problematic, as a problem, something to think about. But by admitting there exist problems, which is not the same as having problems (possibly without being aware of them or without being aware that what I have are *problems*), I give myself the command "Be reasonable: care for truth, care for consistency, beware of falsity, critically evaluate your premisses...". While I am aware of something as a problem, my *norma faciendi* (for to think is to act) is

"You should think, deliberate to the best of your abilities whether it is best to do A or to do B". In most cases, the answer is not given to me - otherwise there would be no problem. But in one case, the case under consideration, to ask the question is to answer it, viz. when the "problem" is whether I should think correctly, judge carefully, seek the truth, act on the best advice, etc. To assume this is a problem is to accept the norm that I ought to be reasonable.

The question, whether I should think or reason correctly and from true premisses, whether I ought to be reasonable and respect my rational nature, is indeed self-answering. The point is not that it is self-contradictory in this case to say, that a) we are dealing with a question and b) the answer is negative. We should not presuppose that the norm, that we ought not to let contradictions go uncorrected, is valid. Rather the point is that *putting* the question presupposes *answering* it - it is therefore a relation between actions which is decisive here. In fact, putting the question *is* answering it positively. The relationship is an identity: there is but one act. If I say A one day and not-A the next, I may be contradicting myself; I may also be correcting myself. In any case, there are two separate intentions to consider, and the question is whether there has been a change of mind between the occurrence of the first and the occurrence of the second. If that is the case, we have to cancel the first statement, at least for purposes of logical evaluation. But with respect to the question, whether we ought to be reasonable or not, it is impossible to answer it at a later moment in the negative, with the intention of cancelling the positive answer "given" at the same moment the question was asked: to do so would destroy the question, and hence also the second answer *as an answer to that question*. The issue is not whether we ought to avoid contradictions; it is a matter of mere logical analysis that, *if you want to reason correctly,* you should avoid contradictions. But our question is whether we ought to reason correctly, whether we ought to make use of our rational abilities. And *that* question is self-answering. In the sense, then, that this "question" is for each of us the ultimate question, the answer to it is the ultimate answer - the first principle.

Thus, not only can we not reasonably deny we ought to be reasonable, meaning that we ought not to deny it, if we want to be reasonable; but also we cannot even maintain it is permissible not to want to be reasonable, for when we think of that as a meaningful piece of information, an answer to a question, we see it is an answer destroying the question itself. Once the question is raised of the validity of the norm, that we ought to be reasonable , there is but one answer: it is valid. To dispute its validity is to recognize its validity. But if it is valid, then *we ought to be reasonable, ought to respect our rational nature.* It is pointless to ask why. There is no way in which one can cast doubt on its validity. One cannot even consciously refuse to raise the question of its validity, for then the question would have to be there already. One can only refuse to think about it: here is a normative rule one can break but cannot contest.

This first principle, that we ought to be reasonable, holds for you as well as for me, for if it holds for me, it must necessarily hold also for you - who are my alter ego in this attempted dialogue. To take a dialogue seriously is to take the other, the "you" seriously; the dialogue will not appear even potentially successful if one does not look upon the other as one whom one can indentify with, without relinquishing one's own identity - an alternative ego; or if one does not present oneself as an alternative ego to the other. This holds true whoever "you", whoever "I" may be, as long as "you" is someone whom "I" can talk to and who can talk back, as long as the "you" is someone who could be the opposite number of the "I" in a dialogue - the writer or the reader, the speaker or the hearer. "You" and "I", being each an "I-You", ought to be reasonable - i.e., w e ought to be reasonable.

## 2. *The fundamental principle of morality*

There are, then, at least two dialectical truths. The first is that you and I are rational creatures; the second that you and I ought to be reasonable. Because of the second, we can say not merely that we cannot reasonably deny the first, but also that we ought not to deny it. If these dialectical propositions are errors, they are irrefutable errors: there is no way for men qua rational creatures to find out what is wrong with them, just as there is no way for men qua rational creatures to cast doubt on their truth. The buck of nihilism stops here; non-tautological, yet irrefutable, these propositions are true sub specie rationis humanae. And that is all we should wish for, when doing philosophy.

As I have remarked already, these truths hold for every "I" and every "you", hence for every "I-You". But who is an I-You? The application of a concept is a distinct matter, and this is no place to go into the difficulties. Let us agree that, at least, every human being ought to respect himself or herself as the rational creature he or she is. But then it follows that every human being ought to have the opportunity to respect himself as a rational creature. As a matter of fact, being a rational creature i s having the opportunity to respect one's rational nature, but as being a rational creature depends on the fulfilment of certain conditions, some of which can be affected by human action, and as one can be deprived of such opportunities without being deprived of one's rational nature, this implied norm means more than that every human being ought to have a rational nature - it means that all human beings ought to respect not only their own, but also every other human being's rational nature. Every human being ought to take care not to destroy or impair any human being's opportunity to be reasonable (which is necessarily also an opportunity to be unreasonable).

This conclusion, that every human being ought to respect every human being, himself as well as others, as the rational creatures they all are, I call the fundamental principle of morality. It is fundamental in the logical sense: capable of serving as the axiom of morality - but it is not fundamental in the sense of dialectical reasoning, as we have seen. I call it a *moral* principle, not only because there are precedents, but also because the *Ought* of the fundamental principle is the absolute and unconditional Ought without which the rules of morality would not only be "words without the Sword", but arbitrary words as well.

Not wishing to go into the question of applying the dialectically established norms and their logical implications to the context of transitive actions, I cannot here dispel the misgivings the reader might have about the moral significance of these precepts of reason. But I can point out that no incongruence is involved in saying the moral is the reasonable, the moral life the intelligent life. The moral point of view is not just another point of view, different from, but otherwise on a par with, say, the point of view of the individual egoist or of the national security zealot.

It has been said that the question "Why should I be moral?" is not self-answering when the 'should' which occurs in it is not taken "in the moral sense"; that, in that case, it is a request for a *reason* (not a motive) why one should adopt the moral point of view rather than any other. But in that case one has already "adopted" the point of view that one ought to be reasonable, and hence has already committed oneself to everything that is implied by it - including the norm that one ought to respect every rational creature's rational nature. The failure to notice the existence of dialectical truths in the realm of the Is as well as of the Ought does not imply the non-existence of these truths or of the connexion between reason and morality.

One important consequence of our arguments should be pointed out: it is quite possible to fail to respect oneself as a rational creature without failing to respect any other rational creature as such, but it is not possible to fail to respect another without failing to respect oneself. This is so because by failing to respect another as a rational creature one acts against the moral Ought, and to act against the moral Ought is to fail to respect oneself as a rational creature: the moral Ought is not an arbitrary, conditional Ought - or rather, if it is conditional, it is conditional only on the existence of rational creatures.

Lack of space forbids me to discuss some of the implications of the existence of non-tautological but non-falsifiable dialectical truths, especially for the methodology of the sciences of human action.[1] I will conclude this short reminder of the fact that the two propositions which have played such an outstanding role in the shaping of Western philosophy are still valid starting-points, with a short discussion of the logic of common morality.

## *3. A dialogical approach to the logic of common morality*

I shall adopt a Lorenzen-Lorenz dialogical approach to the logic of common morality. Such an approach is not only, in some sense, the most "natural"; it is also, in view of my preceding discussion, the most fitting. Let me first introduce the following formulae:

F1) fxy =: x fails to respect y as a rational creature

F2) fxy/dx$\alpha$ =: by doing $\alpha$, x would fail to respect y qua rational creature.[2]

F3) Pdx$\alpha$ =: it is (morally) permissible that x does $\alpha$

F4) Fdx$\alpha$ =: it is (morally) impermissible that x does $\alpha$

F5) Odx$\alpha$ =: it is (morally) obligatory that x does $\alpha$

F6) Rdx$\alpha$ =: x has the right to do $\alpha$

F7) $\bar{R}$dx$\alpha$ =: x does not have the right to do $\alpha$

F8) Ddx$\alpha$ =: x has a duty to do $\alpha$

Assuming that "failing to respect someone as the rational creature he or she is" is not an incoherent concept, we may adopt the following attack-defence rules:

| | A | | B | | A |
|---|---|---|---|---|---|
| (1)[3] | fxy/fxy | :: | I give up | :: | |
| (2)[4] | fxz/-fxy | :: | I win | :: | |
| (3) | fxy/dx$\alpha$ | ⋮⋮ | ? dx$\alpha$ | ⋮⋮ | fxy |

The third rule stipulates that there are two ways to challenge a statement of the form F1: the challenger may choose whether he wants the other to explain just how doing $\alpha$ would amount to failing to respect another as a rational creature, or whether he will try to disprove the other's thesis in the particular case under discussion.

In view of my previous remark that it is is impossible to fail to respect oneself when one is not respecting another, the following should also be accepted as a Win-position for the Logical Validity Proponent in a Lorenzen-Lorenz dialogue:

(4) fxy :: fxx

Let me now turn to the deontic modalities P and R : obviously, in order to challenge the thesis that some action is morally permissible, it is sufficient to show that, by doing that action, one would fail to respect at least one person or rational creature qua rational creature. Thus we have:

(5) $Pdx\alpha$ :: $fxa/dx\alpha$ ::

If the challenger succeeds in defending $fxa/dx\alpha$ , he has established that doing $\alpha$ is morally impermissible for x. But he has not established that x has no right to do $\alpha$ .

(6) $Rdx\alpha$ :: $fxa/dx\alpha$ :: $x = a$

It is morally impermissible to fail to respect oneself as a rational creature, but that cannot mean that one does not have the right to do that. (Remember that to have the opportunity to respect oneself is also to have the opportunity not to respect oneself, and that we ought to respect every other person's opportunity to make his own choices.) Here the challenger has to show that the actor fails to respect a n o t h e r person.

The other rules need even less comment

(7) $Fdx\alpha$ :: $Pdx\alpha$ ::

(8) $\bar{R}dx\alpha$ :: $Rdx\alpha$ ::

(9) $Odx\alpha$ ⋮ $Fdx\alpha$ / $P{\sim}dx\alpha$ ⋮

(10) $Ddx\alpha$ ⋮ $\bar{R}dx\alpha$ / $R{\sim}dx\alpha$ ⋮

A Lorenzen-Lorenz Proponent should be able to defend the following initial positions against all attack-strategies; for all x and y,

(i) Ffxy ( and O-fxy )

(ii) Ffxx ( and O-fxx )

i.e. an LLP should be able to defend the fundamental principle of morality.

(iii) $Pdx\alpha \equiv \sim(\exists y)(fxy/dx\alpha)$

(iv) $Rdx\alpha \equiv \sim(\exists y)(y \neq x \ \& \ fxy/dx\alpha)$

(v) $Pdx\alpha \equiv \sim Fdx\alpha$

(vi) $Rdx\alpha \equiv \sim\overline{R}dx$

(vii) $Odx\alpha \equiv (\exists y)(fxy/\sim dx\alpha) \ \& \sim (\exists y)(fxy/dx\alpha)$

(viii) $Ddx\alpha \equiv (\exists y)(fxy/\sim dx\alpha \ \& \ x \neq y) \ \& \sim (\exists y)(fxy/dx\alpha \ \& \ x \neq y)$

(ix) $Odx\alpha \rightarrow F\sim dx\alpha$

(x) $Pdx\alpha \rightarrow Rdx\alpha$

(xi) $Ddx\alpha \rightarrow Odx\alpha$

(xii) $Odx\alpha \rightarrow Pdx\alpha$

(xiii) $Ddx\alpha \rightarrow Rdx\alpha$

Notice that we do not have as defensible initial positions:

(xiv)* $Pdx\alpha \vee P\sim dx\alpha$

i.e. moral perplexity is not ruled out, and

(xv )* $Fdx\alpha \rightarrow P\sim dx\alpha$

The consistency of a normative system does not imply that a person should never find himself perplexed: it may be morally impermissible to do a given action and morally impermissible not to do it. As Donagan, following Aquinas, notes:"A moral system is inconsistent only if it allows the possibility that, without any wrongdoing on his part, a man may find himself in a situation in which he can only escape doing one wrong by doing another: that is only if it allows the possibility of perplexity *simpliciter* [as opposed to perplexity *secundum quid*]."[5] Let us introduce the predicator"...is morally irreproachable", to be used with respect to persons according to the following attack-defence rule:

(11) Mx :: fxa ::

then we do have, not only that $Mx \equiv \sim(\exists y)fxy$, but also the following

(xiv) $Mx \rightarrow (Pdx\alpha \vee P{\sim}dx\alpha)$

and

(xv ) $Mx \rightarrow (Fdx\alpha \rightarrow P{\sim}dx\alpha)$

so that the morally irreproachable person need not ever be morally perplexed. Also, of course

(xvii) $(Fdx\alpha \ \& \ dx\alpha) \rightarrow {\sim}Mx$

In direct analogy to (11) we may formulate the following:

(12) $Lx :: fxa :: x = a$

with "...is law-abiding" (or some other appropriate formula) for "L..."

## NOTES

(1) Cf. F. van Dun, "Het epistemologisch statuut van de wetenschappen van het menselijk handelen" (The epistemological status of the sciences of human action) in Tijdschrift voor Sociale Wetenschappen 24, 2, 1979, pp.181-192.

(2) Or: "if x would do $\alpha$, he would fail to respect y qua rational creature". I shall not go into the matter of defining the adequate attack-defense rules for conditional statements of the form p/q (if q would be true, p would be true) since that would take me too far afield. For my purpose the attack-defence rules numbered (1), (2) and (3) may suffice.

(3) I.e., if A states that x, by failing to respect y, would fail to respect y, and his opponent B has no other alternative except to challenge A's last statement, B has to concede defeat. Given an adequate attack-defence rule for statements of the form p/q, this rule would obviously be redundant.

(4) I.e., if A can be forced to state that x, by not failing to respect y, would fail to respect some rational creature z, his opponent B may claim victory. The rationale for this rule is that, on the assumption that the system of common morality is coherent, it is impossible that the mere fact that x does not fail to respect y should be adduced as a reason for explaining why he fails to respect someone else. Note that this implies that our formulae should be taken to refer to the action as described. Clearly, my shooting M may be described (rather implausibly) as my not failing to respect N - but that it can be so described does not make it morally permissible. An action is morally impermissible iff there is one true description of it under which it is impermissible.

(5) Alan Donagan, The Theory of Morality. The University of Chicago Press, Chicago and London 1977, p.145.

# THEORY OF ARGUMENTATION: A CHRONOLOGICAL BIBLIOGRAPHY OF SOME IMPORTANT WORKS

## A. CHRONOLOGICAL BIBLIOGRAPHY


1725 Watts, I.

*Logick, or the Right Use of Reason in the Enquiry after Truth, with a Variety of Rules to Guard Against Error, in the Affairs of Religion and Human Life, as well as in the Sciences.*

London: printed for John Clark and Richard Hett.

1824 Bentham, J.

*The Book of Fallacies: From Unfinished Papers of Jeremy Bentham. By a Friend.*

London: Hunt

(Republished under the title: *The Handbook of Political Fallacies*. Revised and edited by Harold A. Larrabee. Baltimore: Johns Hopkins, 1952)

1828 Whately, R.

*Elements of Rhetoric, Comprising an Analysis of the Laws of Moral Evidence and of Persuasion, with Rules for Argumentative Composition and Elocution.*

Edited by Douglas Ehninger. Carbondale

(Southern Illinois University Press, 1963. Photo-offset reprint of the seventh edition)

1830 Schopenhauer,A.
/31 "Eristische Dialektik"

First published in: *Aus Arthur Schopenhauers handschriftlichen Nachlass. Abhandlungen, Anmerkungen, etc hrsg. von Jul. Frauenstädt.*
Leipzig, 1864
Recent publication in: *Der handschriftliche Nachlass.* Dritter Band. Berliner Manuskripte (1818-1830). Herausgegeben von Arthur Hübsche. Frankfurt am Main: Waldemar Kramer, 1970, pp. 666-695

1882 Sidgwick,A.
"The Location of Fallacy."
*Mind*, vol.7,pp.55-64

1884 Sidgwick,A.
*Fallacies. A View of Logic from the Practical Side.*
New York: Appleton

1927 Adler,M.
*Dialectic.*
New York

1938 Naess,A.
"Erkenntnis und wissenschaftliches Verhalten". Entgegnung von A. Naess auf die Bemerkungen von H.J. Pos. (*Theoria,* 3, 1937, pp. 117-124)
*Theoria,* 4,pp.62-68

Naess,A.
*"Truth" as Conceived by those who are not Professional Philosophers.*
Oslo: Det Norske Videnskaps-Akademi i Oslo

1941 Naess, A.
*En del elementaere logiske emner.*
Oslo (mimeographed)

Naess, A.
*En del elementaere logiske emner.*
Oslo, 1947

Naess, A.
*Communication and Argument. Elements of Applied Semantics.*
[translation of Naess 1947]
London, Oslo, 1966

Naess, A.
*Kommunikation und Argumentation. Eine Einführung in die angewandte Semantik.*
Kronberg: Scriptor Verlag, 1975
(translation of: *En del elementaere emner,*
1975: 11th edition)

Naess, A.
*Elementaire argumentatieleer.*
Baarn: Ambo, 1977
(translation of: *En del elementaere emner,*
1976, 11th edition)

1945 Perelman, Ch.
*De la justice.*
Bruxelles: Office de Publicité

1947 Crawshay-Williams, R.
*The Comforts of Unreason. A Study of the Motives behind Irrational Thought.*
London: Kegan Paul

Naess, A.
*Usaklighetsanalyse. En innledning.* (Analysing irrelevance. An intróduction.) *Filosofiske Problemer, nr. 6*
Oslo

1949 Naess, A.
*Innföring i logikk og metodelaere.* (Introduction to logic and methodology.), *Filosofiske Problemer, nr. 14*
Oslo

1950 Baird, A.C.
*Argumentation, Discussion, and Debate.*
New York: McGraw-Hill

1951 Naess, A.
"Analytical Survey of Agreements and Disagreements."
in: R. McKeon (Ed), *Democracy in a World of Tensions. A Symposium prepared by UNESCO.*
Chicago, pp. 447-512

1952 Naess, A.
"Toward a Theory of Interpretation and Preciseness."
in: L. Linsky (ed.), *Semantics and the Philosophy of Language. A Collection of Readings.*
Urbana, Ill., pp. 248-269

Naess, A.
"Mer saklighet i öst-vest debattene!" (More objectivity in the East-West discussion!)
in: A. Haaland, H. Ofstad (eds.) *Tenk en gang til; om fred og forsvar.*
Oslo, pp. 177-188

Perelman,Ch, & Olbrechts-Tyteca,L.
*Rhétorique et philosophie.*
Paris: Presses Universitaires De France

1953 Naess,A.
*Interpretation and Preciseness.A Contribution to the Theory of Communication. Det Norske Videnskaps-Akademi i Oslo, Skrifter* II, *Hist.-Filos. Klasse, 1953,No.1*
Oslo

Naess,A.
*An Empirical Study of the Expressions "True", "Perfectly Certain" and "Extremely Probable". Det Norske Videnskaps-Akademi i Oslo, Avhandlinger* II, *Hist.-Filos. Klasse, 1953*, *No.4*
Oslo

Naess,A.
"Forekomstanalysens grunnproblemer." ( The basic problems of occurrence analysis),
in: *Semantiske problemer*,pp.75-77
(Innledningsforedrag og diskusjonsreferater fra krets 5. Nordisk sommeruniversitet.2.sesjon.Ustaoset 1952.)
Oslo

1955 Beth,E.W.
"Semantic Entailment and Formal Derivability."
*Mededelingen der Kon. Ned. Acad. Wet.*,New Series, vol.18, no.13
Amsterdam

Bird,O.
"Dialectic in Philosophical Inquiry."
*Dialectica*,9,pp.287-304

Lorenzen,P.
"Protologik.Ein Beitrag zum Begründungsproblem der Logik."
*Kantstudien*, Band 47 Heft 4, 1955-56,pp.350-358

Perelman,Ch. & Olbrechts-Tyteca,L.
"Les notions et l'argumentation."
*Archivio di Filosofia, vol. Semantica*,
Rome,pp.249-269

1956 Howell,W.S.
*Logic and Rhetoric in England, 1500-1700.*
Princeton N.J.:Princeton University Press

Naess,A.
*Wie fördert man heute die empirische Bewegung? Eine Auseinandersetzung mit dem Empirismus von Otto Neurath und Rudolph Carnap.* (How should the empirical movement be promoted today? Critical reflections on the empiricism of Otto Neurath and Rudolph Carnap.) *Filosofiske Problemer 19*
Oslo

Naess,A., Christophersen,J.A. and Kvalö,K.
*Democracy, Ideology and Objectivity, Studies in the Semantics and Cognitive Analysis of Ideological Controversy.*
Oslo

1956/58 Naess,A.
"Logical Equivalence, Intentional Isomorphism and Synonymity as Studied by Questionnaires. Dedicated to the Memory of Gerrit Mannoury."
*Synthese*,10, 9 unpag. pp.

1957 Crawshay-Williams,R.
*Methods and Criteria of Reasoning. An Inquiry into the Structure of Controversy.*
London:Kegan Paul

Naess,A.
"Valgkamp og saklighet."(Election campaign and objective relevance), 4 pp. mimeographed. *(Universitetsforlagets kronikktjeneste 1957: 14)*
Oslo

1958 Ong,W.J.
*Ramus, Method and the Decay of Dialogue; from the Art of Discourse to the Art of Reason.*
Cambridge: Harvard University Press

Perelman,Ch.
"L'argument pragmatique."
*Logique et Analyse,* 1,pp. 14-23

Perelman,Ch.
"Les rapports théoriques de la pensée et de l'action."
in: *Entretiens philosophiques de Varsovie,* de l'Institut International de Philosophie, Varsovie, Ossolineum, pp. 23-28

Perelman, Ch. & Olbrechts-Tyteca,L.
"De la temporalité comme caractère de l'argumentation."
*Archivio de Filosofia, vol.* II *Tempo,*
Rome,pp.115-133

Perelman,Ch. & Olbrechts-Tyteca,L.
*La nouvelle rhétorique: traité de l'argumentation.*
Paris: Presses Universitaires de France

Perelman,Ch. & Olbrechts-Tyteca,L.
*The New Rhetoric.A Treatise on Argumentation.*
Notre Dame. London: University of Notre Dame Press, 1969 (translation of: La nouvelle rhëtorique: traité de l'argumentation, 1958)

Toulmin,S.E.
*The Uses of Argument.*
Cambridge: Cambridge University Press

Toulmin,S.E.
*Der Gebrauch von Argumenten.*
Kronberg: Scriptor Verlag, 1975
(translation of: *The Uses of Argument* , 1958)

Wittgenstein,L.
*Philosophische Untersuchungen.*
Oxford: Basil Blackwell

1959 Beth.E.W.
"Considérations heuristiques sur les méthodes de déduction par séquences."
*Logique et Analyse,* NS.2, pp. 153-159

Fearnside, W.W. & Holther, W.B.
*Fallacy: the Counterfeit of Argument.*
Englewood Cliffs, N.Y.: Prentice-Hall

Johnstone,H.W.
*Philosophy and Argument.*
University Park, Pennsylvania: Pennsylvania State Universit Press

Perelman,Ch.
"Les cadres sociaux de l'argumentation."
Rapport présenté au second colloque de l'Association des

sociologues de langue francaise, à Royaumont, le 18 mars 1959.

*Cahiers Internationaux de Sociologie, Paris, vol XXVI,* pp.123-135

1960 Lorenzen,P.

"Logik und Agon."

in: *Atti del XII Congresso Internazionale di Filosofia (Venezia, 12-18 Settembre 1958). Volume quarto.*

Firenze: Sansoni, pp. 187-194

1961 Apostel,L.

"Logic and Ontology."

*Philosophy Today,* 5,pp.40-58

Lorenz,K.

*Arithmetik und Logik als Spiele.*

Kiel (Dissertation)

Lorenzen,P.

"Ein dialogisches Konstruktivitätskriterium."

in: *Infinitistic Methods. Proceedings of the Symposium on Foundations of Mathematics. (Warsaw, 2-9 September 1959).*

Oxford. London. New York. Paris: Pergamon Press, pp. 193-200

Passmore,J.A.

*Philosophical Reasoning.*

New York: Scribners

1962 St. Aubyn,G

*The Art of Argument.*

New York

Hintikka,J.
*Knowledge and Belief.*
Ithaca N.Y.: Cornell University Press

Naess,A.
"L'Emploi de la disjonction chez les adolescents." (Trad. par B. Matalon) in: Implication, formalisation et logique naturelle par E.W. Beth et al.,pp. 151-161
*Etudes d'épistémologie génétique, 16*
Paris

Naess,A.
"Typology of Questionnaires Adopted to the Study of Expressions with Closely Related Meanings."
in: *Logic and Language. Studies Dedicated to Rudolph Carnap on the Occasion of his Seventieth Birthday.*
Dordrecht, pp.206-219

de Rijk,L.M.
"On the Twelfth Century Theories of Fallacies."
in: *Logica Modernorum.A Contribution to the History of Early Terminist Logic.* Vol.I
Assen: van Gorcum

1963 Apostel,L.
"Rhétorique, psycho-sociologie et logique."
*Logique et Analyse, N.S.* 6, n 21-24, pp.236-314

*La théorie de l'argumentation-perspectives et applications.*
Collection published by the Centre Nationale Belge de Recherches de Logique. Louvain, Paris

Drieschner,R.
*Untersuchungen zur dialogischen Deutung der Logik.*
Hamburg, Dissertation

Mittelstaedt, Peter.
*Philosophische Probleme der modernen Physik.*
Mannheim: Bibliographisches Institut; 2nd revised and extended edition: 1966 [translated *Philosophical Problems of Modern Physics,*
Dordrecht: Reidel (1976)].

Naess, A.
"'Rimelig tolkning' i ELE." ("Reasonable interpretation" in ELE/ Communication and Argument.)
in: Filosofiske notater til elementaer logikk, semantikk og metodelaere, 1. *Filosofiske Problemer, 25,* pp.1-9
Oslo

Naess, A.
"Påstandslikhet. En del sitater fra ELE og ILM." (Propositional equality. Some quotations from(1947) and (1949).)
in: Filosofiske notater til elementaer logikk, semantikk og metodelaere,1. *Filosofiske Problemer, 25*, pp. 47-56
Oslo

Naess, A.
"En presiseringsretning av 'Formuleringen T er ullen.'"('The formulation T is fuzzy' made more precise in one possible direction.)
in: Filosofiske notater til elementaer logikk, semantikk og metodelaere, 1. *Filosofiske Problemer,25*, pp. 85-86
Oslo

Naess, A.
"Kriteriene på tendensiöse fremstillinger og sort-hvitt tenkning." (Criteria of biased representation and black-and-white cognition.)

in: Filosofiske notater til elementaer logikk, semantikk og metodelaere, 1. *Filosofiske problemer,25*, pp.86-87 Oslo

Naess,A.
"Kriterier på ikke-ensidighet og mangel på tendens."(Criteria of impartiality and unbiased representation.)
in: Filosofiske notater til elementaer logikk, semantikk og metodelaere, 1. *Filosofiske Problemer,25*, pp.98-100 Oslo

Naess,A.
"Skinnproblemer."(Pseudo-problems)
in: Filosofiske notater til elementaer logikk, semantikk og metodelaere, 1. *Filosofiske Problemer, 25*, pp. 137-139 Oslo

Perelman,Ch.
*The Idea of Justice and the Problem of Argument.*
London: Routledge & Kegan Paul

Perelman,Ch.
*Justice et raison.*
Bruxelles: Presses Universitaires de Bruxelles

1964 Alston,W.P.
*The Philosophy of Language.*
Englewood Cliffs

Naess,A.
"Notat om avgrensninger." (Note on demarcations.)
in: Filosofiske notater til elementaer logikk, semantikk og metodelaere, 2. *Filosofiske Problemer, 26*, pp. 52-59 Oslo

Naess,A.
"Ubestemthet ved formuleringer og utsagn." (Indefiniteness of formulations and statements.)
in: Filosofiske notater til elementaer logikk, semantikk og metodelaere,2. *Filosofiske Problemer,26*, pp. 76-101
Oslo

Naess,A.
"Presisjonsundersökelser ved ekvivalensmetoden." (Investigation of precision by the method of equivalence.)
in: Filosofiske notater til elementaer logikk, semantikk og metodelaere,2. *Filosofiske Problemer,26*, pp.102-104
Oslo

Stegmüller,W.
"Remarks on the Completeness of Logical Systems Relative to the Validity-Concepts of P. Lorenzen and K. Lorenz."
*Notre Dame Journal of Formal Logic*, 5, pp. 81-112

1965 Cole,R.
"A Note on Informal Fallacies."
*Mind*, 74,pp. 432-433

Lorenzen,P.
"Methodisches Denken."
*Ratio*,Bd.VII,pp. 1-23

Natanson, M.& Johnstone, H.W. (eds.)
*Philosophy, Rhetoric and Argumentation.*
University Park: Pennsylvania State University Press

Weinberger,O.
*Der Relativierungsgrundsatz und der Reduktionsgrundsatz-zwei Prinzipien des dialektischen Denkens. Eine logisch-methodologische Studie.*
Pragúe *(Rospravy Československé Akademie Věd. Řada společenských věd. Ročník 75-Sesit 5)*

1966 Lloyd,G.E.R.
*Polarity and Analogy: Two Types of Argumentation in Early Greek Thought.*
Cambridge: Cambridge University Press

Lorenzen,P.
"Logische Strukturen in der Sprache."
*Studium Generale, 19,* Heft 7, pp. 398-401

Miller,G.R. & Nilsen, Th.R. (eds.)
*Perspectives on Argumentation.*
Chicago: Scott, Foresman and Company

Zapffe,P.W.
*Den logiske sandkasse. Elementaer logikk for universitet og selvstudium.* (The logical nursery. Elementary logic for the universities and for private study.)
Oslo, Bergen, Tromsö

1967 Hintikka,J.
"A Programme and a Set of Concepts for Philosophical Logic.
*The Monist,* 51,pp.69-92

Lorenz,K. & Mittelstrass,J.
"Die Hintergehbarkeit der Sprache."
*Kantstudien,* 58, pp. 187-208

Lorenz,K. & Mittelstrass,J.
"On Rational Philosophy of Language. The Programme in Plato's Cratylus Reconsidered."
*Mind,* 76, pp.1-20

Kamlah,W. & Lorenzen,P.
*Logische Propädeutik oder Vorschule des vernünftigen Redens.*
Mannheim: B.I.

Seidler,I.
"The Iconolatric Fallacy. On the Limitations of the Internal Method of Criticism."
*The Journal of Aesthetics and Art Criticism*, 26, pp.9-16

Willard Oliver,J.
"Formal Fallacies and other Invalid Arguments."
*Mind,* 76, pp.463-478

1968 Barth,E.M,
"De algemene Hond en het Niets."
*De Gids,* 131, pp.275-292

Hintikka,J.
"Epistemic Logic and the Methods of Philosophical Analysis."
*The Australian Journal of Philosophy,* 46, pp.37-51

Hintikka,J.
"Behavioral Criteria of Radical Translation."
*Synthese,* 19, pp.69-81

Hintikka,J.
*Language-Games for Quantifiers.*
*American Philosophical Quarterly Monograph Series, no 2: Studies in Logical Theory,* ed. by Nicolas Rescher.
Oxford: Basil Blackwell, pp.46-72

Johnstone,H.W.
"Theory of Argumentation."
in: Klibansky (ed.), *Contemporary Philosophy*, Bd.1, Firenze, 1968, pp.177-184

Kambartel,F.
"Überlegungen zum pragmatischen und argumentativen Fundament der Logik."
in: K.Lorenz (Hrsg.), *Konstruktionen versus Positionen. Beiträge zur Diskussion um die konstruktive Wissenschaftstheorie.*
Berlin

Lorenz,K.
"Dialogspiele als semantische Grundlage von Logikkalkülen."
*Archiv für Mathematische Logik und Grundlagenforschung*, 11,pp.32-55,73-100

Lorenzen,P.
*Methodisches Denken.*
Frankfurt am Main: Suhrkamp Verlag

Mackinnon,W.J.
"Communication, Material Conditions,and Future Sociocultural Development."
*The Philosophical Forum*, 7,pp.41-54

McKeon,R.
"Discourse,Demonstration, Verification, and Justification."
*Logique et Analyse*, 11,pp.37-94

Perelman,Ch.
"Recherches interdisciplinaires sur l'argumentation."
Rapport présenté, le 6 septembre 1966, à Evian, au Congrès Mondial de Sociologie.
*Logique et Analyse*, 11, pp.502-511

Perelman,Ch.
"Rhetoric and Philosophy."
*Philosophy and Rhetoric*,1,pp. 15-24

Perelman,Ch.
"Une théorie philosophique de l'argumentation."
*Archiv für Rechts- und Sozialphilosophie*,54,pp. 141-151

Sesonske,A.
"To Make the Weaker Argument Defeat the Stronger."
*Journal of the History of Philosophy*,6,pp.217-231

1969 Apostel,L.
"A Proposal in the Analysis of Questions."
*Logique et Analyse*,12,pp.376-381

Downie,R.S.
"The Right to Criticize."
*Philosophy*,44,pp. 116-126

Hintikka,J.
*Models for Modalities: Selected Essays.*
Dordrecht: Reidel

Lorenzen,P.
"Logic and Grammar."
*The Monist*,53,pp.195-203

Lorenzen,P.
*Normative Logic and Ethics.*
Mannheim: Hochschultaschenbücher Verlag

Scholuls,P.A.
"Communication, Argumentation, and Presupposition in Philosophy."
*Philosophy and Rhetoric*,2,pp. 183-199

Searle,J.R.
*Speech Acts. An Essay in the Philosophy of Language.*
Cambridge: Cambridge University Press

1970 Angelelli,I.
"The Techniques of Disputation in the History of Logic."
*The Journal of Philosophy*,67,pp. 800-814

Bar-Hillel,Y.
*Aspects of Language.*
Amsterdam

Barth,E.M.
"Enten-eller: de logica van Licht en Donker."
*Algemeen Nederlands Tijdschrift voor Wijsbegeerte*,62, pp.217-240

Brandt,W.J.
*The Rhetoric of Argumentation.*
Indianapolis:Bobbs-Merrill

Fischer,D.H.
*Historian's Fallacies. Towards a Logic of Historical Thought.*
New York:Harper & Row

Hamblin,C.L.
*Fallacies.*
London:Methuen

Perelman,Ch.
*Le champ de l'argumentation.*
Bruxelles:Presses Universitaires de Bruxelles

1971 Apostel,L.
"Assertion Logic and Theory of Argumentation."
*Philosophy and Rhetoric*,4, pp.92-110

Apostel,L.
"Logique inductive, modalités épistémiques et logique de la préférence."
*Revue Internationale de Philosophie*, 25, pp. 78-100

Barth,E.M.
*De Logica van de Lidwoorden in de Traditionele Filosofie.*
Leiden: Universitaire Pers
Dissertation Leiden

Barth,E.M.
*The Logic of the Articles in Traditional Philosophy. A Contribution to the Study of Conceptual Structures.*
Dordrecht/Boston: Reidel, 1974 (translation of dissertation Leiden 1971)

Barth,E.M.
"Arne Naess en de filosofische dialectiek."
*De Gids*, 134, pp.173-186

Hamblin,C.L.
"Mathematical Models of Dialogue."
*Theoria*, 37, pp. 130-155

Howell,W.S.
*Eighteenth-century British Logic and Rhetoric.*
Princeton N.J.: Princeton University Press

*Logique et Analyse*
*Le raisonnement juridique. Actes du congrès mondial de philosophie du droit et de philosophie sociale. Bruxelles, 30 août-3 septembre 1971.*
*Logique et Analyse*, 14, mars-juin 1971

Lorenzen,P.
"Szientismus versus Dialektik."
*Man and World*, 4, pp. 151-168

Perelman,Ch.
*Droit, philosophie et argumentation.*
Zwolle: Tjeenk Willink

1972 Apostel,L.
"Illocutionary Forces and the Logic of Change."
*Mind*, 81, pp. 208-224

Apostel,L.
"Negation: the Tension between Ontological Positivity (Negationless Positivity) and Anthropological Negativity (Positivily Described)."
*Logique et Analyse*, 15, pp. 209-315

Barth,E.M.
*Evaluaties.* Rede uitgesproken bij de aanvaarding van het ambt van gewoon lector in de logica met inbegrip van haar geschiedenis en de wijsbegeerte van de logica in haar relatie tot de wijsbegeerte in het algemeen aan de Rijksuniversiteit te Utrecht op vrijdag 2 juni 1972.
Assen: van Gorcum

van Dun,F.
"On the Modes of Opposition in the Formal Dialogues of P. Lorenzen."
in: L.Apostel (ed), *Negation.*
Louvain-Paris, pp. 103-136
*(=Logique et Analyse, 15, nrs. 57-58, 1972)*

Gühlich,E.& Raible,W.(Hrsg.)
*Textsorten. Differenzierungskriterien aus linguistischer Sicht.*
Frankfurt am Main: Athenäum Verlag.

Kindt,W.
*Eine abstrakte Theorie von Dialogspielen.*
Freiburg, Dissertation

Kummer,W.
"Aspects of a Theory of Argumentation."
in: Gühlich & Raible (Hrsg.), *Textsorten. Differenzierungs-kriterien aus linguistischer Sicht.*
Frankfurt am Main: Athenäum Verlag, pp.25-49

Lorenz,K.
"Der dialogische Wahrheitsbegriff."
*Neue Hefte für Philosophie*, 2/3,pp. 111-123

Mittler,J.R.
"Indirection: a Rhetorical Technique in Philosophical Argumentation."
*Dialogue (Phi Sigma Tau)*, 14,pp. 39-45

Rotenstreich,N.
"Argumentation and Philosophical Clarification."
*Philosophy and Rhetoric*, 5,pp. 12-23

Woods,J. & Walton,D.
"On Fallacies."
*Journal of Critical Analysis*, 4,pp. 103-112

1973 van Dun,F.
"Entailment."
*Philosophia*, 12,pp.122-130

Habermas,J.
"Wahrheitstheorien."
in: H. Fahrenbach (Hrsg.), *Wirklichkeit und Reflexion. Walter Schulz zum 60. Geburtstag.*
Pfullingen, pp.211-265.

Hintikka,J.
"Quantifiers, Language-Games, and Transcendental Arguments."
in: J.Hintikka, *Logic, Language-Games and Information. Kantian Themes in the Philosophy of Logic.*
Oxford:Clarendon

Hintikka,J.
*Logic, Language-games and Information. Kantian Themes in the Philosophy of Logic.*
Oxford:Clarendon

Lorenz,K.
"Die dialogische Rechtfertigung der effektiven Logik."
in: Friedrich Kambartel und Jürgen Mittelstrass(eds.), *Zum normativen Fundament der Wissenschaft.*
Frankfurt am Main:Athenäum Verlag,pp. 250-280

Lorenz,K.
"Rules versus Theorems: A New Approach for Mediation between Intuitionistic and Two-Valued Logic."
*Journal of Philosophical Logic*, 2, pp.352-367

Lorenzen,P. & Schwemmer,O.
*Konstruktive Logik, Ethik und Wissenschaftstheorie.*
Mannheim, Wien, Zürich: B.I.

Sagal,P.T.
"Predicates, Concepts, and Ontological Neutrality in Lorenzen.
*Ratio*, 15,pp. 320-324

Wetlesen,J.
*Praktisk argumentasjon. En innföring i etikk.* I. *Med tekstutvalg fra Platon, Aristoteles, Spinoza, Hume, Bentham og Kant.*
(Practical argumentation. An introduction to ethics.I. With selected texts from Plato, etc.)
Oslo, Bergen, Tromsö

Wetlesen,J.
*Praktisk argumentasjon. En innföring i etikk.* II. *Oppgave- og eksempelsamling samt annet studiemateriale.*
(Practical argumentation. An introduction to Ethics.II.A collection of exercises and examples and other material for instruction)
Oslo, Bergen, Tromsö

1974 Apostel,L.(ed.)
*Negation.*
Gent:Communication and Cognition Press

Cizek,F.
"The Problem of Fallacies."
*Teorie a Metoda*,6,pp. 101-115

Günther,A.
"On Evaluating Argumentation in a Natural Language."
in: *Kommunikationsforschung und Phonetik: Festschrift zum fünfzigjährigen Bestehen des Instituts für Kommunikationsforschung und Phonetik der Universität Bonn.*
Hamburg: Buske, pp. 115-124

Hintikka,J.
"Quantifiers versus Quantification Theory."
*Linguistic Inquiry*,5,pp. 153-177

Lorenzen,P.
"Regeln vernünftigen Argumentierens."
in: *Konstruktive Wissenschaftstheorie.*
Frankfurt am Main,pp. 47-97

1975 *Der Deutschunterricht.*
*Logik,Rhetorik,Argumentationslehre* I.
*Der Deutschunterricht,Jg.27.Hft.2.*
Verantwortlich für dieses Heft:Robert Ulshöfer

Gerhardus,D.,Kledzik,S.M.,Reitzig,G.H.
*Schlüssiges Argumentieren.Logisch-Propädeutisch Lehr- und Arbeitsbuch.*
Göttingen:Vandenhoeck & Ruprecht

Hintikka,J.
"Quantifiers in Logic and Quantifiers in Natural Language."
in: S. Körner (ed.), *Philosophy of Logic.*
Oxford: Blackwell, pp. 208-232

Hintikka,J.
*The Intentions of Intentionality and Other New Models for Modalities.*
Dordrecht: Reidel

Kruger,A.N.
"The Nature of Controversial Statements."
*Philosophy and Rhetoric,*8,pp. 137-158

Mooij,J.J.A.
"Polemiek en overreding."
in: P.J. Roscam Abbing (red), *Conflict en Harmonie; opstellen over -al dan niet vruchtbare- tegenstellingen in het maatschappelijke leven.*
Meppel: Boom

1976 Crable,R.E.
*Argumentation as Communication: Reasoning with Receivers.*
Columbus, Ohio: Charles E. Merril

*Der Deutschunterricht.*
*Logik, Rhetorik und Argumentationslehre* II.
*Der Deutschunterricht, Jg.28, Hft.4.*
Verantwortlich für dieses Heft:Robert Ulshöfer

Giles,R.
"A Non-Classical Logic for Physics."
*Studia Logica,* 33, part 4, pp.397-415

Giles,R.
"A Logic for Subjective Belief."
in: W.L. Harper & C.A. Hooker (eds.)
*Foundations of Probability Theory, Statistical Inference, and Statistical Theories of Science* .I.
Dordrecht: Reidel, pp.41-47

Grize,J.B. (ed.)
*Recherches sur le discours et l'argumentation.*
Genève:Libraire Droz S.A.

Günther,A. & Lutz-Hensel,M.
"Konstruktion eines formalen Modellschemas für Dialoge."
in: *Forschungsberichte des IKP ,Bd.53*-I,pp. 141-180
Hamburg: Buske

Habermas,J.
"Was heisst Universalpragmatik."
in: K-O. Apel (Hrsg.),*Sprachpragmatik und Philosophie.*
Frankfurt am Main, pp.174-272

Heidrich,C.H.
"Grundlagen für Modelle von situationsabhängigem Handeln."
in: *Forschungsberichte des IKP, Bd. 53*-I, pp. 181-200
Hamburg: Buske

Heidrich,C.H. (ed.)
*Formale Betrachtungen in Sprach- und Kommunikationstheorie* I.
Hamburg: Buske

Hintikka,J.
*The Semantics of Questions and the Questions of Semantics.*
*(Acta Philosophica Fennica, vol. 28, no. 4)*
Amsterdam: North-Holland Publ. Comp.

Hintikka,J.
"Language Games."
in: Hintikka, J. et al. (eds.), *Essays on Wittgenstein in Honour of G.H. von Wright.*
Amsterdam, pp. 105-125.

Naess,A.
*Equivalent Terms and Notions in Spinoza's Ethics.*
Oslo: University Press

Stachow,E-W.
"Completeness of Quantum Logic."
*J. Phil. Logic, 5*, pp. 237-280

Woods,J. & Walton,D.
"Fallaciousness without Invalidity."
*Philosophy and Rhetoric*, 9, pp. 52-54

1977 van Asperen,G.M.
*Het ongedwongen gesprek. Over de waardevrijheid van een meta-ethische theorie.* (On unconstrained discourse.)
Rede uitgesproken ter gelegenheid van de aanvaarding van het ambt van gewoon lector in de sociale ethiek aan de Rijksuniversiteit te Groningen op dinsdag 18 januari 1977.

Barth,E.M.
"Phenomenology, Grammar, or Theory of Argumentation?:A Plea for Meta-Philosophical Change,Applied to the Problems of Nominalization and of Negation."
*Cultural Hermeneutics*,4,pp. 163-182

Barth,E.M.
"The Logical Paradigm in Dialectical Philosophy and Science."
*Erkenntnis*, 11, pp. 291-322

Barth,E.M. & Krabbe,E.C.W.
"Formal Dialectics: Language-Invariant Systems of Rules for Conflict-Resolution Pertaining to Conflicting Propositional Attitudes."
Pre-publication

Barth, E.M. & Martens,J.L.
"Argumentum ad Hominem: From Chaos to Formal Dialectic."
*Logique et Analyse*, 20, no 77-78, pp.76-96

Føllesdal,D. & Walløe,L.
*Argumentasjonsteori og vitenskapsfilosofi.* (Theory of argumentation and philosophy of science.)
Oslo, Bergen, Tromsö

Günther,A.
"Der Begriff der Dialogbasis."
in: C.H.Heidrich (Hrsg.), *Konstituenten dialogischer Kommunikation.*
Hamburg: Buske

Günther,A.
"Dialoge zu Ableitungen."
in: C.H.Heidrich (Hrsg.), *Konstituenten dialogischer Kommunikation.*
Hamburg: Buske

Günther,A.
*Dialogkonstruktionen auf der Basis logischer Ableitungen.*
Hamburg: Buske

Heidrich,C.H.(Hrsg.)
*Konstituenten dialogischer Kommunikation.*
Hamburg: Buske

Heidrich,C.H.
*Intensionale Analysen von Sprechhandlungen.*
Hamburg: Buske

Hintikka,J.
"Quantifiers in Natural Languages: Some Logical Problems II."
*Linguistics and Philosophy*,1,pp. 153-172

Hottois,G.
"Philosophie du langage et philosophie de l'argumentation."
*Revue de Metaphysique et de Morale*,82,pp. 471-510

Inhetveen,R.
"Die konstruktive Interpretation der modallogischen Semantik."
in: A. Conte, R. Hilpinen und G.H. von Wright (Hrsg.)
*Deontische Logik und Semantik.*
Wiesbaden, pp. 89-100.

Koch,H.J.
"Ansätze einer juristischen Argumentationstheorie?"
*Archiv für Rechts- und Sozialphilosophie*, 63,pp. 355-378

Lorenz,K.
"Die Überzeugungskraft von Argumenten.Bemerkungen über die Fundierung des Geltungsbegriffs im Dialogbegriff."
*Archiv für Rechts- und Sozialphilosophie.Beiheft N.F.9*, pp. 15-22

Martens,J.L.
*Drogredenen.*
Doctoraalscriptie,R.U. Utrecht, Centrale Interfaculteit

Naess,A.
"Notes on the Methodology of Normative Systems."
*Methodology and Science*, 10,pp. 64-79

Perelman,Ch.
*L'Empire rhétorique. Rhétorique et argumentation*
Paris

Perelman,Ch.
*Retorica en argumentatie*
Baarn: Ambo, 1979 (translation of Perelman 1977)

Rescher,N.
*Dialectics. A Controversy-Oriented Approach to the Theory of Knowledge.*
Albany, New York: State University of New York Press

Woods,J.
"Towards a Theory of Argument."
*Metaphilosophy*, 8,pp. 298-315

978 Apostel,L.
"The Elementary Theory of Collective Action."
*Philosophica*, 21,pp. 129-157

Barth,E.M. & Krabbe,E.C.W
"Formele$_3$ dialectiek: instrumenten ter beslechting van conflicten over geuite meningen."
*Spektator,Tijdschrift voor Neerlandistiek*,7,pp. 307-341
(translation of Barth & Krabbe 1977)

van Eemeren,F.H.,Grootendorst,R.,Kruiger,T.
*Argumentatietheorie.*
Utrecht.Antwerpen:het Spectrum

Inhetveen,R.
"Die semantische Vollständigkeit der Gegenformelmethode."
in: I. Tammelo und H. Schreiner (Hrsg.),*Strukturierungen und Entscheidungen im Rechtsdenken.*
Wien, New York,pp. 95-98

Krabbe,E.C.W.
"The Adequacy of Material Dialogue-Games."
*Notre Dame Journal of Formal Logic*,19,pp. 321-330

Lorenzen,P. & Lorenz,K.
*Dialogische Logik.*
Darmstadt:Wissenschaftliche Buchgesellschaft

Maneli,M.
"The New Theory of Argumentation and American Jurisprudence."
*Logique et Analyse*,21,pp. 19-50

Mittelstaedt, Peter.
*Quantum Logic.*
Dordrecht: Reidel

de Rivera,J.R.
*Kommunikationsstrukturen in den geistlichen Exerzitien des Ignatius von Loyola.*
Hamburg:Buske

*Spektator.*
Themanummer Argumentatietheorie. (Special issue: Theory of Argumentation)
*Spektator, Tijdschrift voor Neerlandistiek,* 7, pp.262-356
Gastredactie: F.H. van Eemeren, R. Grootendorst en T. Kruiger.
Groningen:Wolters-Noordhoff

Stachow,E.-W.
"Quantum Logical Calculi and Lattice Structures."
*J.Phil. Logic,7,* pp. 347-386.

1979 Apostel,L.
"What is the Force of an Argument?"
*Revue Internationale de Philosophie,*33,pp. 99-109

Apostel,L.
*Communication et action.*
Gent:Communication and Cognition Press

Apostel,L.
"Persuasive Communication as Metaphorical Discourse under the Guidance of Conversational Maxims."
*Logique et Analyse,*87,pp.265-320

Barth,E.M.
*Perspectives on Analytic Philosophy.*
*Mededelingen der Kon. Ned. Akad. Wet.*,New Series, vol. 42-no.2
Amsterdam.

Gethman,C.F.
*Protologik. Untersuchungen zur formalen Pragmatik von Begründungsdiskursen.*
Frankfurt am Main: Suhrkamp

Hintikka,J. & Saarinen,E.
"Information-Seeking Dialogues: Some of Their Logical Properties."
*Studia Logica*, 32, pp. 355-363

Hintikka,J. & Carlson,L.
"Conditionals, Generic Quantifiers, and Other Applications of Subgames."
in: E. Saarinen(ed.), *Game Theoretical Semantics.*
Dordrecht.Boston: Reidel, pp. 179-214

Inhetveen,R.
"Dialogische Logik in der Jurisprudenz: Dialogregeln und Prozessordnungen."
in: *Rechtstheorie- Beiheft 1:* Argumentation und Hermeneutik in der Jurisprudenz.
Berlin, pp. 231-238

Jacques,F.
"Logique ou rhétorique de l'argumentation."
*Revue Internationale de Philosophie*, 33, pp. 47-68

Leopold-Wildburger,U.
"Spieltheoretische Aspekte von sozialen Entscheidungsprozessen."
in: Berghel, H., Hübner, A., Köhler, E. (eds.)
*Wittgenstein, the Vienna Circle and Critical Rationalism, Proceedings of the 3rd International Wittgenstein-Symposium.*
Wien, pp. 496-499

Lorenzen,P.
"Das Problem wissenschaftlicher Prinzipien der Politik."
(Lecture held for the Friedrich Ebert Stiftung.)
unpublished (mimeographed)

Saarinen,E. (ed.)
*Game Theoretical Semantics.*
Dordrecht/Boston: Reidel

Zyskind,H.
"The New Rhetoric and Formalism."
*Revue Internationale de Philosophie,* 33,pp. 18-32

1980 Gethmann, C.F. (Hrsg.)
*Theorie des wissenschaftlichen Argumentierens.*
Frankfurt a.M.: Suhrkamp

Heidrich, C.H. (ed.)
*Formale Betrachtungen in Sprach- und Kommunikationstheorie* II.
Hamburg: Buske (in preparation)

Heidrich,C.H.
"Formal Capacity of Montague-grammars."
in: Los & Pfeiffer(eds.), *Proceedings of the 6th International Congres of Logic.*
Amsterdam

Hofstee,W.K.B.
*De empirische discussie.*
Meppel:Boom.

Naess,A.
"The Empirical Semantics of Key Terms, Phrases and Sentences."
in: S. Kanger & S. Öhman (eds.)
*Philosophy of Grammar.*
Dordrecht: Reidel,pp. 133-151
(In press)

Leopold-Wildburger,U.
"Spieltheoretische Überlegungen in Dialogspielen."
in: Becker,W.,Essler, W.(eds.),*Konzepte der Dialektik*.
Frankfurt am Main: Klostermann (In press)

1981 Apostel,L.
"Nominalistise en intensionele logika op praxeologise grondslag."
(to appear)

Apostel,L.
"Logique et action."
(to appear)

1982 Barth,E.M. & Krabbe,E.C.W.
*From Axiom to Dialogue*. A Text-book in Logic for Students of Philosophy and Human Communication.
New York/Berlin: De Gruyter (In Press)

van Eemeren, F.H. & Grootendorst, R.
*Regels voor redelijke discussies, Een bijdrage tot de theoretische analyse van argumentatie ter oplossing van geschillen.*
Dissertation, Amsterdam

Lorenzen,P.
"Politische Anthropologie."
in: Oswald Schwemmer (Hrsg.), *Vernunft, Handlung und Erfahrung. Über die Grundlagen und Ziele der Wissenschaften.*
München: Beck

## B INDEX OF NAMES TO CHRONOLOGICAL BIBLIOGRAPHY